SIXTH EDITION

STUDY GUIDE
FOR CROOKS AND BAUR'S
Our Sexuality

LAUREN KUHN
Portland Community College

Brooks/Cole Publishing Company
I(T)P™ An International Thomson Publishing Company

Pacific Grove • Albany • Bonn • Boston • Cincinnati • Detroit • London • Madrid • Melbourne
Mexico City • New York • Paris • San Francisco • Singapore • Tokyo • Toronto • Washington

Sponsoring Editor: *Faith B. Stoddard*
Editorial Associate: *Laura Donahue*
Production Coordinator: *Dorothy Bell*

Cover Design: *Jeanne Calabrese*
Cover Photo: *Robert Farber*
Printing and Binding: *Patterson Printing*

For more information, contact:

BROOKS/COLE PUBLISHING COMPANY
511 Forest Lodge Rd.
Pacific Grove, CA 93950
USA

International Thomson Editores
Campos Eliseos 385, Piso 7
Col. Polanco
11560 México D. F. México

International Thomson Publishing Europe
Berkshire House 168-173
High Holborn
London, WC1V 7AA
England

International Thomson Publishing GmbH
Königswinterer Strasse 418
53227 Bonn
Germany

Thomas Nelson Australia
102 Dodds Street
South Melbourne, 3205
Victoria, Australia

International Thomson Publishing Asia
221 Henderson Road
#05-10 Henderson Building
Singapore 0315

Nelson Canada
1120 Birchmount Road
Scarborough, Ontario
Canada M1K 5G4

International Thomson Publishing Japan
Hirakawacho Kyowa Building, 3F
2-2-1 Hirakawacho
Chiyoda-ku, Tokyo 102
Japan

Printed in the United States of America

10 9 8 7 6 5 4

ISBN 0-534-32096-1

To The Student

Crooks and Baur's sixth edition of *Our Sexuality* provides an exciting and informative exploration of the psychological, biological, social, cultural, and historical dimensions of human sexuality. This study guide is designed to assist you in maximizing your learning experience as you read through this text.

Each study guide chapter consists of several different features that, when used together, will help you successfully integrate the factual and conceptual material in the text. Each chapter begins with a brief introductory paragraph and a list of chapter objectives. Key terms and concepts are provided in the form of flash cards at the end of each chapter which may easily be removed and used for review. The following chapter overview with fill-ins provides a concise yet thorough summary of material presented in the text that will enable you to actively test your knowledge of the material once you have finished reading the chapter. When appropriate, a matching exercise will follow the chapter overview. In the next section, a series of short answer questions will enable you to elaborate in greater depth on your understanding of the chapter. Subsequent multiple choice questions will allow you to test your recall. Finally, at the end of each chapter are several insight and application questions, exercises and/or activities. The purpose of these items is to encourage you to think about and apply what you have read within the framework of your own background, values, and personal experiences.

In order to maximize your study time, you may find it helpful to use the following system. Begin by reading the chapter summary which is at the end of each chapter in the text. This will give you a brief overview of what to anticipate. Then read through the chapter itself, a major section at a time, underlining definitions, key concepts, research conclusions, and summary paragraphs when appropriate. When you have finished, refer to the flash cards at the end of the study guide chapter and test your recall of key terms and concepts.

At this point, proceed to the chapter overview with fill-ins. You will notice that the overview is organized according to the same headings that are in the text. After reading each of the major sections in the chapter, check your retention by **mentally** filling in each of the blanks in the corresponding sections. Cover the answers in the margin as you go along, and write the answers in the space provided only when you are doing your final review. If you have a basic understanding of the overall concepts and definitions of the chapter, you should be able to complete the majority of the fill-ins without referring to your text. If you find yourself struggling with a particular section in the chapter overview, go back and review the corresponding material in your book. Return again to the overview when you feel you understand the material. This process may be repeated at a later time to test your recall.

When you have completed the overview, proceed to the matching exercises, which are included in most, but not all chapters. Following that are the short answer questions, which are listed in the order in which the material is presented in the text. The study guide is designed so that you may write your answers in the book itself, unless you prefer or your instructor requires you to write them on a separate sheet of paper. In many ways, these short answer questions are the "heart" of the study guide. Taking the time to go back, cover up your answers and then recite them aloud is a key part of the learning process which will pay off handsomely for you later.

After completing the short answer questions, you will find a number of multiple choice items. Complete these and check your answers with the key provided at the end of the chapter. Mark the questions you missed, and then go back to the chapter and review the appropriate section.

Finally, there are several insight and application questions and activities, referred to earlier, that you may wish to take the time to answer for yourself.

Prior to your chapter exam, reread the text, paying particular attention to what you have underlined. Review the various sections of your study guide, covering up your answers to test your recall. Once again, remember that recitation is critical to your retention.

Keep in mind that the suggestions above are **guidelines**; variations that are tailored to what works best for you are encouraged.

Taking a human sexuality course can be a very powerful learning experience. There is the potential to expand your knowledge and awareness on a number of levels: intellectual, personal, emotional, social, and cultural. You are investing your time, your money, and your energy. Make it count.

Lauren Kuhn

Contents

1

Perspectives on Sexuality

Introduction

The psychosocial orientation of the text is discussed, and the authors state their opposition to two long-standing sexual themes in Western cultures: sex-for-reproduction and the rigid distinction between male and female roles. The importance of viewing sexual attitudes and behaviors from a cross-cultural perspective is also presented, and a profile of two societies with diverse sexual values and practices exemplifies the range of sexual expression throughout the world. The diversity that exists within the United States is discussed as well. The chapter concludes with an overview of current social and legal trends that affect our sexual decision-making processes.

Objectives

After studying this chapter, you should be able to:

emotional motivational attitudinal

1. Define the term "psychosocial" as it applies to the orientation of the text, and explain why ↑ the authors choose to emphasize this perspective. *The perspective that includes psychosocial and social conditioning instead of biological factors. (instincts, hormones)* *Societies norms* *factors*

2. Discuss how the sex-for-reproduction and gender-role legacies have evolved historically, and explain how those themes affect sexual attitudes and behaviors today.

3. Describe the difficulty in determining what constitutes "normal" sexual behavior, citing specific cross-cultural examples to support your explanation.

4. Explain what ethnographers do, and discuss some of the limitations of their work, especially as it relates to the study of human sexual behavior. *anthropologists you study the cultures of different societies,*

5. Discuss the sexual attitudes and behaviors of the people in Mangaia and Inis Beag. *Mangaia → horny, sex is good   Inis Beag → virgins til marriage, it's dirty*

6. List several examples that illustrate how diversity exists in various subcultures within the United States.

7. Give examples of specific psychological, scientific and social advances within the last century that have affected sexual values and behavior in our society today.

Key Terms and Concepts

"Flash cards" listing key terms and concepts on one side and their corresponding definitions and explanations on the other side are provided at the end of the chapter.

Chapter Overview With Fill-Ins

After reading each of the major sections in the chapter, check your retention by **mentally** filling in each of the blanks in the corresponding sections below. Cover the answers in the margin as you go along, and write the answers in the space provided only when you are doing your final review.

The Authors' Perspectives

psychosocial   The book has a _____ orientation, reflecting the authors' view
                    that human sexuality is influenced more by social conditioning and
                    psychological factors than by hormones or instincts.

                    Two long-standing sexual themes that the authors oppose are: the sex-
intercourse   for-reproduction legacy, which places emphasus on _____, and
                    as a result devalues other kinds of sexual behavior; and the
gender-role   _____-_____ legacy, which limits human potential and
negative   produces a _____ impact on our sexuality.

The Sex-for-Reproduction Legacy

                    The idea of sex-for-reproduction is associated with both
Judaic   _____ and Christian traditions. Christian writers such as
Augustine   Paul of Tarsus, _____, and Thomas Aquinas contributed to
                    the view of sex as sinful, legitimized only for the purposes of
procreation   _____ within a marriage.

                    In the sixteenth century, leaders of the Protestant Reformation, such
Martin Luther   as _____ _____ and John Calvin challenged the
nonreproductive   view of _____ sex as sinful.

Hindu   In contrast to Western traditions, ancient Taoists, _____
sexual   and Islamic cultures placed a high value on _____ behavior
                    within marriage, not just for procreation.

contraception   Although the availability of modern _____ has allowed
                    people to separate sexuality from procreation to a degree not possible
                    in earlier times, the sex-for-reproduction legacy maintains a powerful
                    influence in twentieth century Western culture.

The Gender-Role Legacy

gender-role   Rigid _____-_____ differences between men and
                    women go far back in Western history. In ancient Hebraic culture,
children   women were required to manage the household, bear _____,
Paul of Tarsus   and be obedient to their husbands. The writings of _____ in
                    the New Testament emphasized the importance of women being
submissive   _____.

                    During the Middle Ages, two contradictory images of women evolved:
                    the pure and unattainable woman revealed in the cult of the
Virgin Mary   _____ _____ and in courtly love; and the evil
Eve   temptress represented by _____ and by the women persecuted
witches   as _____.

eighteenth   Women enjoyed increased respect for a brief time in the _____
Mary Wollstonecraft century. _____ _____ of England wrote a book
                    asserting women's rights, emphasizing the importance of women being
                    well-educated and claiming that women were entitled to
sexual   _____ satisfaction as well as men.

Victorian   During the _____ era, women were viewed as asexual. The
                    lives of men and women were sharply dichotomized, and men often
prostitutes   sought _____ for sex and companionship.

sexes

A number of events in the twentieth century have contributed to more equality between the _____. However, the legacy of Victorianism and earlier traditions in gender roles limits the full potential of men and women in our society.

A Cross-Cultural Perspective: Social Norms and Sexual Diversity

ethnographers

Irish

The information we have on sexual expression in other societies has been derived from the fieldwork of _____, anthropologists who specialize in studying the cultures of different societies. The authors discuss the sexual attitudes and behaviors of two different societies: the Polynesian island of Mangaia and the _____ island known as Inis Beag.

superincision

night-crawling

oral-genital

In Mangaia, children receive extensive information on and exposure to sexuality. At adolescence, boys undergo an operation called _____, where the tissue on top of the penis is cut and folded back, exposing the glans. Sex occurs in "public privacy" as young men engage in a practice called _____-_____, which allows a boy to be sexually intimate with a young woman in her family home with her parents' covert approval. Sexual interest and activity occurs frequently for both unmarried and married men and women. A wide variety of sexual behavior, including _____-_____ sex and a considerable amount of touching is encouraged.

breast-feeding
masturbation

intercourse; orgasm

On the Irish island of Inis Beag (a pseudonym), sexual expression is discouraged throughout the population and at all ages. Mothers avoid _____-_____ their children, nudity is considered repugnant, and religious leaders teach that _____ , sex play, and discussion of premarital sex is sinful. Sex during marriage focuses only on _____. Female _____ is unknown or considered a deviant response.

Diversity Within the United States

premarital
chastity

Some examples of diversity that exist within the United States include: Asian-Americans, who are generally less likely to engage in _____ intercourse than other subcultures; and Latinos, who endorse sexual exploration for men but value _____ before marriage for women.

acculturation

education

The degree to which traditional beliefs and behaviors are replaced with those of the dominant culture, known as _____, also creates differences within subcultures. Socioeconomic status and _____ also influence sexual attitudes and behaviors.

Sexuality: Personal or Public Domain?

twentieth

Kinsey

response cycle

The sexual freedoms and responsibilities that men and women currently enjoy are largely the result of psychological, scientific and social advances that have taken place in the _____ century. Many individuals have made contributions in the area of human sexuality, including Alfred _____ , whose research brought greater acceptance of masturbation, homosexuality, and non-marital intercourse as normal expressions of sexuality. The research of Masters and Johnson contributed to a greater understanding of the sexual _____ _____ in men and women.

oral contraceptive pill

abortion
homosexuality
AIDS

The invention of the _____ _____ _____ in the early 1960s, as well as the increased availability of other reliable contraceptive devices, helped bring sexual decisions even more firmly into the personal realm. In 1973, the U.S. Supreme Court ruled that _____ is a woman's choice, and in the late 1960s and 1970s attitudes regarding another traditional taboo, _____, began to change. The onset of the _____ crisis in the 1980s increased both negative and positive public sentiment toward homosexuality.

sexually transmitted
adolescent

AIDS

Although young men and women have more information, contraceptive choices, and medical care available to them than ever before, there has been an epidemic of _____ _____ diseases, an increase in the birth rate among unmarried _____ women, and extensive confusion regarding personal values. On the other hand, the risk of contracting a terminal disease — _____ — has prompted many people to be much more cautious and conservative in their sexual behavior.

personal

Some people believe _____ choice should be the foundation for decisions related to sexuality, while others believe that personal control should be limited and brought back to the public domain.

Matching

Match the people below with their ideas or contributions.

a.	Paul of Tarsus	g.	Mary Wollstonecraft
b.	Augustine	h.	Sigmund Freud
c.	Thomas Aquinas	i.	Havelock Ellis
d.	Martin Luther	j.	Theodore Van de Velde
e.	John Calvin	k.	Alfred Kinsey
f.	William Masters and Virginia Johnson		

_____1.   A reformer who wrote that marital sex was permissible "… to ease the cares and sadness of household affairs, or to endear each other."

_____2.   Lived from 1856 to 1939; recognized sexuality in both men and women as natural

_____3.   Lived from 353 to 430 AD; formalized the idea that intercourse was for procreation only within the context of marriage.

_____4.   Published research that resulted in increased understanding of the sexual response cycle.

_____5.   Wrote *Summa Theologica;* maintained that oral-genital sex and anal intercourse was against God's will.

_____6.   A contemporary of Freud's who recognized that individuals have different sexual needs.

_____7.   Saw celibacy as superior to marriage; his writings were incorporated into the New Testament.

_____8.   Lived from 1483 to 1546; recognized the value of sex in marriage.

_____9.   Wrote a book in the late 1700s that asserted, among other things, that premarital and extramarital affairs were not sinful.

_____10. Published scientific information that resulted in greater acceptance of masturbation, homosexuality, etc.

_____11. Lived from 1873 to 1937; emphasized the importance of sexual satisfaction and pleasure.

Short Answer

1.   What is meant by "a psychosocial orientation"? (Obj. #1)

2.   Why do the authors oppose the sex-for-reproduction legacy? (Obj. #2)

3.   What effects do rigid gender-role conditioning have on men and women? (Obj. #2)

4.   How is the sex-for-reproduction legacy related to Judaic and Christian traditions? (Obj. #2)

5.   What were some of the themes in the writings of Paul of Tarsus? (Obj. #2)

6.   How were the philosophies of Augustine and Thomas Aquinas related? (Obj. #2)

7.   Briefly describe the sexual perspectives of Martin Luther and John Calvin during the Protestant Reformation. (Obj. #2)

8.   Briefly compare and contrast ancient Taoist, Hindu and Islamic philosophies regarding sexual activity. (Obj. #2)

9.   List five methods of contraception that were used in ancient times. (Obj. #2)

10.   According to the Book of Proverbs, what were the responsibilities of a good wife? (Obj. #2)

11.   Describe the two contradictory images of women that evolved during the Middle Ages. (Obj. #2)

12.   What contributions did Mary Wollstonecraft make regarding equal rights for women? (Obj. #2)

13.   Explain the nature of sex roles for men and women during the Victorian era. (Obj. #2)

14.   Briefly explain why it is difficult to define what is normal sexual behavior. (Obj. #6)

15. Why is the data we have on sexual expression in other cultures rather limited? (Obj. #4)

16. Define the terms "superincision" and "night-crawling." (Obj. #5)

17. Describe the sexual attitudes and behaviors of the inhabitants of Inis Beag. (Obj. #5)

18. How does the practice of oral-genital sex differ between college-educated whites and blacks as well as people with less education? (Obj. #6)

19. What developments in the twentieth century led to greater equality for women? (Obj. #7)

20. Briefly describe how the works of Sigmund Freud, Havelock Ellis, and Theodore Van de Velde led to new definitions of sexuality. (Obj. #7)

21. How did the research of Kinsey, and Masters and Johnson contribute to our knowledge and understanding of human sexuality? (Obj. #7)

22. What events have occurred in the last 100 years that have resulted in making sexual decision-making a more personal matter? (Obj. #7)

Multiple Choice

Select the best alternative. Check your answers with the answer key at the end of the chapter.

1. The textbook has a _____ orientation.
   a. biological
   b. sociological
   c. biosocial
   d. psychosocial

2. Which of the following is the **best** example of a potential effect of the **sex-for-reproduction** legacy as opposed to rigid gender-role conditioning?
   a. Men may feel compelled to initiate social and sexual interaction.
   b. Women may be more passive sexually.
   c. Men and women may view masturbation as sinful.
   d. Men may feel obligated to be sexually knowledgeable.

3. Which of the following cultural themes would **most likely** result in men feeling pressure to initiate social or sexual interaction?
   a. sex-for-reproduction legacy
   b. the gender-role legacy
   c. "sex" is synonymous with penile-vaginal intercourse
   d. goal-oriented sexual expression

4. Which of the following is **not** associated with Paul of Tarsus?
   a. viewing celibacy as superior to marriage
   b. explaining why women should be submissive
   c. writing his *Summa Theologica*
   d. associating sex with sin

5. During the Protestant Reformation, _____ disagreed with church doctrine on celibacy and chastity.
    a. Martin Luther
    b. Thomas Aquinas
    c. Augustine
    d. Paul of Tarsus

6. The writing of Mary Wollstonecraft
    a. emphasized sex for procreation.
    b. elaborated on courtly love.
    c. asserted women's rights.
    d. discussed women's roles during the Victorian era.

7. A woman who feels guilty because she is sexually more knowledgeable and experienced than her male partner is a victim of
    a. the equal rights movement.
    b. rigid gender-role conditioning.
    c. a psychosocial orientation.
    d. the sex-for-reproduction legacy.

8. Which of the following statements about ethnographers is **true**?
    a. They are sociologists who specialize in studying the cultures of different societies.
    b. They administer detailed questionnaires to the people they study.
    c. Their fieldwork has provided relatively little information on sexual expression.
    d. Their research allows them to make direct cause-and-effect statements regarding human behavior.

9. _____ is practiced in Mangaia.
    a. Clitoridectomy
    b. Genital infibulation
    c. Superincision
    d. Labiotomy

10. The most extreme example of sexual repression would be found in
    a. Mangaia.
    b. Haiti.
    c. New Guinea.
    d. Inis Beag.

11. Which of the following statements regarding night-crawling is **false**?
    a. Parents approve of this practice.
    b. It is initiated by young men.
    c. If awakened, other family members alert the head of the household.
    d. This practice occurs in Mangaia.

12. Compared to European settlers, Native American sexual customs
    a. were quite similar.
    b. were more restrictive.
    c. were more permissive.
    d. were very similar in most respects but radically different in others.

13. The inhabitants of Inis Beag
    a. believe that intercourse before a strenuous job gives a man extra energy.
    b. practice oral and manual stimulation more than intercourse.
    c. have similar values to Mangaians.
    d. avoid breast-feeding their children.

14. What was the focus of Masters' and Johnson's research?
    a. a broad survey of people's sexual attitudes and behaviors
    b. a study of adolescent sexuality
    c. sexual response patterns in men and women
    d. case studies of atypical sexual behavior

15. The individual who has provided an explanation for the shift in power from female deities to male deities over the course of history is
    a. Merlin Stone.
    b. Havelock Ellis.
    c. Theodore Van de Velde.
    d. Alfred Kinsey.

Insight and Application

Throughout this course and as you read the assigned chapters in the text, you will have the opportunity to examine your values regarding a range of issues related to human sexuality. The following exercise is designed to help you begin this "values clarification" process. The topics below represent some of the more sensitive and controversial issues you will be addressing as you read this book. The questions beneath each topic are designed to stimulate your thoughts related to the subject, but they are not comprehensive, so feel free to digress on your own. In addition, for each topic, ask yourself:

1. What is my knowledge base regarding this subject? What facts do I have to support my view?

2. How have my values evolved on this issue? Have they always been the same, or have they changed over time? If there has been a shift in my attitude over time, what factors have contributed to that?

3. To what extent am I open to exploring my values on this topic as I progress through this course?

Sex education

To what extent do I feel this should be taught at home, if at all? Why? What are some specific ways parents might assume more responsibility for sex education at home? To what extent do I feel sex education should be taught in school, if at all? Why? If I support sex education in school, at what grade level should sex education begin? What topics should be addressed in a sex education curriculum in grade school? Junior high school? High school?

Premarital sexual intercourse

How do I feel about this **for me**? Under what circumstances or conditions is this acceptable? Unacceptable? Why? How do I feel about my partner having experience with premarital sexual intercourse? Why?

Masturbation

How do I feel about this **for myself**? What are the benefits and drawbacks? Do I feel this is more acceptable at some age levels than others? Would I feel comfortable with this practice for myself or my partner if we were married or living together? Under what circumstances would I be or am I uncomfortable with this practice?

Cohabitation

Under what circumstances would I consider living with a partner, if at all? What do I perceive as the benefits and drawbacks? Do I feel that living together would result in a potentially more successful marital relationship? Why or why not?

Homosexuality

How do I feel about people with a homosexual orientation? Why? Do I feel that sexual orientation can be altered or changed? Do I believe that people with a homosexual orientation should have the same rights and freedoms as people with a heterosexual orientation? Why or why not?

Abortion

Under what circumstances would I consider having an abortion or support my partner in having one, if any (e.g., contraceptive failure, in cases of rape or incest, high risk of birth defects, etc.)? How do I feel about abortion being available to women in the community? Under what conditions or circumstances, if any? How do I feel abortion should be funded?

Love and sex

How do I feel about the relationship between love and sex? Are they related? If so, in what way? Is it or would it be possible **for me** to have a good sexual relationship without being in love? Under what circumstances, if at all? Do I think men and women perceive the relationship between love and sex in similar or different ways? Elaborate.

Extramarital sexual intercourse

Under what circumstances, if any, would extramarital sex be acceptable for me or my partner (e.g., different values or priorities regarding sex, prolonged illness, extended absence, etc)? Have my partner or I ever experienced this, now or in a previous relationship? What impact did it have?

Pornography

How do I define "pornography"? To what degree, if at all, have I been exposed to pornography? Do I feel that it does or would enhance my sexual experience — alone or with a partner? Or detract from it? Do I think that viewing pornography would affect sexual attitudes and behavior — for myself or for others? Why or why not?

Sexual harassment

Have I ever experienced sexual harassment as a perpetrator and/or victim? How do I feel about the increased focus on this subject in recent years? What impact has that had on my attitudes and behavior, if any?

- You may wish to expand the list of issues above as you proceed through the course.

- You may wish to do this assessment again after you have finished reading the text and/or completed the class to see how your values have changed, if at all.

- As a variation on this activity, after completing it alone, you may wish to sit down with a partner, friend, group of friends or family members to discuss your values with one another. It can be especially challenging if you select people whose values you know are different than your own. The ground rules are:

    1. Listen to each other with the intent to more fully **understand** each other's view, **not** to attempt to **change** it.

    2. Ask questions to get more information to help you better understand how and why the person happens to view the issue in a certain way, **not** to challenge the person's position or to make the person defend his or her view.

Matching Answers

1. e	2. h	3. b	4. f	5. c	6. i	7. a	8. d
9. g	10. k	11. j					

Multiple Choice Answers

1. d	2. c	3. b	4. c	5. a	6. c	7. b	8. c
9. c	10. d	11. c	12. c	13. d	14. c	15. a	

polygyny	**acculturation**
revisionism	**berdache**

replacing traditional beliefs and behaviors with those of the dominant culture	one man having multiple wives simultaneously
men and women in some Native American groups who pursued traditional roles of the other sex	a process whereby an ethnic group tries to recapture an aspect of their culture

2

Sex Research: Methods and Problems

Introduction

Understanding how sex research is conducted and becoming familiar with several classic research studies will help lay the groundwork for integrating and appreciating much of the information presented in the text. This chapter describes four research methods used in studying sexuality and outlines advantages and limitations of each.

Objectives

After studying this chapter, you should be able to:

1. Define sexology and describe three of its goals, providing examples of each goal.

2. Describe when and how the discipline of sexology originated.

3. Describe each of the following research methods, including advantages and disadvantages of each method, and provide an example of each type of research:
   a. case study
   b. survey
   c. direct observation
   d. experimental

4. Define each of the following and distinguish among them: survey sample, target population, representative sample, and random sample.

5. Discuss two types of survey methods, and the strengths and limitations of each.

6. Explain how nonresponse, self-selection, demographic bias and inaccuracy present problems in sex survey research.

7. Summarize the available research on "volunteer bias."

8. Describe the research studies of Alfred Kinsey and his associates, including research methods used, subject populations studied, and strengths and limitations of this work.

9. Describe the results of surveys on violent pornography and alcohol use.

10. Describe Masters and Johnson's research, including the research method used, subject populations studied, and the strengths and limitations of this work.

11. Distinguish between independent and dependent variables, providing examples of each.

12. Describe how the experimental method has been used to study the effects of alcoholism on sexual arousal.

13. Identify some criteria that would be helpful in evaluating various kinds of research.

14. Discuss some of the ethical considerations in conducting sex research.

15. Describe how sexual arousal is measured in men and women in a research setting.

Key Terms and Concepts

"Flash cards" listing key terms and concepts on one side and their corresponding definitions and explanations on the other side are provided at the end of the chapter.

Chapter Overview With Fill-Ins

After reading each of the major sections in the chapter, check your retention by **mentally** filling in each of the blanks in the corresponding sections below. Cover the answers in the margin as you go along, and write the answers in the space provided only when you are doing your final review.

The Goals of Sexology

scientists
predicting

Sexologists share certain goals with _____ in other disciplines and these include understanding, _____ and controlling events that are the subject matter of their fields.

Nonexperimental Research Methods

case studies
flexible
control

in depth

In-depth explorations of single cases or small groups of people who are examined individually are called _____ _____. This research method allows for _____ data gathering procedures, and while it sacrifices some _____ , it offers opportunities to explore specific behaviors, thoughts and feelings _____ _____.

survey

interviews
questionnaires

Most of our information about human sexuality has been obtained by a second research method, the _____ , in which people are asked about their sexual attitudes or experiences. Surveys take the form of face-to-face _____ or written _____ .

representative

target
random

Researchers strive to select a _____ sample, in which various subgroups are represented proportionate to their incidence in the _____ population. Another kind of sample, called a _____ sample, is selected by randomization procedures, but this does not necessarily ensure a representative sample.

nonresponse

self-selection

demographic

accuracy

A common problem encountered in sex survey research is that of _____ , the refusal to participate in a research study. Even if the researcher has been careful in selecting the sample population, _____-_____ , also called "volunteer bias", may distort the sample. Another problem that affects sex surveys is _____ bias, which occurs when one group of people is disproportionately represented. Because survey respondents may consciously or unconsciously distort information regarding their sexual experiences, _____ of information is still another problem that plagues sex research.

Alfred Kinsey

A very well-known example of sex survey research is the work conducted by _____ _____ in the late 1940s and early 1950s on male and female sexuality.

direct observation

A third method for studying human sexual behavior is _____ _____ , where researchers observe and record responses of participating subjects. A classic research study using this method is

Masters; Johnson
physiological

the work of _____ and _____ , who observed the _____ changes that men and women experience during sexual arousal.

The Experimental Method

experimental

A fourth method, _____ research, involves presenting subjects with certain specific stimuli under controlled conditions so that their reactions can be reliably measured. The major advantage is

control
causal

having _____ over variables thought to influence the behavior being studied, so that _____ relationships between variables may be explored.

Evaluating Research: Some Questions To Ask

credentials
media
methodology
bias
findings

When evaluating a particular piece of research, first determine the _____ of the researchers. Note the type of _____ in which the results were published. Examine the type of _____ used, check the sample size of the group, and consider the possibility of _____ in the selection of subjects. Compare the _____ of the study to those of other reputable studies.

Matching

Match the research method below with the appropriate description.

    a.   survey method
    b.   case study method
    c.   direct observation
    d.   experimental research

_____1.   Sexual response patterns were studied in this way by Masters and Johnson.

_____2.   This method has been used to explore the relationship between sexually violent media and rape.

_____3.   Questionnaires or interviews are two ways in which this method may be used.

_____4.   This method is being used with increasing frequency to study human sexual behavior.

_____5.   If this method is used, it is difficult to make generalizations about the rest of the population.

_____6.   This is the way in which most of our information regarding human sexuality has been obtained.

_____7.   This method allows sex to be studied under controlled conditions.

_____8.   Using this method, cause-and-effect relationships may be explored in detail.

_____9.   Kinsey used this method.

_____10. Much current information about transsexuals and sex offenders has been obtained through this approach.

Short Answer

1. List and briefly describe three goals of sexology. (Obj. #1)

2. Briefly describe how and when human sexual behavior became the subject of serious study. (Obj. #2)

3. In what kinds of research would use of the case study method be most appropriate? Cite an example of research that has used the case study method. (Obj. #3)

4. List the advantages and disadvantages of the case study method. (Obj. #3)

5. List the two types of survey methods and describe advantages and limitations of each. (Obj. #3, 5)

6. Define and give an example of a representative sample. (Obj. #4)

7. Summarize the most recent research on self-selection. (Obj. #7)

8. Define and give an example of demographic bias. (Obj. #6)

9. Explain how the problems of nonresponse and inaccuracy may affect the findings in a study of human sexual behavior. (Obj. #6)

10. Briefly describe the nature of Kinsey's research: (Obj. #8)

    a. What was the purpose of his research?

    b. Who were the subjects of his study?

    c. What research method did he use?

    d. Why is his research considered to be so important?

    e. On what basis has his research been criticized?

11. In what ways was the National Health and Social Life Survey significant? (Obi. #9)

12. Briefly describe the nature of Masters and Johnson's research: (Obj. #10)

    a. What was the purpose of their research?

b.   Who were the initial subjects in the study? The final subjects?

c.   What research method did they use?

d.   What stimulus situations were used to observe sexual response?

13. List advantages and limitations of the direct observation method of research. (Obj. #3, 10)

14. What method is being used with increasing frequency in studying human sexual behavior? Why? (Obj. #3)

15. Provide an example that demonstrates the difference between an independent and a dependent variable. (Obj. #11)

16. Briefly list seven criteria to consider in evaluating a piece of research. (Obj. #13)

17. Briefly describe several ethical and legal considerations in conducting research on human sexuality. (Obj. #14)

18. How do low levels of alcohol consumption affect sexual arousal in men and women? (Obj. #12)

19. Name the device used to measure penile tumescence. (Obj. #15)

20. What does a vaginal photoplethysmograph do? (Obj. #15)

Multiple Choice

Select the best alternative. Check your answers with the answer key at the end of the chapter.

1. Sexual behavior became the subject of serious study
   a. shortly after the Renaissance.
   b. in the early 1800s.
   c. in the late 1800s.
   d. within this century.

2. Which of the following statements regarding the survey method is **true**?
   a. The researcher is able to explore cause and effect relationships.
   b. Masters and Johnson used this method in their research.
   c. This would be a good method to use in studying the physiological effects of alcohol consumption on sexual arousal.
   d. Most of our scientific knowledge of human sexuality has been obtained by this method.

3. The ideal sample is called a/an _____ sample.
   a. random
   b. representative
   c. survey
   d. equivalent

4. In conducting a survey, a researcher may choose to conduct interviews rather than administer a survey because interviews are
   a. cheaper.
   b. more anonymous.
   c. more flexible.
   d. easier to administer.

5. Self-selection is another term for
   a. volunteer bias.
   b. demographic bias.
   c. ethnocentrism.
   d. the primacy effect.

6. Disproportionate representation of certain groups of people (i.e., college students, white-collar workers) illustrates the problem of
   a. geographic discrimination.
   b. demographic bias.
   c. data discrimination.
   d. ethnocentrism.

7. A limitation of the case-study method is that
   a. data gathering procedures are very structured.
   b. generalizations can rarely be drawn to the rest of the population.
   c. it does not allow for in-depth exploration of a person or social group.
   d. cause-and-effect relationships cannot be explored.

8. A penile strain gauge
   a. measures the slightest change in penis size.
   b. is a flexible "ruler" that is attached to the penis and measures changes in length during arousal.
   c. measures the time between arousal and orgasm.
   d. measures subjective reports of sexual arousal in men.

9. Which of the following is a limitation of the direct observation method of research?
   a. data falsification through memory deficits
   b. having to rely on subjective reports of past experiences
   c. inability to see and measure sexual behavior firsthand
   d. the degree to which a subject's behavior may be influenced by an observer

10. The studies cited on the effects of alcohol on sexual arousal used which research method?
    a. survey
    b. case study
    c. direct observation
    d. experimental

11. Which of the following statements concerning experimental research is **false**?
    a. This method is being used with increasing frequency in studying human sexual behavior.
    b. The studies cited on how alcohol consumption affects physiological sexual arousal used this method.
    c. Cause-and-effect relationships cannot be explored when using this method.
    d. This method allows the researcher to control variables thought to influence the behavior being studied.

12. Two devices for measuring sexual arousal include
    a. a penile strain gauge and vaginal photoplethysmograph.
    b. a tumescent thermometer and vaginal photoplethysmograph.
    c. a penile strain gauge and vaginal dilator.
    d. a tumescent thermometer and vaginal dilator.

13. If you wished to do an in-depth study of individuals seeking sex-change surgery, which of the following research methods would be **most** appropriate?
    a. experimental research
    b. direct observation
    c. case study
    d. survey

14. A _____ variable is a condition of the experiment that is under control of the researchers.
    a. dependent
    b. independent
    c. representative
    d. random

15. Which of the following groups of people were **omitted** from Kinsey's survey?
    a. better-educated, city-dwelling Protestants
    b. older people
    c. people living in rural communities
    d. blacks

16. Masters and Johnson's research has made a major contribution to the understanding of
    a. men's and women's sexual values, attitudes and behavior.
    b. the sexual behavior of adolescent males and females.
    c. the effects of alcohol on sexual arousal.
    d. physiological changes that occur during sexual arousal.

17. In the research study for which they are most well-known, Masters and Johnson used which of the following groups in their **final** sample population?
    a. volunteers from the academic community
    b. prostitutes
    c. people who had difficulty responding sexually
    d. men and women contacted at random through the telephone directory

18. Which of the following is **not** one of the criteria cited for evaluating a piece of research?
    a. Examine the methodology used and consider possible limitations of this method.
    b. Note the size of the sample group and consider possible bias in the selection of subjects.
    c. See if the researchers are considered to be reputable professionals.
    d. Check to see if the results of the study have been published in a popular magazine.

19. One of the **more controversial** ethical issues in human sexual research involves
    a. potential physical harm to subjects.
    b. potential psychological harm to subjects.
    c. the issue of deception.
    d. the issue of anonymity.

Insight and Application

1. Assume that you were given the opportunity to research any aspect of human sexual attitudes and/or behavior that interested you. What would you choose to investigate? What questions would you pose? Once you have established an hypothesis, what research method would you use for your study? Why? How would you determine your sample population?

2. Assume that you are a researcher who is interested in gathering information on childhood sexuality (i.e., the level of sexual knowledge and awareness that children possess at various ages, sources of sexual information, masturbatory activity in which children might engage, orgasmic response, sex play with siblings or other children, etc.). What method(s) would you choose to obtain this information? What problems might you encounter in doing this type of research? How might you deal with them?

Matching Answers

1. c	2. b	3. a	4. d	5. b	6. a	7. d	8. b
9. a	10. b						

Multiple Choice Answers

1. d	2. d	3. b	4. c	5. a	6. b	7. b	8. a
9. d	10. d	11. c	12. a	13. c	14. b	15. d	16. d
17. a	18. d	19. c					

survey	representative sample
random sample	nonresponse
self-selection	demographic bias
sexology	case study
direct observation	experimental research

a type of research sample in which every person in the total population about which one wishes to draw a conclusion has an equal chance, or probability, of being included	a research method in which a sample of people are questioned about their attitudes or behaviors, either through their response to a written questionnaire or a face-to-face interview
the number of people who choose NOT to participate in survey research, and the problems this creates in interpreting the results of the survey	a type of survey sample that is selected by indiscriminate or random procedures; this sample may or may not be the same as a representative sample
research in which the survey samples contain a disproportionately higher number of one group of individuals as opposed to another	the degree to which research results may be distorted by the individuals who choose to participate in a study as opposed to those who do not
a research method that involves in-depth study of one or more subjects who are examined individually	the study of sexuality
a research method in which the subject's reactions and behaviors can be reliably measured under controlled laboratory conditions	a research method in which subjects are observed as they go about their activities

penile strain gauge	**vaginal photoplethysmograph**
independent variable	**dependent variable**

a device used in sex research to measure the increases in vaginal blood volume that occurs as a woman becomes sexually aroused	a device used in sex research that can measure even the slightest changes in penis size as the result of sexual arousal
the outcome that the experimenter observes but does not control	a condition of the experiment that is under the control of the researcher

3

Gender Issues

Introduction

This chapter examines the complex process whereby our maleness and femaleness are determined and the extent to which they influence our social and sexual behavior. Both the biological and social-learning aspects of gender-identity formation are discussed as well as some of the variations that may occur as a result of abnormal prenatal differentiation. Finally, the authors explore a number of gender-based societal stereotypes and how these may inhibit our growth and development.

Objectives

After studying this chapter, you should be able to:

1. Define the key terms and concepts listed in the "flash card" section of the study guide.

2. Distinguish between gender identity and gender role and provide examples of each.

3. List and describe the six different levels of gender-identity formation from a biological perspective.

4. Discuss some of the abnormalities that may occur in prenatal sex differentiation, making specific reference to the following:
   a. androgen insensitivity syndrome
   b. fetally androgenized females
   c. DHT-deficient males

5. Explain how social-learning factors influence gender-identity formation.

6. Define the interactional model of gender-identity formation.

7. Discuss transsexualism, making specific references to the following:
   a. the characteristics of transsexualism
   b. various theoretical explanations regarding what causes gender dysphoria
   c. treatment options for people with gender dysphoria
   d. the various phases involved in sex reassignment surgery
   e. what studies have revealed regarding post-operative follow-up of the lives of transsexuals

8. Define and give examples of gender-based stereotypes.

9. Explain how parents, peers, schools, textbooks, television and religion contribute to the socialization of gender roles, making reference to relevant research.

10. List and describe five gender-role assumptions and explain how these stereotypes affect sexual attitudes and behaviors in men and women.

11. Define the term "androgyny" and discuss research comparing androgynous individuals to people who are gender-typed masculine or feminine.

Key Terms and Concepts

"Flash cards" listing key terms and concepts on one side and their corresponding definitions and explanations on the other side are provided at the end of the chapter.

Chapter Overview With Fill-Ins

After reading each of the major sections in the chapter, check your retention by **mentally** filling in each of the blanks in the corresponding sections below. Cover the answers in the margin as you go along, and write the answers in the space provided only when you are doing your final review.

Male and Female, Masculine and Feminine

Sex

genetic

anatomical

Gender

Gender-identity

role

_____ refers to our biological maleness or femaleness. There are two aspects of biological sex: _____ sex, which is determined by our sex chromosomes, and _____ sex, the obvious physical differences between males and females. _____ refers to the psychosocial meanings added to our biological maleness or femaleness. _____ _____ refers to our subjective sense of being male or female, while gender _____ refers to the attitudes and behaviors that are appropriate in a specific culture for people of a particular sex.

Gender-Identity Formation

biological

six

gonadal

brain

Gender-identity formation involves both _____ and social-learning factors. Our physical maleness or femaleness is the result of processes that occur at _____ different levels of sexual differentiation. These are: chromosomal sex, _____ sex, hormonal sex, sex of the internal reproductive structures, sex of the external genitals, and sex differentiation of the _____.

sperm

ovum

male

female

Y

At the first level of differentiation, our biological sex is determined by the chromosomal makeup of the _____ (male reproductive cell) which fertilizes an _____ (female reproductive cell). Fertilization of the ovum by a Y-bearing sperm produces an XY combination, resulting in a _____ child. Fertilization by an X-bearing sperm results in an XX combination and a _____ child. The _____ chromosome must be present to ensure the complete development of internal and external male sex organs.

gonads

six

During the first few weeks of prenatal development, the _____ - structures that will become the reproductive organs - are the same in males and females. Differentiation begins about _____ weeks after conception.

estrogens
androgens
testosterone
testes

female

At this point, the hormones become the critical factor in further differentiation. The ovaries produce two classes of hormones: _____ and progestational compounds. The primary hormone products of the testes are the _____, the most important of which is _____. The appropriate amount of androgens, secreted by the _____, stimulates the development of male structures. In the absence of male hormones, the fetus develops _____ structures.

Wolffian

Müllerian-inhibiting

female

female

At about eight weeks after conception, internal reproductive structures begin to differentiate from two paired internal duct systems, the Müllerian ducts and the _____ ducts. If the embryo is chromosomally male, and if the gonads have previously differentiated into testes, the testes will begin secreting two substances: _____-_____ substance, which causes the Müllerian ducts to shrink rather than develop into _____ structures; and androgens (testosterone), which stimulate the development of the Wolffian ducts into internal male reproductive structures. If the Müllerian ducts are not suppressed by MIS and testosterone, they develop into internal _____ structures.

dihydrotestosterone

testosterone

When testosterone begins circulating in the bloodstream of males, it is converted in some tissues into a hormone called _____ which causes the tissues to differentiate into male genitals. In the absence of _____ , the external female genitals evolve.

brains
prenatal

hypothalamus;
cerebral

verbal

psychosocial

Research suggests that important functional and structural differences exist in the _____ of human males and females that result in part from _____ sex differentiation. These differences appear to involve at least two major brain areas: the _____, and the left and right _____ hemispheres. Sex differences in the structure of the two cerebral hemispheres suggest a possible biological basis for differences in the _____ and spatial abilities of males and females. However, other theorists argue that these differences are largely due to _____ factors.

androgen; fetally
males

Abnormal prenatal development may occur for a variety of reasons. Three examples of abnormal prenatal differentiation are: _____ insensitivity syndrome; _____ androgynized females; and DHT-deficient _____.

social-learning

In addition to the biological explanation for the formation of gender identity, there is also the _____-_____ interpretation that suggests that gender identity results from social and cultural models and influences we are exposed to during our early development. There are numerous studies to support the fact that in

differently

our culture boys and girls are treated _____ from the moment they are born. Anthropological studies of other cultures also

learning
New Guinea

support the social-_____ interpretation. For example, Margaret Mead studied three societies in _____ _____, two of which demonstrated minimal differences

Tchambuli

between the sexes, while another, the _____, demonstrated a reversal of our typical masculine and feminine roles. The research of

John Money

_____ _____ and his colleagues has also provided evidence in support of the social-learning perspective.

interactional

Today almost all researchers and theorists support the _____ model of gender-identity formation, which acknowledges both biology and experience in the development of gender identity.

transsexual
gender dysphoria
normal

A person whose gender identity is opposite to his or her biological sex is called a _____; this condition is also referred to as _____ _____. For the most part, these individuals are biologically _____, and as yet there is no clear understanding of what causes transsexualism. There are several steps involved for the individual who wants to pursue sex change

interviews
identity
hormone

surgery: extensive screening _____; living a lifestyle consistent with their gender _____ (dress and behavior patterns); _____ therapy; and finally, the surgical procedure itself. Although post-operative follow-ups of transsexuals' lives have revealed contradictory findings, more recent findings have

positive

indicated a much higher incidence of _____ outcomes.

Gender Roles

stereotype

A _____ is a generalized notion of what a person is like based only on the person's sex, race, religion, etc. Common gender-

men

based stereotypes regarding _____ in our culture state that they are aggressive, logical, unemotional, independent, dominant, competitive, etc., while gender stereotypes concerning

women

_____ state that they are passive, illogical, emotional, dependent, subordinate, and nurturing.

Socialization
Parents

_____ is the process by which individuals learn society's expectations for behavior. _____ play a strong role in the socialization of gender roles in their children by the behaviors they encourage or discourage, the roles they model, and how they interact with their children on the basis of their sex. In addition to parents, the

peer group

_____ _____ is influential in the socialization of gender roles, particularly during the adolescent years.

Schools _____ may also play a strong role in the socialization of
gender roles. Teachers often respond to students on the basis of their

stereotypes; text-
books
own _____ about males and females. The _____
used in schools have also tended to perpetuate gender-role

Television
religion
stereotypes. _____ is another powerful agent of gender role
socialization, and organized _____ also influences views
regarding gender roles.

The authors discuss several gender-role assumptions that are common
in our society and the effects that these assumptions have on our
intimate relationships with one another. One assumption, women as

undersexed; over-
sexed
_____, men as _____, makes it difficult for women
to openly acknowledge their sexual interest for fear of being labeled
"slut," "sleaze," etc. On the other hand, men who don't behave like sex
machines — always ready, always responsive — may feel inadequate
in their male role. In a second gender-role assumption,

initiators; recipients
men as _____, women as _____, men may feel the
constant burden and pressure to initiate social and sexual interaction,
while women, due to their more passive role, never have
the opportunity to choose, to deal with possible rejection, or to take
control of their social or sexual relationships. The pressure on men to
be sexually knowledgeable and experienced is a result of another

sexperts
gender-role assumption, men as "_____". A woman who
feels she must constantly control her partner's raging sexual lust, and
in the process of doing that may suppress her own sexual feelings, is a

controllers
movers
nurturing; support-
ive
victim of the gender stereotype of women as _____, men as
_____. The last stereotype discussed, men as unemotional
and strong, women as _____ and _____, makes
it difficult for men to develop emotionally satisfying relationships; and
furthermore, women may find their designated role rather tiresome,
especially when there is little reciprocity.

Androgyny _____ is a term used to describe flexibility in gender roles.

Matching

Match each term below with the appropriate numbered description. Note that each term below may be used more than once, and there may be more than one term for each description.

    a.   transvestites
    b.   fetally androgenized females
    c.   individuals with androgen-insensitivity syndrome
    d.   DHT-deficient males
    e.   transsexuals

_____1.   the problem is usually discovered when menstruation fails to commence

_____2.   their external genitals begin to appear at puberty

_____3.   individuals who cross dress for the purpose of sexual arousal

_____4.   an example of abnormal prenatal differentiation

_____5.   chromosomally normal; as infants, external genitals resemble those of a male to
            varying degrees

_____6.   prenatal exposure to excessive amounts of male hormones may precipitate this
            condition

_____7.   these individuals experience gender dysphoria

_____8.   there is currently no definitive explanation for what causes this condition

_____9.   social-learning factors appear to be significant in determining how these
            individuals behave

_____10.   sociocultural factors appear to facilitate gender identity change in these
            individuals at puberty

Short Answer

1.   Distinguish between the terms "sex" and "gender." (Obj. #1)

2.   Distinguish between the terms "gender identity" and "gender role." (Obj. #2)

3.   List the six different levels of sexual differentiation. (Obj. #3)

4. Briefly explain what occurs at the level of chromosomal sex differentiation under normal conditions. (Obj. #3)

5. What is the function of SRY and DHT? (Obj. #1, 3)

6. Identify the following: (Obj. #1)

    a. endocrine system

    b. estrogens

    c. progestational compounds

    d. androgens

7. Briefly describe how the Müllerian and the Wolffian ducts may develop into internal female or male structures. (Obj. #3)

8. Name the homologous male equivalents to each of the following: clitoris, labia minora, labia majora, ovaries, Skene's ducts, and Bartholin's glands. (Obj. #3)

9. Describe the consequences of prenatal sex differentiation of the hypothalamus for both males and females. (Obj. #3)

10. What do we know about sex differences in the cerebral hemispheres of the brain? (Obj. #3)

11. What are the effects of androgen insensitivity syndrome? (Obj. #4a)

12. In females who are fetally androgenized, what are two possible sources of the androgen? (Obj. #4b)

13. What are the effects of excessive prenatal androgen exposure in females? (Obj. #4b)

14. Summarize Money and Ehrhardt's findings (1972) regarding fetally androgenized females. (Obj. #4b)

15. When males are DHT-deficient, what is the result? (Obj. #4c)

16. What is a possible explanation for why the individuals in the Dominican study of DHT-deficient males converted to a male identity? (Obj. #4c)

17. How may the apparent inconsistencies in the results of the studies of hormone-based differentiation errors be explained? (Obj. #4c, 5, 6)

18. According to one study, how soon after birth may parents communicate to their children their preconceived ideas of how boys and girls differ? (Obj. #5)

19. Describe the gender-role behaviors of males and females in the following New Guinea cultures studied by Margaret Mead. (Obj. #5)

    a. Mundugumor

    b. Arapesh

    c. Tchambuli

20. According to Money's research, what kind of gender identity did children develop whose assigned sex did not match their chromosomal sex? (Obj. #5)

21. Describe the interactional model of gender identity. (Obj. #6)

22. How is transvestism different from transsexualism? (Obj. #7a)

23. Briefly discuss two theories of the causes of transsexualism. (Obj. #7b)

24. List the stages an individual must go through in order to have a sex change. (Obj. #7d)

25. Summarize the recent research findings on the postoperative follow-up of transsexuals' lives. (Obj. #7e)

26. List some common gender-role stereotypes for men and women. (Obj. #8)

27. Briefly describe how each of the following contribute to gender-role socialization. (Obj. #9)
    a.   parents

    b.   peers

    c.   schools

d.   television

e.   religion

28. According to various researchers, how may parents interact differently with their little
    boys and little girls? (Obj. #9)

29. Briefly summarize how the following gender-role assumptions may limit men and women
    regarding their social and sexual behavior. (Obj. #10)

    a.   women as undersexed, men as oversexed

    b.   men as initiators, women as recipients

    c.   men as "sexperts"

    d.   women as controllers, men as movers

    e.   men as unemotional and strong, women as nurturing and supportive

30. Define "androgyny." (Obj. #11)

31. Summarize research findings regarding how androgynous people tend to differ from
    people who are strongly gender-typed. (Obj. #11)

Multiple Choice

Select the best alternative. Check your answers with the answer key at the end of the chapter.

1. Gender refers to
    a. having characteristics of both sexes.
    b. our biological maleness or femaleness.
    c. flexibility in male/female roles.
    d. the psychosocial concept of our maleness or femaleness.

2. _____ refers to our own personal, subjective sense that "I am a male" or "I am a female."
    a. Gender
    b. Gender assumptions
    c. Gender identity
    d. Gender role

3. In the 1950s, assuming that an American man would work to support his family while his wife would stay home to care for their children would be an example of
    a. gender identity.
    b. gender dysphoria.
    c. gender role expectations.
    d. androgyny.

4. Biological sex is determined by the _____ present in the reproductive cells at the moment of conception.
    a. autosomes
    b. chromosomes
    c. hormones
    d. DHT

5. To ensure the complete development of external male sex organs, _____ must be present.
    a. the X chromosome
    b. the Y chromosome
    c. DHT
    d. the primary autosome

6. _____ appears to be responsible for initiating the development of male gonads.
    a. The testis-determining gene (SRY)
    b. Androgen
    c. Estrogen
    d. Dihydrotestosterone (DHT)

7. The structures that contain the future reproductive cells are called
    a. gonads.
    b. bipotential chromosomes.
    c. genes.
    d. Müllerian ducts.

8. Hormones stimulate the development of the Wolffian ducts into
    a. internal female reproductive structures.
    b. internal male reproductive structures.
    c. external female sexual structures.
    d. external male sexual structures.

9. The labia minora in the female is homologous to the _____ of the male.
   a. shaft of the penis
   b. scrotal sac
   c. prostate gland
   d. glans of the penis

10. In a female-differentiated hypothalamus, sex hormones are released
    a. at random.
    b. steadily.
    c. in a cyclic fashion.
    d. once every three months.

11. Money's study of genetic males with androgen-insensitivity syndrome who were raised as girls revealed that most of them were
    a. interested in traditionally masculine activities.
    b. interested in traditionally feminine activities.
    c. androgynous in their attitudes and behavior.
    d. interested in changing their sex.

12. _____ helps regulate the menstrual cycle and stimulates development of the uterine lining in preparation for pregnancy.
    a. Estrogen
    b. Progesterone
    c. Androgen
    d. Müllerian-inhibiting substance

13. Which of the following **least** supports the importance of social-learning factors in gender identity?
    a. Margaret Mead's research on cultures in New Guinea
    b. John Money's research on children whose assigned sex didn't match their chromosomal sex
    c. Rubin's research on how parents respond to their newborn babies
    d. Money's research on fetally androgenized females

14. Androgen insensitivity syndrome is the result of
    a. a rare genetic defect.
    b. a chromosomal abnormality.
    c. steroid abuse.
    d. gender dysphasia.

15. A person whose gender identity is opposite to his or her biological sex is called a/an
    a. transvestite.
    b. bisexual.
    c. androgynous person.
    d. transsexual.

16. Which of the following statements regarding transsexualism is **true**?
    a. Most transsexuals have the appropriate XX or XY chromosomes.
    b. There are currently more men than women requesting sex change surgery.
    c. Transsexualism is caused by a prenatal hormonal imbalance.
    d. Most transsexuals have malformed or nonexistent internal reproductive structures.

17. **Most** female-to-male transsexuals would desire a sexual relationship with a
    a. lesbian.
    b. heterosexual woman.
    c. gay man.
    d. heterosexual man.

18. Which of the following statements regarding male-to-female transsexuals is **false**?
    a. Intercourse is not possible after surgery.
    b. Surgical procedures for these individuals are more effective than female to male transsexuals.
    c. Many report postsurgical capacity to experience arousal and orgasm.
    d. All of the above.

19. The majority of researchers today support a _____ explanation for how gender identity is acquired.
    a. biological
    b. social learning
    c. biological and social learning
    d. sociobiological

20. Which of the following statements regarding stereotypes is **false**?
    a. Stereotypes do not take individuality into account.
    b. There is strong evidence that gender-role stereotypes are pervasive in our culture.
    c. "Women are aggressive" is an example of a stereotype.
    d. Research suggests that women may be less entrenched in gender-role stereotypes than men.

21. The process whereby society conveys behavioral expectations to the individual is called
    a. imprinting.
    b. gender identification.
    c. stereotyping.
    d. socialization.

22. Which of the following is **not** one of the gender-role assumptions discussed by the authors?
    a. women as controllers, men as movers
    b. women as undersexed, men as oversexed
    c. women as initiators, men as recipients
    d. women as nurturing, men as unemotional

23. A man feels pressure to demonstrate sexual interest in a woman early on in the relationship, in spite of his personal inclination to take his time and go more slowly. This man is a victim of which of the following gender-role assumptions?
    a. women as undersexed, men as oversexed
    b. men as "sexperts"
    c. women as controllers, men as movers
    d. men as unemotional and strong, women as nurturing and supportive

24. Androgyny refers to
    a. flexibility in gender role.
    b. an asexual orientation.
    c. a condition where people have both male and female genitalia.
    d. gender dysphoria.

25. Research on androgyny has demonstrated that
    a. androgynous males demonstrate better overall emotional adjustment than masculine-typed males.
    b. androgynous college professors exhibit less job-related stress than those who are more gender-typed.
    c. some college students associate the presence of masculine personality characteristics with being versatile more than they do with androgynous traits.
    d. gender-typed individuals have more positive attitudes toward sexuality than androgynous individuals.

Insight and Application

1. What messages did you receive as you were growing up regarding specific expectations or behaviors appropriate to your gender? Think in terms of academic/career expectations, social and sexual behavior, emphasis on competition (in sports or in school), household chores required of you, recreational activities in which you participated, etc.

2. If you had siblings of the other sex, how were they treated differently, if at all? Think in terms of household chores required of you, curfew limits, messages regarding appropriate social or sexual behavior, educational and/or career goals, etc.

3. You have seen how your father/mother has lived his/her life as a man/woman. What would you do differently? What would you want to remain the same? Cite specific examples.

4. How do you feel that your life would be different, if at all, if you were a member of the other sex? Think in terms of your recreational interests, education, work/career interests, relationship involvement, parenting experiences, etc. Do you think the pressures, fears, and anxieties would be the same?

5. How do you view your current relationships with men and women? Do you perceive your behavior as more gender-typed or more androgynous? Give specific examples. Do you have attitudes or behaviors regarding gender roles that you would like to change? If so, what are they?

Matching Answers

1. c	2. d	3. a	4. b–d	5. b	6. b	7. e	8. e
9. c	10. d						

Multiple Choice Answers

1. d	2. c	3. c	4. b	5. c	6. a	7. a	8. b
9. a	10. c	11. b	12. b	13. d	14. a	15. d	16. a
17. b	18. a	19. c	20. c	21. d	22. c	23. a	24. a
25. c							

Tchambuli of New Guinea	**sex**
gender	**gender identity**
gender role (sex role)	**chromosomal sex**
gonadal sex	**hormonal sex**
endocrine system	**estrogens**

our biological maleness or femaleness, two aspects of which are genetic sex (determined by sex chromosomes) and anatomical sex (the physical differences between males and females)	a society in which traditional masculine and feminine behavior patterns are complete opposites of those that characterize American society
how one psychologically perceives oneself as being either male or female	the psychosocial aspects of being masculine or feminine
the first level of sex differentiation, whereby our biological sex is determined by the sex chromosomes (XX or XY) present in the reproductive cells at the moment of conception	a collection of attitudes and behaviors that are considered normal and appropriate in a specific culture for people of a particular sex
the third level of sex differentiation, whereby the testes secrete androgens, causing development of male sex structures. Without androgens, female structures develop.	the second level of sex differentiation, whereby the presence of TDF triggers the transformation of the gonads into testes, and the absence of TDF causes the gonads to develop into ovaries
ovarian hormones, the most important of which is estradiol, which influence the development of female sex characteristics and help regulate the menstrual cycle	several ductless glands located throughout the body that produce hormones. The major endocrine glands include the pituitary, gonads, thyroid, parathyroids, adrenals and pancreas.

Chapter 3 53

progestational compounds | androgens

Müllerian ducts | Wolffian ducts

Müllerian inhibiting substance (MIS) | dihydrotestosterone (DHT)

hypothalamus | cerebral hemispheres

sperm | ovum

the primary hormone products of the testes, most importantly testosterone, which influences both the development of male physical sexual characteristics and sexual motivation	ovarian hormones, most importantly progesterone, which help regulate the menstrual cycle and stimulate the development of the uterine lining in preparation for pregnancy
the internal duct system of the embryo that develops into male reproductive organs	a pair of ducts in the embryo that develop into female reproductive organs
a hormone in the fetal bloodstream that stimulates the labioscrotal swelling to become the scrotum, and the genital tubercle and genital folds to differentiate into the penis	a substance secreted by the fetal testes that causes the Müllerian ducts to shrink rather than develop into internal female structures
the left and right sides of the cerebrum, the largest part of the brain	a brain structure that plays a major role in controlling the production of sex hormones and the regulation of fertility and menstrual cycles through its interaction with the pituitary gland
female reproductive cell	male reproductive cell

fetally androgenized females	**androgen insensitivity syndrome**
DHT-deficient males	**interactional model**
transsexual	**gender dysphoria**
stereotypes	**socialization**
gender assumptions	**androgyny**

a condition resulting from a genetic defect that causes chromosomally normal males to be insensitive to the action of testosterone and other androgens	chromosomally normal females exposed to excessive levels of androgens during prenatal sex differentiation, resulting in external genitals resembling those of male infants to varying degrees
the perspective whereby gender identity is considered to be a result of both biological and social learning factors	a genetic disorder that prevents conversion of testosterone into dihydro-testosterone (DHT), a hormone that is necessary for normal development of male external genitals
another term for transsexualism, the condition where an individual feels trapped in the body of the wrong sex	a person whose gender identity is opposite to his or her biological sex
the process whereby society conveys behavioral expectations to the individual	a generalized notion of what a person is like based only on that person's sex, religion, ethnic background or similar criterion
possessing behavioral characteristics of both sexes; also used to describe gender role flexibility	beliefs regarding how people are likely to behave, based on their maleness or femaleness

SRY **gonads**

the reproductive organs
(testes in men and ovaries in
women)

the maleness (testis
determining) gene

4

Female Sexual Anatomy and Physiology

Introduction

Becoming more aware of our bodies and how they function helps us in taking a more active, responsible role in our health care, as well as feeling more comfortable with ourselves and with our partners. This chapter deals with female sexual and reproductive structures and functions, with an emphasis on relevant health care concerns.

Objectives

After studying this chapter, you should be able to:

1. List the reasons for doing a genital self-exam.

2. Briefly describe the process of doing a genital self-exam.

3. Define the terms "gynecology" and "vulva".

4. Identify and briefly describe the following structures of the vulva:
    a. mons veneris
    b. labia majora
    c. labia minora
    d. clitoris
    e. vestibule
    f. urethral opening
    g. introitus and hymen
    h. perineum

5. Discuss the following in reference to urinary tract infections:
    a. incidence of
    b. causes of
    c. symptoms of
    d. preventative measures

6. Identify the location, structure, and function of the following:
    a. vestibular bulbs
    b. Bartholin's glands
    c. vagina
    d. cervix
    e. uterus
    f. fallopian tubes
    g. ovaries

7. Explain when and for what purpose Kegel exercises were developed.

8. Describe the steps involved in practicing Kegel exercises, and explain the benefits of doing these exercises.

9. Discuss the source and function of vaginal lubrication.

10. List several factors that may inhibit vaginal lubrication, and explain how those situations might be remedied.

11. Identify the location and function of the Grafenberg spot.

12. Describe what function vaginal secretions serve.

13. Describe the chemical balance of the vagina, and discuss ways in which this balance may be altered.

14. Define vaginitis and discuss the following in relation to it:
    a. symptoms
    b. factors increasing the susceptibility to vaginitis
    c. ways to help prevent vaginitis

15. Discuss the following in relation to a Pap smear:
    a. what purpose it serves
    b. how it is done
    c. how often it should be done
    d. what steps may be taken if the results of a Pap smear are not normal

16. Describe which women may be at higher risk of cervical cancer, and discuss available treatment options for women who receive this diagnosis.

17. Explain how an ectopic pregnancy may occur, the incidence of ectopic pregnancy and discuss who is most susceptible.

18. Define the following terms:
    a. hysterectomy
    b. oophorectomy

19. Describe how a hysterectomy may affect a woman sexually, physically and emotionally.

20. Discuss the following in relationship to the breasts:
    a. structure of
    b. self-exam — when, how and why
    c. mammography
    d. three types of breast lumps that may occur
    e. treatment alternatives; options available for women with breast cancer
    f. high and low risk factors for breast cancer

21. Discuss the following in regard to menstruation:
    a. attitudes toward it in American society
    b. when it typically begins
    c. the extent to which young men and women are informed about it
    d. the length of the menstrual cycle
    e. menstrual synchrony
    f. the relationship among the hypothalamus, pituitary gland and adrenal glands
    g. the proliferative, secretory and menstrual phases of the menstrual cycle
    h. sexual activity and the menstrual cycle
    i. premenstrual syndrome
    j. primary and secondary dysmenorrhea
    k. primary and secondary amenorrhea
    l. toxic shock syndrome
    m. self-help for menstrual problems

22. Describe three types of genital mutilation, the reasons for doing them, the health consequences that may result and the current controversy that surrounds it.

23. Explain how some other cultures have viewed menstruation, including American culture.

Key Terms and Concepts

"Flash cards" listing key terms and concepts on one side and their corresponding definitions and explanations on the other side are provided at the end of the chapter.

Chapter Overview With Fill-Ins

Genital Self-Exam

Gynecology

medical

_____ is the medical specialty for female sexual and reproductive anatomy. Genital self-exam serves at least two purposes: to help women learn about and feel more comfortable with themselves, and to augment routine _____ care.

The Vulva

vulva
mons veneris
labia majora
labia minora

glans
vestibule

urethra

The _____ refers to the female external genital structures. This includes the _____ _____, which is the area covering the pubic bone; the _____ _____, or large outer lips; the _____ _____, or inner lips that join at the prepuce, or clitoral hood; the clitoris, which is composed of the external shaft and _____, and the internal crura; the _____ which is the area of the vulva inside the labia minora that includes the urinary and vaginal openings; and the _____, which is the short tube connecting the bladder to the urinary opening.

hymen
introitus; perineum

The _____ is a fold of tissue partially covering the _____, or vaginal opening. The _____ is the smooth area of skin located between the introitus and the anus.

Underlying Structures

vestibular bulbs

Bartholin's

The _____ _____ are located on each side of the vagina, and they fill with blood during sexual arousal, causing the vagina to increase in length. The _____ glands are located on each side of the vaginal opening, and they typically produce a drop or two of fluid just prior to orgasm.

Kegel

urination
genital

Pelvic floor muscles can be strengthened by doing _____ exercises, which were developed in the early 1950s as a way of help-ing women gain control of _____ after childbirth. An added benefit is that women usually report an increase in _____ sensitivity as a result of practicing these exercises.

Internal Structures

vagina
mucous

vasocongestion

In its nonaroused state, the _____ is three to five inches in length. It contains three layers of tissue: _____, muscle, and fibrous tissue. Vaginal lubrication is the result of _____, the blood engorgement that occurs in the pelvic area.

anterior
glands

The Grafenberg spot is located within the _____ wall of the vagina. It consists of a system of _____ and ducts that surround the urethra, and is believed to be the female counterpart to

prostate gland

the male _____ _____.

cervix

The _____ is the small end of the uterus and is located at the back of the vagina. The opening in the center of the cervix is

os
Pap smear
cryosurgery
biopsy
hysterectomy

called the _____. The screening test for cervical cancer is called the _____ _____, and treatments for cervical cancer include _____ (freezing of tissues), removing malignant tissue by means of a _____, or in more severe cases, a complete _____ (surgical removal of cervix and uterus).

uterus
fallopian tube
zygote
uterus

The _____, or womb, is a thick, pear-shaped organ. Fertilization usually occurs in the _____ _____, and then the united sperm and egg, called the _____, travel down and become implanted in the _____.

uterus
fimbriae

ovary

ectopic pregnancy

The fallopian tubes extend from the _____ into the pelvic cavity. Fringe-like projections called _____ at the outside end of each tube wave the newly released egg inside. Fertilization occurs while the egg is still close to the _____. Sometimes the fertilized egg will implant in some place other than the uterus, a condition known as an _____ _____.

ovaries
ovulation

The _____ are endocrine glands that produce two classes of sex hormones. Egg maturation and release, or _____, occurs as a result of the complex chain of events known as the menstrual cycle.

uterus

Hysterectomy, or removal of the _____, is the most frequently performed major operation in the United States.

The Breasts

secondary
fatty tissue
mammary glands

areola

The breasts are _____ sex characteristics and are composed of _____ _____, which accounts for variation in breast size among women, and _____ _____, which produce breast milk after childbirth. The nipple is the center of the _____, which contains oil-producing glands that help lubricate the nipples during breast feeding.

Mammography

fibroadenomas
malignant

_____ is an X-ray screening test for cancerous breast lumps. Three types of lumps can occur in the breasts. Cysts and _____ are benign tumors, and they are most common. A third type of lump, a _____ tumor, is cancerous.

Menstruation

menarche
21; 35

synchrony

The first menstrual bleeding is called the _____. Cycle length can vary from _____ to _____ days, depending upon the woman. When women who live together develop similar menstrual cycles it is referred to as menstrual _____.

There are three stages in the menstrual cycle: the menstrual phase,

proliferative

the _____ phase, and the the secretory phase. The cycle is regulated by hormonal interaction among the hypothalamus, the

pituitary

_____ gland, the adrenal glands, the ovaries and the uterus. During the menstrual phase, the uterus sheds the

endometrium
reduced
pituitary
FSH
proliferative

_____ , which is discharged as menstrual flow. This discharge is triggered by _____ hormone levels. As the hormone levels fall, the hypothalamus stimulates the _____ to release _____ , and this action initiates the _____ phase of the menstrual cycle. During the proliferative phase of the menstrual cycle, the pituitary gland

follicle-stimulating
Estrogen

increases production of _____-_____ hormone. _____ causes the endometrium to thicken. When the level of ovarian estrogen reaches a peak, the pituitary gland depresses the

luteinizing
14

release of FSH and stimulates the production of _____ hormone. Approximately _____ days before the onset of the next menstrual period, ovulation occurs. In response to the

LH

_____ secreted by the pituitary gland, the mature follicle ruptures and the ovum is released. Some women experience

mittelschmerz

_____, a twinge, pain or cramping in their abdomen at ovulation.

During the secretory phase, the ruptured follicle develops into a

corpus luteum
estrogen

yellowish bump called the _____ _____, which secretes progesterone. Progesterone, combined with _____ produced by the ovaries, causes the endometrium to thicken and

implantation
pituitary

engorge with blood in preparation for _____ of a fertilized egg. If implantation does not occur, the _____ gland responds by shutting down production of FSH and LH. This causes

corpus luteum

the _____ _____ to degenerate, and estrogen and progesterone production decrease. This reduction of hormone levels triggers the sloughing off of the endometrium, initiating the

menstrual

_____ phase once again.

physical
psychological

Premenstrual syndrome refers to the _____ and _____ symptoms that occur before each menstrual period and are severe enough to interfere with some aspects of life. While there is speculation that fluctuations in sex hormones may affect this

unknown

condition, at this time the causes of PMS are _____.

dysmenorrhea

Painful menstruation is called _____. Primary dysmenorrhea occurs during menstruation and is usually caused by the

prostaglandins
menstruation

overproduction of _____. Secondary dysmenorrhea occurs prior to or during _____ and is characterized by lower abdominal pain that can extend to the back and thighs.

amenorrhea
Primary amenorrhea
Secondary
amenorrhea

Another common menstrual difficulty is _____, the absence of menstruation. _____ _____ is the failure to begin to menstruate at puberty. _____ _____ involves the disruption of an established menstrual cycle, with the absence of menstruation for three months or more.

Toxic shock
syndrome

superabsorbent

_____ _____ _____ is a rare disease that is associated with the use of tampons and is most likely to occur in menstruating women. Using sanitary napkins instead of tampons or using regular instead of _____ tampons have been suggested to help prevent this condition.

Identification

Label the various parts of the female sexual anatomy indicated below. Check your answers with the key at the end of the chapter.

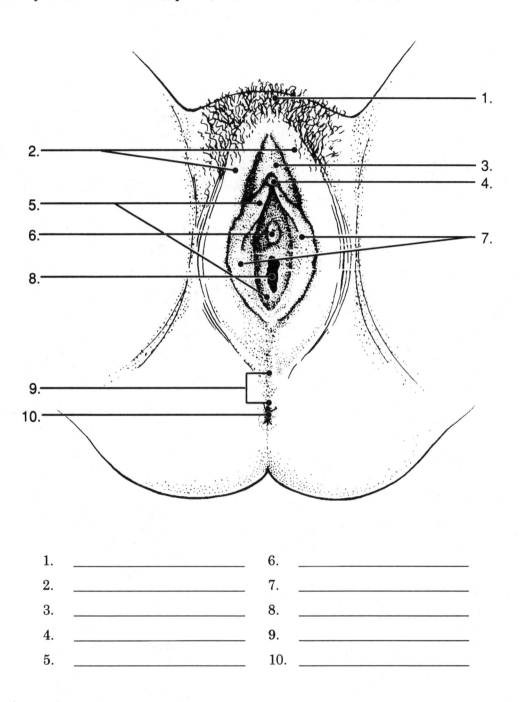

1. _____   6. _____
2. _____   7. _____
3. _____   8. _____
4. _____   9. _____
5. _____   10. _____

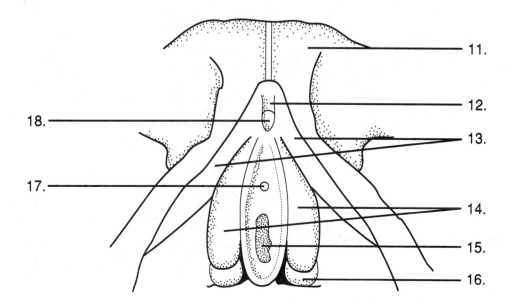

11. _____

12. _____

13. _____

14. _____

15. _____

16. _____

17. _____

18. _____

31. _____
30. _____
29. _____
28. _____
27. _____
26. _____

19. _____
20. _____
21. _____
22. _____
23. _____
24. _____
25. _____
32. _____

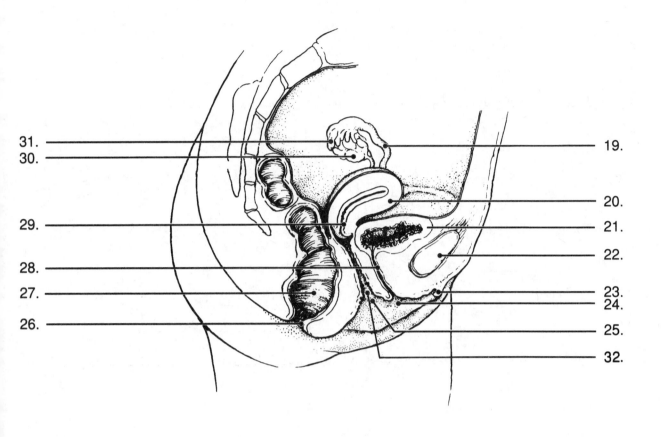

19.	_____	26.	_____
20.	_____	27.	_____
21.	_____	28.	_____
22.	_____	29.	_____
23.	_____	30.	_____
24.	_____	31.	_____
25.	_____	32.	_____

Short Answer

1. List some of the reasons for doing a genital self-exam. (Obj. #1)

2. List and briefly describe the structures of the vulva. (Obj. #4a–h)

3. Explain the structure of the clitoris. (Obj. #4d)

4. What role does the clitoris play in sexual arousal and orgasm? (Obj. #4d)

5. Describe how nerves are distributed in the vagina. (Obj. #6c)

6. List the factors that may contribute to urinary infections in women. (Obj. #5b)

7. What are some symptoms of urinary tract infections? (Obj. #5c)

8. List six precautions that may help prevent urinary tract infections. (Obj. #5d)

9. What is the function and significance of the hymen? (Obj. #4g)

10. What is an imperforate hymen? How is this condition treated? (Obj. #4g)

11. What changes in the vestibular bulbs and the Bartholin's glands occur during sexual arousal? (Obj. #6a, b)

12. What are the benefits of Kegel exercises? (Obj. #8)

13. List and describe the three layers of vaginal tissue. (Obj. #6c)

14. Describe the source of vaginal lubrication during sexual arousal. (Obj. #9)

15. List the two functions of vaginal lubrication. (Obj. #9)

16. What may inhibit vaginal lubrication? (Obj. #10)

17. What is the Grafenberg spot and where is it located? (Obj. #11)

18. Describe the natural chemical balance of the vagina and how douching may affect this. (Obj. #13)

19. List six factors that increase susceptibility to vaginitis. (Obj. #14b)

20. List six ways that vaginitis might be prevented. (Obj. #14c)

21. Briefly describe the procedure for a Pap smear. How frequently should this procedure be done?(Obj. #15b, c)

22. Identify three treatments for cervical cancer. (Obj. #16)

23. List four factors that increase the risk of developing cervical cancer. (Obj. #16)

24. Briefly describe the structure of the uterus. (Obj. #6e)

25. Where does fertilization occur? (Obj. #6f)

26. What is an ectopic pregnancy? Why is it difficult to diagnose? (Obj. #17)

27. Briefly explain the structure and function of the ovaries. (Obj. #6g)

28. Describe the effects of hysterectomy on a woman's sexuality. (Obj. #19)

29. What accounts for the difference in size in women's breasts? (Obj. #20a)

30. When is the best time to do a breast self-exam? (Obj. #20b)

31. What is a mammogram and when is it indicated? (Obj. #20c)

32. List and describe the three types of breast lumps. (Obj. #20d)

33. List several factors that may minimize fibrocystic breast disease. (Obj. #20d)

34. Name at least eight high risk factors for breast cancer. (Obj. #20f)

35. List several forms of treatment for breast cancer. (Obj. #20d)

36. To what does the timing of menarche appear to be related? (Obj. #21b)

37. Identify two factors which may trigger menstrual synchrony. (Obj. #21e)

38. Describe the role of the hypothalamus in the menstrual cycle. (Obj. #21f)

39. Briefly explain what occurs in each of the following phases of the menstrual cycle. (Obj. #21g)

    a.   menstrual phase

    b.   proliferative phase

    c.   secretory phase

40. How does our culture view intercourse during menstruation? (Obj. #21a)

41. List several examples that indicate how other cultures have viewed menstruation. (Obj. #23)

42. What is the relationship between menstrual cycle changes and sexual behavior? (Obj. #21h)

43. Define premenstrual syndrome. What causes it and how is it treated? (Obj. #21i)

44. What is the difference between primary and secondary dysmenorrhea? (Obj. #21j)

45. What type of disorder may cause secondary amenorrhea? (Obj. #21k)

46. Twenty percent of all TSS cases are nonmenstrual. In what situations do these cases occur? (Obj. #21l)

47. List five suggestions that may help minimize menstrually-related problems. (Obj. #21m)

48. Name three types of genital mutilation. What are the various rationales for performing these mutilations? (Obj. #22)

49. For couples who make love during a woman's menstrual period, what things need to be taken into consideration? (Obj. #21m)

Multiple Choice

Select the best alternative. Check your answers with the answer key at the end of the chapter.

1. The term for the female external genital structures is the
    a. vestibule.
    b. vagina.
    c. vulva.
    d. mons veneris.

2. Which of the following statements regarding the labia minora is **false**?
    a. They are hairless.
    b. They are surrounded by the labia majora.
    c. They have nerve endings and fatty tissue similar to that of the mons.
    d. They join at the prepuce over the clitoris.

3. The clitoris
    a. is comprised of the external shaft and glans, and internal crura.
    b. has several different reproductive and sexual functions.
    c. is located in the vestibule.
    d. all of the above.

4. The formation of _____ can be prevented by drawing back the hood while washing the vulva.
    a. Bartholin's glands secretions
    b. smegma
    c. venereal discharge
    d. clitoral adhesions

5. Smegma
    a. is released from the Bartholin's glands.
    b. may accumulate in the urethra.
    c. can be surgically removed by a physician if necessary.
    d. may cause pain during sexual activity if allowed to accumulate.

6. The _____ is the short tube connecting the bladder to the urinary opening.
    a. introitus
    b. urethra
    c. vestibular bulb
    d. vagina

7. A (an) _____ _____ completely covers the vaginal opening.
    a. introital membrane
    b. perineal adhesion
    c. imperforate hymen
    d. clitoral transudate

8. The _____ _____ engorge with blood during sexual arousal, causing the vagina to increase in length.
    a. Bartholin's glands
    b. Kegel muscles
    c. labia majora
    d. vestibular bulbs

9. Which of the following is **not** part of the vulva?
    a. clitoris
    b. labia minora
    c. mons veneris
    d. pelvic floor muscles

10. _____ is one option for treating cervical cancer in which the cancerous cells are removed from the cervix by freezing the tissue.
    a. Cryosurgery
    b. Laparoscopy
    c. Hysterotomy
    d. Colposcopy

11. The vagina
    a. contains mucous, muscle and fibrous tissue.
    b. is approximately twelve inches long in its nonaroused state.
    c. has a high concentration of nerve endings in the back near the cervix.
    d. is a part of the vulva.

12. Vaginal lubrication
    a. helps to make the chemical balance of the vagina more acidic.
    b. occurs within five to ten minutes after effective stimulation begins.
    c. is derived primarily from the Bartholin's glands.
    d. prepares the vagina for entry of the penis.

13. Which of the following statements regarding the Grafenberg spot is **false**?
    a. It consists of a system of glands and ducts that surround the perineum.
    b. It can be stimulated through the anterior wall of the vagina
    c. It is believed to be the female counterpart of the male prostate gland.
    d. Some women ejaculate following Grafenberg spot stimulation.

14. Which of the following may increase susceptibility to vaginitis?
    a. a high protein diet
    b. using a sterile lubricant during intercourse
    c. wearing cotton underwear
    d. using antibiotics

15. Which of the following may help prevent urinary tract infections?
    a. having a woman's partner wash hands and genitals before sexual contact
    b. wiping from back to front after urination and defecation
    c. using intercourse positions that gently massage the urethral wall
    d. drinking coffee or tea on a regular basis

16. The _____ is located at the back of the vagina and contains mucous-secreting glands.
    a. Grafenberg spot
    b. cervix
    c. endometrium
    d. perineum

17. Which of the following statements regarding the cervix is **false**?
    a. It is located at the back of the vagina.
    b. The opening to the cervix is called the os.
    c. It contains many nerve endings which make it sensitive to touch.
    d. Cells are removed from the cervix when a Pap smear is taken.

18. A woman who has had genital warts as well as a large number of sexual partners may be at increased risk for developing
    a. fibroadenomas.
    b. cervical cancer.
    c. endometriosis.
    d. clitoral adhesions.

19. Cryosurgery, biopsy and hysterectomy are all treatments for
    a. fibroadenomas.
    b. myometriosis.
    c. cervical cancer.
    d. cystitis.

20. Increased risk of cervical cancer has been associated with all of the following **except**
    a. high-fat diet.
    b. smoking cigarettes.
    c. having a husband who has occupational contact with toxic materials.
    d. having had genital warts.

21. Which of the following statements regarding the uterus is **false**?
    a. It is suspended in the pelvic cavity by ligaments.
    b. It is normal for the uterus to be in different positions, depending upon the woman.
    c. The top area of the uterus is called the fundus.
    d. It is the site of an ectopic pregnancy.

22. Which of the following statements regarding hysterectomy is **false**?
    a. It does not affect sexual response.
    b. It refers to the removal of the uterus.
    c. It is the most frequently performed major surgery for women in the United States.
    d. It may be used to treat ovarian or cervical cancer.

23. Which of the following is **not** one of the types of lumps that can occur in the breasts?
    a. cysts
    b. mammary lesions
    c. fibroadenomas
    d. malignant tumors

24. Which of the following places a woman at lower risk for breast cancer?
    a. no pregnancies
    b. menopause after 50
    c. early onset of menstruation (before age 12)
    d. low-fat diet

25. _____ may contribute to benign breast lumps.
    a. Eating red meat
    b. Drinking caffeine
    c. Eating chocolate
    d. all of the above

26. Research indicates that sexual adjustment is better following _____ than _____ mastectomy.
    a. partial; radical
    b. radical; partial
    c. aspirated; radial
    d. radial; aspirated

27. _____ percent of women may develop cancer from flaws in a gene.
    a. One
    b. Five
    c. Eleven
    d. Seventeen

28. Menarche refers to
    a. painful menstruation.
    b. absence of menstruation.
    c. pain at ovulation.
    d. the first menstrual bleeding.

29. Which of the following statements regarding menstruation is **false**?
    a. The average cycle length is 21 to 35 days.
    b. Women who live together may develop similar menstrual cycles.
    c. Time differences in cycle length occur in the phase after ovulation.
    d. The menstrual cycle is divided into three phases.

30. The hypothalamus stimulates the _____ to release hormones.
    a. pituitary gland
    b. corpus luteum
    c. endometrium
    d. fimbriae

31. The corpus luteum
    a. develops during the proliferative phase.
    b. produces the hormone progesterone.
    c. produces FSH.
    d. causes the endometrium to thicken.

32. Which of the following occurs during the proliferative phase of the menstrual cycle?
    a. The corpus luteum develops.
    b. Ovulation occurs.
    c. The amount of estrogen and progesterone are at low levels.
    d. Menstruation occurs.

33. Around ovulation there is an increase and change in cervical mucous secretions due to increased levels of
    a. progesterone.
    b. estrogen.
    c. FSH.
    d. LH.

34. To date, studies regarding the relationship between menstrual cycle changes and sexual behavior
    a. show no significant variations in arousal at different points in the cycle.
    b. indicate an increase in sexual feelings and behavior during ovulation.
    c. indicate an increase in sexual feelings and behavior prior to and during menstruation.
    d. Different studies demonstrated all of the above.

35. Which of the following is **not** a symptom of PMS?
    a. depression
    b. irritability
    c. fever
    d. breast tenderness

36. _____ causes premenstrual syndrome.
    a. Hormonal imbalance.
    b. Vitamin deficiency.
    c. High-stress lifestyle.
    d. There is a lack of consistent data in support of any single cause.

37. The average age of menarche in the United States is _____ years old.
    a. 10.2
    b. 12.8
    c. 14.5
    d. 16.7

38. Overproduction of prostaglandins is usually the cause of
    a. mittelschmerz.
    b. amenorrhea.
    c. primary dysmenorrhea.
    d. secondary dysmenorrhea.

39. Endometriosis refers to
    a. a condition in which cells from the uterine lining implant in the abdominal cavity.
    b. chronic infection of the reproductive organs.
    c. benign tumors present in the uterus.
    d. a type of ovarian cancer.

40. Which of the following statements regarding amenorrhea is **false**?
    a. It may be caused by an imperforate hymen.
    b. It is more common among athletes than the general population.
    c. Primary amenorrhea is a normal condition during pregnancy and breast feeding.
    d. It may be caused by hormonal imbalances or problems with the reproductive organs.

41. Which of the following would **least** likely be associated with toxic shock syndrome?
    a. a menstruating woman using superabsorbent tampons
    b. a woman with venereal warts
    c. a woman with a postoperative wound
    d. a postmenopausal woman

42. Which of the following is **not** a type of female genital mutilation?
    a. clitoridectomy
    b. vulval extraction
    c. circumcision
    d. genital infibulation

Insight and Application

For Women:

1. Have you ever taken the time to leisurely touch and explore your body with the goal of becoming more knowledgeable and accepting of your body and how it functions? If not, why not? In considering the possibility of doing so, what thoughts or feelings come up for you? If you have taken the time to do some body exploration, what was your experience in doing so? What were the benefits? The drawbacks?

2a. Set aside an hour or more when you can have some uninterrupted time alone. Take a leisurely bath or shower, and then select some lotion or massage oil that is pleasing to you. As you apply the lotion or oil to all parts of your body, experiment with different types of pressure, rhythm and touch. Explore your face, neck, arms, hands, breasts, abdomen, buttocks, legs, feet and toes. Notice what kinds of touch your body responds to. Notice what parts of you body you appreciate or find attractive as well as the parts you criticize or find unattractive. How have you developed the relationship you have with your body? Are you comfortable with that relationship or is it something you would like to change? What are your personal standards for health and attractiveness? What do you base them upon? Are they realistic?

b. Using a mirror, touch and explore all the different parts of your vulva: the mons, clitoris, inner and outer lips, urethral and vaginal openings. What words do you use to refer to your vulva or to your vagina? Are you comfortable using these words? In looking at and touching your vulva, what thoughts or feelings come up for you as you do this? What are the sources of these thoughts or feelings? How do they affect your sexual self-esteem, the way in which you care for your body, and your relationship with a partner or potential partner?

c. Is there anything you would like to change regarding the way in which you think or feel about your body, or are you comfortable just as you are? List specific things you do or could do to enhance the acceptance, comfort and pleasure you feel in relationship to your body.

For women and men:

1. In addition to self-exam, how might women be encouraged to become more comfortable with and accepting of their bodies, and more specifically, their genitals? Think in terms of messages and information provided by parents, teachers, the media, health care providers, and partners.

2. A substantial percentage of young men and women receive inadequate information regarding menstruation. What might parents and educators do to change this? Discuss at what age and in what type of format and environment this information would be most effectively transmitted.

3. If you had to do it over again, how would you change or improve the way in which you learned about female genital anatomy? What factors might have contributed to more awareness or comfort with this subject?

Identification Answers

1.	mons veneris	17.	urethral opening
2.	labia majora	18.	clitoral glans
3.	clitoral hood or prepuce	19.	fallopian tubes
4.	clitoris	20.	uterus
5.	vestibule	21.	bladder
6.	urethral opening	22.	pubic bone
7.	labia minora	23.	clitoris
8.	introitus	24.	urethral opening
9.	perineum	25.	introitus
10.	anus	26.	anus
11.	pubic bone	27.	rectum
12.	clitoral shaft	28.	urethra
13.	crura of clitoris	29.	cervix
14.	vestibular bulbs	30.	ovary
15.	introitus	31.	fimbriae
16.	Bartholin's glands	32.	vagina

Multiple Choice Answers

1. c	2. c	3. a	4. b	5. d	6. b	7. c	8. d
9. d	10. a	11. a	12. d	13. a	14. d	15. a	16. b
17. c	18. b	19. c	20. a	21. d	22. a	23. b	24. d
25. d	26. a	27. b	28. d	29. c	30. a	31. b	32. b
33. b	34. d	35. c	36. d	37. b	38. c	39. a	40. c
41. b	42. b						

gynecology	vulva
mons veneris	labia majora
labia minora	prepuce
clitoris	clitoral shaft
clitoral glans	crura

all external female genital structures	the medical specialty for female sexual and reproductive anatomy
the outer lips that extend downward from the mons on each side of the vulva; they surround the labia minora and urethral and vaginal openings	literally "mound of Venus"; refers to the pads of fatty tissue covering the pubic bone
clitoral hood, or skin that covers the clitoris	the inner lips, located within the labia majora, that consist of hairless folds of skin that join at the clitoral hood
the length of the clitoris between the glans and the body	a highly sensitive structure of the female external genitals, the only purpose of which is sexual pleasure
the innermost tips of the cavernous bodies that connect to the pubic bones	the head of the clitoris, richly endowed with nerve endings

smegma	cavernous bodies
vestibule	urethra
introitus	hymen
imperforate hymen	perineum
episiotomy	vestibular bulbs

the two small spongy structures in the shaft of the clitoris that engorge with blood during sexual arousal	genital secretions, skin cells and bacteria which may accumulate under the clitoral hood
the short tube connecting the bladder to the urinary opening, located between the clitoris and the introitus	the area of the vulva inside the labia minora where both the urinary and vaginal openings are located
a fold of tissue partially covering the vaginal opening	the opening of the vagina, located between the urinary opening and the anus
the area of smooth skin between the vaginal opening and the anus	in rare instances, when the hymen completely covers the vaginal opening
two bulbs, one on each side of the vaginal opening, that engorge with blood during sexual arousal	an incision that is sometimes made in the perineum to prevent the ragged tearing of tissues that may occur during the birth process

Bartholin's glands

Kegel exercises

vagina

mucosa

rugae

vasocongestion

Grafenberg spot

douching

vaginitis

speculum

a series of exercises developed by Arnold Kegel that strengthen the muscles underlying the external male or female genitals	two small glands located on each side of the vaginal opening that secrete a few drops of fluid during sexual arousal
the layer of mucous membrane that a woman feels when she inserts a finger inside her vagina	an expandable canal in the female that opens at the vulva and extends about four inches into the pelvis, consisting of mucous, muscle and fibrous tissue
the engorgement of blood vessels in particular body parts in response to sexual arousal	the soft, moist, folded walls of the vagina
rinsing out the vagina with plain water or solutions; usually unnecessary. Excessive douching may result in vaginal irritation.	the system of glands and ducts surrounding the urethra which can be located by stimulating the anterior wall of the vagina below the urethra
an instrument used to hold open the vaginal walls during a gynecological exam	inflammation of the vaginal walls caused by a variety of vaginal infections

cervix	**os**
Pap smear	**uterus**
myometrium	**perimetrium**
endometrium	**fallopian tubes**
fimbriae	**ectopic pregnancy**

the opening in the cervix that leads to the interior of the uterus

the small end of the uterus, located at the back of the vagina

a pear-shaped organ inside the female pelvis, within which the fetus develops

a screening test for cervical cancer

the thin membrane covering the outside of the uterus

the smooth muscle layer of the uterine wall

two four-inch tubes that extend from the uterus in the pelvic cavity where the egg and sperm travel

the tissue that lines the inside of the uterine walls

implantation of a fertilized ovum in a location other than the uterus, usually in the fallopian tubes

fringe-like ends of the fallopian tubes into which the released ovum enters

ovaries	secondary sex characteristics
ovulation	hysterectomy
oophorectomy	breasts
mammary glands	nipple
areola	mammography

the physical characteristics other than genitals that indicate sexual maturity, such as body hair, breasts, and deepened voice	female gonads that produce ova and sex hormones
the surgical removal of the uterus	the release of a mature ovum from the graafian follicle of the ovary
secondary sex characteristics, composed of fatty tissue and mammary glands	the surgical removal of the ovaries
the central pigmented area of the breast, which contains numerous nerve endings. In women, the nipple also contains the milk ducts	milk glands in the female breast
a highly sensitive x-ray test for the detection of breast cancer	the darkened circular area surrounding the nipple of the breast

cysts	**fibroadenomas**
malignant tumor	**menstruation**
menarche	**menstrual synchrony**
proliferative phase	**secretory phase**
menstrual phase	**follicle stimulating hormone (FSH)**

a common, benign, solid, rounded tumor which may occur in the breasts

a common, benign, fluid-filled lump that may occur in the breasts

the sloughing off of the built-up uterine lining that takes place if conception has not occurred

a lump made up of cancer cells that may occur in the breasts

the development of congruent menstrual cycle timing that sometimes occurs among women who live in close proximity

the initial onset of menstrual periods in a young woman

the phase of the menstrual cycle in which the corpus luteum develops and secretes progesterone

the phase of the menstrual cycle in which the ovarian follicles mature

a pituitary hormone secreted by a female during the secretory phase of the menstrual cycle that stimulates the development of ovarian follicles

the phase of the menstrual cycle when menstruation occurs

luteinizing hormone
(LH)

corpus luteum

premenstrual syndrome

dysmenorrhea

prostaglandins

endometriosis

amenorrhea

toxic shock syndrome

ovulation

a yellowish body that forms
on the ovary at the site of
the ruptured graafian follicle
and secretes progesterone

the hormone secreted by
the pituitary gland that
stimulates ovulation
in the female

pain or discomfort that
occurs before or
during menstruation

physical and/or psychological
symptoms that women may
experience before each
menstrual period

a condition in which cells
from the uterine lining
adhere to the fallopian
tubes or other parts of
the abdominal cavity

hormones produced by
body tissues that cause
the muscles of the uterus
to contract

a disease caused by toxins
produced by the bacterium
staphylococcus aureus that
may induce a person to go
into shock, occurring
most commonly in
menstruating women

the absence of menstruation

the release of a mature
ovum from the graafian
follicle of the ovary

5

Male Sexual Anatomy and Physiology

Introduction

The key structures of male sexual anatomy are discussed, including explanations of how these structures affect sperm, hormone, and seminal fluid production. Both the physiological and psychological aspects of erection, ejaculation, penis size and circumcision are also addressed. Regular genital self-exams are encouraged as a way to assume more responsibility for health care.

Objectives

After studying this chapter, you should be able to:

1. Describe the structure and function of the following parts of the male sexual anatomy:
   a. the scrotum
   b. the testes
   c. the vas deferens
   d. the seminal vesicles
   e. the prostate gland
   f. the Cowper's glands
   g. semen
   h. the penis

2. Define cryptorchidism, including its incidence and how it is treated.

3. Discuss the possible relationship between heat and sperm production.

4. Define the cremasteric reflex, and discuss what types of situations may provoke this response.

5. Discuss several reasons why male genital self-exam is recommended.

6. Describe the incidence of, symptoms of and treatment alternatives for testicular cancer, prostate cancer **and** prostatitis.

7. Explain how and where sperm production and storage takes place.

8. Describe how Kegel exercises are done, and give three possible benefits of doing them.

9. Discuss in detail the functions of erection and ejaculation.

10. Explain why penis size has historically been so important, and how that has affected men's masculinity and/or self-image. Describe the physiological facts of sexual interaction and penis size.

11. Discuss various practices regarding male genital modification and mutilation, referring specifically to the following:
    a. under what circumstances it is practiced
    b. advantages and disadvantages of these procedures
    c. how these procedures relate to sexual pleasure and function
    d. cross-cultural beliefs and practices

Key Terms and Concepts

"Flash cards" listing key terms and concepts on one side and their corresponding definitions and explanations on the other side are provided at the end of the chapter.

Chapter Overview With Fill-Ins

After reading each of the major sections in the chapter, check your retention by **mentally** filling in each of the blanks in the corresponding sections below. Cover the answers in the margin as you go along, and write the answers in the space provided only when you are doing your final review.

Sexual Anatomy

scrotum

testicle
spermatic
vas deferens

The _____ is a loose pouch of skin that is an outpocket of the abdominal wall in the groin area. Inside the scrotal sac are two separate compartments, each of which contains a single _____. Each testis (or testicle) is suspended within the compartment by the _____ cord, which contains the _____ _____ (sperm-carrying tube), as well as other blood vessels, nerves, and fibers.

hormones; sperm

cryptorchidism

testicular

The testicles have two major functions: the secretion of male sex _____ and the production of _____. Sometimes one or both of the testes fail to descend into the scrotum, a condition known as _____. Self-examination of the genitals is encouraged in order to prevent or provide early treatment for _____ cancer, sexually transmitted diseases, and other infections.

sperm
seminiferous tubules
interstitial
androgen
epididymis

Within and adjacent to the testes are two separate areas involved in the production and storage of _____. The first of these, the _____ _____, is where sperm production takes place. The _____ cells, or Leydig's cells, are located between the tubules and are the major source of _____. The second important area for sperm processing is the _____, a C-shaped structure that adheres to the back of each testicle.

vas deferens

vasectomy

The sperm move through the epididymis and drain into the _____ _____, a long thin duct that travels up through the scrotum inside the spermatic cord. This is where the male sterilization procedure, _____, takes place.

seminal vesicles

70

The _____ _____ are two small glands adjacent to the terminals of the vas deferens. They secrete an alkaline fluid that constitutes up to _____ percent of seminal fluid.

prostate

urethra; Prostatitis

cancer

The _____ gland is a structure about the size of a walnut and is located at the base of the bladder. The ejaculatory ducts and the _____ pass through this organ. _____, a condition in which the prostate may become inflamed as a result of various infections, may occur in men at any age. Some men may also develop prostate _____, and so they should be aware of early symptoms and have annual check-ups with their physicians at age 40 and older.

Cowper's	The _____ glands, or bulbourethral glands, are located on each side of the urethra just below where it emerges from the prostate gland. When a man is sexually aroused, these organs secrete an
alkaline	_____ fluid that helps buffer acidity of the urethra and provides lubrication for the flow of seminal fluid through the penis.
semen	The _____ that is ejaculated through the opening of the penis comes from the seminal vesicles, the prostate, and the Cowper's glands.
penis	The _____ consists of nerves, blood vessels, fibrous tissue,
cavernous	and three parallel cylinders of tissue: two _____ bodies
root	and one spongy body. The _____ of the penis is the part that extends into the pelvic cavity. The external, pendulous portion
shaft	(excluding the head) is called the _____, and the head of
glans	the penis is called the _____. Some of the skin covering the penile shaft folds over the glans, and this is called the
foreskin; Circum-cision	_____, or prepuce. _____ involves the permanent removal of this sleeve of skin. The greatest concentration
glans	of nerve endings in the penis is in the _____. Two areas in
corona	particular are sensitive to stimulation: the _____, or rim of
frenum	the penis; and the _____.
	There is a network of muscles surrounding the root of the penis, the
pubococcygeus	most important of which is the _____ muscle (PC). Men
Kegel	may strengthen these muscles by doing _____ exercises.
Urology	_____ is the medical specialty that focuses on male reproductive structures.

Male Sexual Functions

erection	An _____ is a process coordinated by the autonomic
rapid-eye	nervous system. Nighttime erections occur during the _____-_____ movement, or dreaming, stage of sleep.
Ejaculation	_____ is the process whereby the semen is expelled through the penis to the outside of the body. Ejaculation occurs in two
emission	stages: the _____ phase and the expulsion phase. Some
retrograde	men experience _____ ejaculation, in which the semen is expelled into the bladder rather than through the penis. Sometimes a man will experience orgasm without direct genital stimulation, an
nocturnal emission	occurrence which is usually referred to as a _____ _____, or "wet dream".

Some Concerns About Sexual Functioning

size	Historically, there has been a preoccupation with the _____ of a man's penis. For many men, penis size has played a part in
masculinity	defining their _____ or worth as a lover. In fact, from a physiological standpoint, the nerve endings in a woman's vagina are
outer	concentrated in the _____ portion, and while some women do find pressure and stretching deep within the vagina to
sexual	be pleasurable, it is not usually essential for female _____ gratification.

Circumcision   _____ is the surgical removal of the foreskin, and there are arguments for and against this procedure. The glands located in the foreskin secrete an oily, lubricating substance, and if these secretions are allowed to accumulate they combine with sloughed-off dead skin

smegma   cells to form a substance called _____. Routine

hygiene   _____ can prevent this substance from accumulating.

Matching

Match each term below with the appropriate description. Each term is used only once.

a.	inguinal canal	g.	seminal vesicles
b.	cremasteric muscle	h.	prostate gland
c.	seminiferous tubules	i.	Cowper's glands
d.	interstitial cells	j.	seminal fluid
e.	epididymis	k.	cavernous and spongy bodies
f.	vas deferens		

_____1.   a C-shaped structure that serves as a storage chamber for sperm

_____2.   the major source of androgen

_____3.   their secretions constitute a major portion of seminal fluid

_____4.   its amount is influenced by the length of time since last orgasm, among other factors

_____5.   the place from which the testes descend

_____6.   they often secrete an alkaline fluid when a man is sexually aroused

_____7.   the coils found within the testes where sperm production occurs

_____8.   they engorge with blood when a man gets an erection

_____9.   located at the base of the bladder, it is checked for cancer by means of a rectal exam

_____10. sudden fear may cause it to contract

_____11. the duct that carries sperm from the scrotal sac and is severed during a vasectomy

Identification

Label the various parts of the male sexual anatomy indicated below. Check your answers with the key at the end of the chapter.

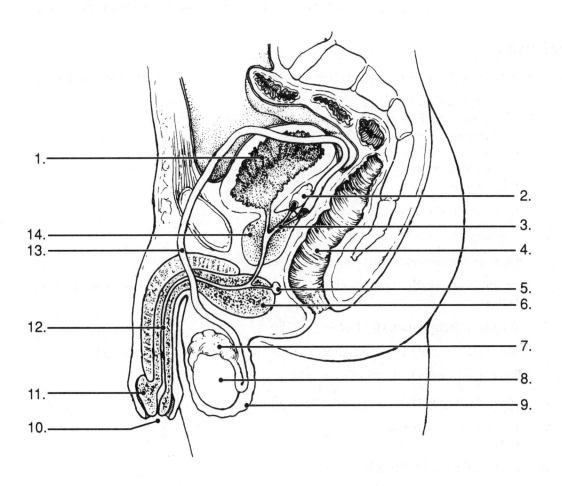

1. _____

2. _____

3. _____

4. _____

5. _____

6. _____

7. _____

8. _____

9. _____

10. _____

11. _____

12. _____

13. _____

14. _____

Short Answer

1. Briefly describe the **structure** and **function** of the following: (Obj. #1a–h)

    a. scrotum

    b. testes

    c. vas deferens

    d. seminal vesicles

    e. prostate gland

    f. Cowper's glands

    g. semen

    h. penis

2. Define cryptorchidism. How is it treated? What may happen if it is not treated? (Obj. #2)

3. How may scrotal temperature be related to male infertility? (Obj. #3)

4. Name three types of stimuli that will provoke the cremasteric reflex. (Obj. #4)

5. List three reasons why genital self-exam is important. (Obj. #5)

6. How common is testicular cancer? What are some of the symptoms? (Obj. #6)

7. Define prostatitis and list some of the symptoms. (Obj. #6)

8. How common is prostate cancer? At what age and how frequently should men be examined for this? (Obj. #6)

9. List three factors that influence the amount of seminal fluid a man ejaculates. (Obj. #9)

10. Identify the two areas of the glans of the penis that are most responsive to stimulation. (Obj. #1h)

11. What are three potential benefits men may experience as a result of practicing Kegel exercises? (Obj. #8)

12. Briefly discuss the sexual self-health practices that a man may utilize in the preventive care of his penis. (Obj. #5)

13. Physiologically, what does a penis fracture involve? How can this happen and how might it be prevented? (Obj. #1h)

14. Describe the **physiological** and **psychological** components of an erection. (Obj. #9)

15. List several nonsexual stimulus situations that cause erections in men. (Obj. #9)

16. List and briefly describe the two stages of ejaculation. (Obj. #9)

17. What is retrograde ejaculation? Under what circumstances does it occur? (Obj. #9)

18. How may a man experience orgasm without direct penile stimulation? (Obj. #9)

19. Explain how the size of a man's penis may affect his female partner's sexual pleasure during intercourse. (Obj. #10)

20. List the arguments for and against circumcision. (Obj. #11a, b)

21. What are the differences in sexual responsiveness between men who are circumcised and those who are not? (Obj. #11c)

22. List and briefly describe **three** types of male genital modification/mutilation. (Obj. #11d)

Multiple Choice

Select the best alternative. Check your answers with the answer key at the end of the chapter.

1. The _____ is a loose pouch of skin that is an outpocket of the abdominal wall in the groin area.
    a. foreskin
    b. epididymis
    c. scrotum
    d. vas deferens

2. Which of the following is **not** associated with the testicles?
   a. sperm production
   b. Cowper's glands
   c. inguinal canal
   d. storage of sperm

3. Which of the following statements concerning cryptorchidism is **false**?
   a. This is a condition where one or both testicles fail to descend from the abdominal cavity.
   b. Approximately 15 percent of boys demonstrate this condition at birth.
   c. This condition may result in infertility.
   d. This condition may be associated with increased risk for developing testicular cancer.

4. The cremasteric reflex
   a. is characterized by the strain and pressure of the testicles when they are exposed to extreme heat.
   b. is revealed by the movement of the testes away from the body when the room temperature increases.
   c. is manifested as an upward movement of the testes toward the body wall when the inner thighs are stroked.
   d. is manifested as a scream of pain when a male falls on the crossbar of a bike.

5. The _____ are thin, highly coiled structures where sperm production takes place.
   a. seminal vesicles
   b. Cowper's glands
   c. interstitial cells
   d. seminiferous tubules

6. The epididymis
   a. is where sperm processing takes place.
   b. is the major source of androgen.
   c. is where sperm production takes place.
   d. is located at the base of the prostate gland.

7. Which of the following statements concerning the vas deferens is **false**?
   a. It is located inside the spermatic cord.
   b. It is the tube that is severed in a vasectomy.
   c. It is the tube through which urine passes from the bladder to the outside of the body.
   d. sperm drain into it from the epididymis

8. The prostate gland
   a. is the major source of seminal fluid.
   b. releases alkaline secretions during sexual arousal that buffer the acidity of the urethra.
   c. is a C-shaped structure located along the back of each testicle.
   d. is a source of male sex hormones

9. Which of the following is **not** a symptom of prostatitis?
   a. pain in the pelvic area
   b. a mass within the testicle
   c. a burning sensation while urinating
   d. a cloudy discharge from the penis

10. Which of the following **best** describes the function of Cowper's glands secretions?
    a. buffers the acidity of the urethra and facilitates flow of semen through the urethra
    b. facilitates flow of semen through the urethra and helps to lubricate the vagina
    c. helps to lubricate the vagina and buffers the acidity of the urethra
    d. buffers the acidity of the urethra and makes up the largest portion of the fluid in semen

11. Which of the following is **not** a factor in the amount of seminal fluid a man ejaculates?
    a. the length of time since last orgasm
    b. the duration of arousal time prior to ejaculation
    c. a man's age
    d. how physically fit a man is

12. Which of the following is found in the penis?
    a. the seminal vesicles
    b. extensive muscular tissue
    c. a cylinder-shaped bone
    d. three chambers of spongy tissue

13. The _____ and _____ are two places on the glans of the penis that many men find especially responsive to stimulation.
    a. prepuce; corona
    b. shaft; frenum
    c. corona; frenum
    d. shaft; prepuce

14. Which of the following is **not** one of the benefits that men may experience as a result of doing Kegel exercises?
    a. stronger, more pleasurable orgasms
    b. better ejaculatory control
    c. increased pelvic sensation during sexual arousal
    d. shorter refractory period over time

15. _____ is a medical specialty that focuses on the male reproductive structures.
    a. Urology
    b. Gonadotology
    c. Gynecology
    d. Proctology

16. On rare occasions during intercourse, too much weight is placed on the penis when attempting to gain or regain vaginal penetration. This may result in a
    a. glans decapitation.
    b. penile fracture.
    c. coronal collapse.
    d. frenulum fissure.

17. The first stage of ejaculation is the _____ phase while the second stage is called the _____ phase.
    a. emission; expulsion
    b. expulsion; emission
    c. REM; nocturnal emission
    d. nocturnal emission; REM

18. Which of the following statements concerning retrograde ejaculation is **false**?
    a. It results from a reversed functioning of the two urethral sphincters.
    b. This condition sometimes occurs in men who have had prostate surgery.
    c. This condition is potentially fatal if not treated.
    d. Certain tranquillizers can cause this reaction.

19. Nocturnal emissions
    a. are also known as "wet dreams."
    b. occur when semen is expelled into the bladder.
    c. occur during the emission stage of ejaculation.
    d. refer to Cowper's glands secretions that occur during sleep.

20. The size of a man's penis tends to be related to
    a. the length of his fingers.
    b. his race.
    c. his body build.
    d. none of the above

21. Circumcision is the surgical removal of the
    a. frenulum.
    b. foreskin.
    c. tunica dartos.
    d. scrotal sac.

22. Smegma
    a. may harbor organisms that can cause infections in women.
    b. is a watery gray discharge.
    c. may accumulate in the vas deferens.
    d. may result in urethral constriction.

23. Which of the following statements concerning circumcision is **true**?
    a. Recent research has suggested that the incidence of ovarian cancer is more frequent in women who have sex with uncircumcised partners.
    b. In recent years, the incidence of circumcision in the United States has increased.
    c. Circumcision is widely practiced throughout the world for religious or hygienic reasons.
    d. It appears that urinary tract infections occur more frequently among circumcised boys.

24. Generally speaking, a circumcised male responds
    a. more quickly during intercourse than an uncircumcised male.
    b. less quickly during intercourse than an uncircumcised male.
    c. about the same during intercourse as an uncircumcised male.
    d. Research results and subjective reactions have not been consistent.

25. Sperm production in the male requires a temperature that
    a. is higher than body temperature.
    b. is lower than body temperature.
    c. is the same as body temperature.
    d. varies from high to low temperatures from day to day.

Insight and Application

For Men:

1. Have you ever taken the time to leisurely touch and explore your body with the goal of becoming more knowledgeable and accepting of your body and how it functions, as well as to explore the feelings and sensations in various parts of your body without the goal of orgasmic release? If not, why not? In considering the possibility of doing so, what thoughts or feelings come up for you? If you find yourself feeling disgusted, embarrassed, defensive or confused at the prospect of doing so, why do you think that is? If you have taken the time to do some body exploration, what was your experience in doing so? What were the benefits? The drawbacks?

2. Set aside an hour or more when you can have some uninterrupted time alone. Take a leisurely bath or shower, and then select some lotion or massage oil that is pleasing to you. As you apply the lotion or oil to all parts of your body, experiment with different types of pressure, rhythm and touch. Explore your face, neck, arms, hands, chest, nipples, abdomen, buttocks, legs, feet and toes. Notice what kinds of touch your body responds to. Notice what parts of your body you appreciate or find attractive as well as the parts you criticize or find unattractive. How have you developed the relationship you have with your body? Are you comfortable with that relationship or is it something you would like to change? What are your personal standards for health and attractiveness? What do you base them upon? Are they realistic?

3. Touch and explore the different parts of your genitals: the glans and shaft of your penis, your scrotum, and the perineum (the area between the scrotum and the anus). What words do you use to refer to your genitals? What words would you prefer your partner or potential partner to use? In doing this exercise, what thoughts or feelings come up for you? How do you feel about the size, shape or color of the various parts of your sexual anatomy? What are the sources of these feelings? How do they affect your sexual self-esteem, the way in which you care for your body, and your relationship with a partner or potential partner? Are you comfortable with these thoughts and feelings? If not, what would you like to change?

For Men and Women:

1. If you had it to do over again, how would you change or improve the way in which you learned about male sexual anatomy and function? What factors might have contributed to more awareness or comfort with this subject? Give specific examples.

2. If you had a newborn son, would you choose to have him circumcised? Why or why not?

3. From your perspective, how important is penis size to a woman's sexual satisfaction? Think in terms of coital satisfaction as well as psychological stimulation. Has penis size been an issue for you and/or for your partner? How have you dealt with that?

Matching Answers

1. e	2. d	3. g	4. j	5. a	6. i	7. c	8. k
9. h	10. b	11. f					

Identification Answers

1.	bladder	8.	testis
2.	seminal vesicle	9.	scrotum
3.	ejaculatory duct	10.	urethral opening
4.	rectum	11.	glans of penis
5.	Cowper's gland	12.	urethra
6.	root of penis	13.	vas deferens
7.	epididymis	14.	prostate gland

Multiple Choice Answers

1. c	2. b	3. b	4. c	5. d	6. a	7. c	8. b
9. b	10. a	11. d	12. d	13. c	14. d	15. a	16. b
17. a	18. c	19. a	20. d	21. b	22. a	23. c	24. d
25. b							

scrotum

tunica dartos

spermatic cord

testes

inguinal canal

cryptorchidism

cremastic reflex

epididymis

seminiferous tubules

phimosis

the second layer of the scrotal sac, composed of smooth muscle fibers and fibrous connective tissue	the pouch of skin of the external male genitals that encases the testicles
male gonads inside the scrotum that produce sperm and sex hormones	a firm, rubbery tube that contains the vas deferens and from which a testicle is suspended
a condition in which the testicles fail to descend from the abdominal cavity to the scrotal sac	during fetal development, the route the testes take from inside the abdomen to the scrotum
the structure along the back of each testicle in which sperm maturation occurs	involuntary contractions of the major scrotal (cremasteric) muscle, causing the scrotum to draw closer to the body
a condition characterized by an extremely tight penile foreskin	thin, highly coiled structures in the testicles in which sperm are produced

interstitial cells	vas deferens
vasectomy	ejaculatory duct
seminal vesicles	cilia
prostate gland	urethra
prostatitis	Cowper's glands

a sperm-carrying tube that begins at the testicle and ends at the urethra	(Leydig's cells) cells located between the seminiferous tubules that are the major source of androgen in males
two, short ducts located within the prostate gland	male sterilization procedure that involves removing a section from each vas deferens
hairlike filaments that line the inner walls of the vas deferens	two, small glands adjacent to the terminals of the vas deferens that secrete an alkaline fluid conducive to sperm motility
the tube through which urine passes from the bladder to the outside of the body	a gland located at the base of the bladder whose secretions comprise about 30 percent of the seminal fluid released during ejaculation
(bulbourethral glands) two pea-sized glands located alongside the base of the urethra in the male that secrete an alkaline fluid during sexual arousal	inflammation and enlargement of the prostate gland as a result of various infectious agents

semen

penis

root

shaft

glans

cavernous bodies

spongy body

smegma

corona

frenum

a male sexual organ
consisting of the internal
root and external shaft
and glans

a fluid ejaculated through
the penis that contains sperm
and fluids from the prostate,
seminal vesicles, and
Cowper's glands

the external, pendulous
portion of the penis,
excluding the head

the portion of the penis that
extends internally into the
pelvic cavity

the structures in the shaft of
the penis that engorge with
blood during sexual arousal

the smooth, acorn-shaped
head of the penis

a cheesy substance of
glandular secretions and
skin cells that sometimes
accumulates under the
foreskin of the penis

an internal chamber that
forms a bulb at the base of
the penis, extends up into
the penile shaft and forms
the penile glans

(frenulum) a highly sensitive,
thin fold of skin that
connects the foreskin
with the underside of
the penile glans

the rim of the glans
of the penis

pubococcygeus muscle | Kegel exercises

urology | erection

ejaculation | emission phase

circumcision | urethral bulb

expulsion phase | retrograde ejaculation

a series of exercises that strengthen the muscles underlying the external female or male genitals	one of the major muscles surrounding the root of the penis which can be strengthened by doing Kegel exercises
coordinated by the autonomic nervous system, the process whereby the three erectile chambers of the penis engorge with blood causing it to increase in size	the medical specialty that focuses on male reproductive structures
the first stage of male orgasm, in which the seminal fluid is gathered in the urethral bulb	the process whereby semen is expelled through the penis to the outside of the body
the portion of the urethra between the urethral sphincters in the male	surgical removal of the foreskin of the penis
process by which semen is expelled into the bladder instead of out of the penis	the second stage of male orgasm, during which the semen is expelled from the penis by muscular contractions

nocturnal emissions

involuntary ejaculation during sleep, also known as a "wet dream"

6

Sexual Arousal and Response

Introduction

Our sexual arousal and response are influenced by a myriad of psychological, cultural and biological factors. In this chapter, the focus is on the biological aspects of arousal and response: hormones, brain functions, sensory processes, foods, drugs and chemicals. In addition, the physiological changes that men and women experience throughout sexual arousal and response are also discussed.

Objectives

After studying this chapter, you should be able to:

1. Explain the role of hormones in male sexual behavior, and include the following in your discussion:
   a. definition of androgens and their source
   b. definition of orchidectomy and what research has revealed regarding the effects of this procedure on sexual functioning
   c. definition of antiandrogens and what research has demonstrated regarding the use of antiandrogens in the treatment of sex offenders
   d. definition of hypogonadism and how research on this condition has contributed to our understanding of the relationship between androgens and sexual motivation

2. Explain the role of hormones in female sexual behavior, making specific reference to estrogens and androgens, and citing relevant research studies.

3. Discuss the role of the brain in sexual arousal.

4. Describe the role of the following senses in sexual arousal: touch, vision, smell, taste and hearing.

5. Assess each of the following in regard to their aphrodisiac effects:
   a. various foods (oysters, eggplant, etc.)
   b. alcohol
   c. amphetamines
   d. barbiturates
   e. cantharides
   f. cocaine
   g. psychedelic drugs
   h. marijuana
   i. amyl nitrate
   j. L-dopa
   k. yohimbine hydrochloride

6. List at least four substances that inhibit sexual behavior.

7. Describe Kaplan's three-stage model of sexual response.

8. List the four phases of Masters and Johnson's sexual response cycle and briefly describe the physiological changes that occur in each stage for women and men.

9. Discuss how female orgasmic response has been analyzed and explained over time, beginning with Freud's interpretation.

10. Define the Grafenberg spot and explain the controversy surrounding it.

11. Identify at least three significant differences in sexual response between men and women.

12. Discuss sexual arousal from a cross-cultural perspective, citing specific examples.

Key Terms and Concepts

"Flash cards" listing key terms and concepts on one side and their corresponding definitions and explanations on the other side are provided at the end of the chapter.

Chapter Overview With Fill-Ins

After reading each of the major sections in the chapter, check your retention by **mentally** filling in each of the blanks in the corresponding sections below. Cover the answers in the margin as you go along, and write the answers in the space provided only when you are doing your final review.

Sexual Arousal

hormones
brain
drugs

This section explores the role of several factors that affect human sexual arousal: the role of _____; the impact of _____ functions; sensory input and how individuals interpret it; and the effects of certain foods and _____.

testosterone
adrenal
orchidectomy

psychological

About 95 percent of the androgens produced by the male are secreted by the testes in the form of _____. The remaining 5 percent are produced by the _____ glands. In medical terms, castration is called _____. In studies of men who have been castrated, it is difficult to distinguish between the physical (hormonal) effects of castration and the _____ effects of this procedure.

antiandrogens

prostate

A class of drugs called _____ drastically reduces the amount of testosterone circulating in the bloodstream. These drugs have been used to treat sexual offenders and certain medical conditions such as advanced _____ cancer.

Hypogonadism

_____ is a state of androgen deprivation that occurs when hormone production in the testes is impaired.

female
Estrogens

ovarian

androgens

The role of hormones in _____ sexual functioning still remains unclear. _____ help maintain vaginal elasticity and contribute to the production of vaginal lubrication. However, the role that _____ estrogens play in female sexual motivation, arousal and behavior is controversial. In contrast, the evidence implicating _____ in female sexuality is more substantial, although even the available research in this area is not without contradictions.

brain

The fact that sexual arousal can occur without any sensory stimulation at all — that arousal and even orgasm may be produced by fantasy alone — demonstrates the important role of the _____ in our sexuality.

touch
Primary

Secondary

Of the major senses, _____ tends to predominate during sexual sharing. _____ erogenous zones contain dense concentrations of nerve endings and include the genitals, buttocks, anus, perineum, breasts, inner thighs, armpits, navel, neck, ears and mouth. _____ erogenous zones include all other areas of the body that become endowed with erotic significance through sexual conditioning.

vision

similarities

women
men

Next to touch, _____ is second in the hierarchy of stimuli that people view as sexually arousing. Current research has demonstrated strong _____ in the responses of males and females to visual erotica. However, when sexual arousal is measured by self-reports rather than physiological devices, _____ are less inclined than _____ to report being sexually aroused by visual erotica.

pheromones

In regard to the sense of smell, the females of many species secrete certain substances called _____ during their fertile periods that appear to play a role in sexual arousal.

Taste

_____ seems to play a relatively minor role in human sexual arousal.

variable

Whether people make sounds during sexual sharing and how they respond to their partner making them is highly _____.

aphrodisiac

An _____ is a substance that supposedly arouses sexual desire or increases a person's capacity for sexual activities.

genitals

A variety of foods, especially those resembling male external _____, have been ascribed various aphrodisiac qualities, but aside from a person's subjective assessment, there have been no objective data to substantiate these claims.

Alcohol

increased
reduced

_____ has been viewed as a sexual stimulant, although it actually has a depressing effect on higher brain centers. Research has demonstrated that with _____ levels of alcohol intake, both men and women experience _____ sexual arousal (as measured physiologically), decreased pleasure and intensity of orgasm, and increased difficulty in attaining orgasm.

drugs

enhance

There are a number of other _____ and chemicals such as marijuana, amphetamines, cocaine, amyl nitrate, L-dopa, barbiturates and psychedelics, that many people claim _____ their sexual arousal or performance.

yohimbine
rats
humans

A crystalline alkaloid derived from the sap of a tree that grows in West Africa, _____ hydrochloride, apparently induces intense sexual arousal and performance in _____, although recent research regarding similar effects on _____ has been inconclusive.

anaphrodisiacs

nicotine

Substances that inhibit sexual behavior are called _____. These include: opiates, tranquilizers, antihypertensives, and _____, one of the most widely used and least recognized anaphrodisiacs.

Sexual Response

desire

Kaplan's model of sexual response contains three stages: _____, excitement and orgasm.

plateau
refractory
male

Masters and Johnson outline four phases in the sexual response cycle: excitement, _____, orgasm and resolution. They also include a _____ period — a recovery stage in which there is a temporary inability to reach orgasm — in the _____ resolution phase.

vasocongestion
myotonia

Two fundamental physiological responses to effective sexual stimulation occur in both men and women: _____, or the blood engorgement that occurs; and _____, the increased muscle tension that occurs throughout the body.

differences

variation
refractory

multiple

Despite many similarities, there are several major _____ of sexual response in men and women. For one, women tend to have more _____ in their sexual response patterns than men. The presence of a _____ period in men represents a second major difference. Finally, women have the capacity to achieve _____ orgasms to a far greater degree than men, although recent research suggests that men may be capable of training themselves to experience a series of orgasms as well.

Matching

Match the phases below with the appropriate descriptions of various changes that occur in the sexual response cycle. Note that each phase may be used more than once, and there may be more than one answer for each description.

a.	female excitement	f.	male emission phase of orgasm
b.	male excitement	g.	male expulsion phase of orgasm
c.	female plateau	h.	female resolution
d.	male plateau	i.	male resolution
e.	female orgasm	j.	male refractory

_____1. formation of orgasmic platform

_____2. testicles return to unstimulated size

_____3. onset of "sex flush"

_____4. labia minora increase in size and begin to deepen in color

_____5. breast size increases

_____6. penis becomes erect, but the erection is not necessarily stable

_____7. contraction of orgasmic platform

_____8. testicles begin to swell and elevate

_____9. Cowper's glands become active

_____10. prostate gland and seminal vesicles contract

_____11. uterus is fully elevated

_____12. onset of vaginal lubrication

_____13. clitoris slowly descends from beneath hood

_____14. vestibular bulbs increase in size

_____15. nipples become erect

_____16. clitoral glans is retracted under hood

_____17. areola increases in size, causing nipple to appear less erect

_____18. penile urethra and rectal sphincter contract

_____19. stable erection

_____20. temporary inability to reach orgasm

_____21. labia majora separate away from vaginal opening

_____22. uterus contracts

_____23. Bartholin's glands may secrete fluid

Short Answer

1. Define orchidectomy and describe its effects on sexual interest and activity. (Obj. #1b)

2. Name two sources of androgens in men. (Obj. #1a)

3. How do antiandrogens work? List two ways in which they have been used. (Obj. #1c)

4. Define hypogonadism. Describe the effects of hypogonadism in preadolescent males as well as in adult males. (Obj. #1d)

5. Name two functions that estrogens serve in women. (Obj. #2)

6. What hormones appear to play the strongest role in female sexuality? Briefly summarize research to support this. (Obj. #2)

7. What parts of the brain are associated with sexual motivation and activity. (Obj. #3)

8. Describe the effects of pleasure center stimulation in rats and in humans. (Obj. #3)

9. Distinguish between primary and secondary erogenous zones. (Obj. #4)

10. Contrast current research findings with Kinsey's research on how men and women respond to visual erotica. (Obj. #4)

11. List two pheromones and describe their sources. (Obj. #4)

12. What is the function of the vomeronasal system? (Obj. #4)

13. In one research study, what effect did the silence of their male partners have on women's sexual arousal? (Obj. #4)

14. Describe the effects of alcohol consumption on sexual arousal and orgasm from both a subjective and objective (physiological) point of view. (Obj. #5b)

15. Briefly assess the objective aphrodisiac properties of the following drugs or chemicals: (Obj. #5)

    a. cantharides (Spanish fly)

    b.   marijuana

    c.   amphetamines

    d.   cocaine

    e.   amyl nitrate

    f.   L-dopa

    g.   barbiturates

    h.   yohimbine hydrochloride

    i.   psychedelic drugs

    j.   alcohol

16. List three types of drugs that are anaphrodisiacs. (Obj. #6)

17. Name two ways in which nicotine retards sexual motivation. (Obj. #6)

18. What distinguishes Kaplan's model of sexual response from Masters and Johnson's? (Obj. #7)

19. For the excitement phase in Masters and Johnson's sexual response cycle, briefly summarize the physiological changes that take place in both sexes, in women and in men. (Obj. #8)
(For questions 18 through 21, refer to Figures 6.5 through 6.8 in the text.)

both sexes:

female responses:

male responses:

20. For the plateau phase in Masters and Johnson's sexual response cycle, briefly summarize the physiological changes that take place in both sexes, in women and in men. (Obj. #8)

both sexes:

female responses:

male responses:

21. For the orgasm phase in Masters and Johnson's sexual response cycle, briefly summarize the physiological changes that take place in both sexes, in women and in men. (Obj. #8)

both sexes:

female responses:

male responses:

22. For the resolution phase in Masters and Johnson's sexual response cycle, briefly summarize the physiological changes that take place in both sexes, in women and in men. (Obj. #8)

    both sexes:

    female responses:

    male responses:

23. Define vasocongestion and myotonia. (Obj. #8)

24. How have each of the following individuals described female orgasm? (Obj. #9)
    a. Freud

    b. Masters and Johnson

    c. Singer and Singer

25. Where is the Grafenberg spot located? How may it be stimulated? (Obj. #10)

26. What is the source of the female ejaculate? Of what is this fluid composed? (Obj. #10)

27. Briefly describe the differences in sexual response patterns between men and women. (Obj. #11)

28. Briefly outline three possible explanations for the existence of a refractory period in men. (Obj. #8)

29. Even though most women have the capacity for multiple orgasm, why is it that such a small percentage of women report having them? (Obj. #11)

30. It appears that some men may be capable of experiencing a series of orgasms within a short time. How do they do this? (Obj. #11)

Multiple Choice

Select the best alternative. Check your answers with the answer key at the end of the chapter.

1. Which of the following statements concerning androgens is **true**?
   a. Most of the androgens produced by men are secreted by the adrenal glands.
   b. Estrogen is a type of androgen.
   c. A number of studies have linked androgens with sexual activity.
   d. Orchidectomy would eliminate about half of the androgens that men produce.

2. For which of the following reasons would castration be **least** likely to be performed?
   a. as a treatment for genital tuberculosis
   b. for sex offenders who agree to it
   c. as a treatment for prostate cancer
   d. as a treatment for hypogonadism

3. Depo-Provera is
   a. a type of androgen.
   b. a type of antiandrogen.
   c. a type of estrogen.
   d. used to treat hypogonadism.

4. Hypogonadism is
   a. the surgical removal of the testes.
   b. treated with Depo-Provera.
   c. when the testicles become infected and swollen.
   d. a state of androgen deprivation.

5. Which of the following statements regarding hypogonadism is **true**?
   a. If it occurs in adulthood, loss in sexual desire and function is always impaired.
   b. If it occurs before puberty, the effects are highly variable depending upon the individual.
   c. Androgen insensitivity is one of the effects of this condition.
   d. Diseases of the endocrine system can result in this condition.

6. At the present time, the evidence linking _____ with female sexuality is more substantial than that which supports _____.
   a. androgens; estrogens
   b. estrogens; androgens
   c. progesterones; androgens
   d. estrogens; progesterones

7. Researchers have reported increased sexual activity in rats when the anterior and posterior regions of the _____ are stimulated.
   a. gonads
   b. adrenal glands
   c. hypothalamus
   d. cerebellum

8. Which of the following statements concerning the cerebral cortex is **true**?
   a. Key structures include the septal area, amygdala and parts of the hypothalamus.
   b. When certain parts of it are surgically destroyed, there may be a significant reduction in sexual behavior of males and females.
   c. This is referred to as the "pleasure center" of the brain.
   d. Strictly mental events like fantasies are produced here.

9. Amyl nitrate
   a. is used in the treatment of a variety of mental and physical conditions; can heighten arousal and orgasm.
   b. has frequently been used to treat Parkinson's disease; can heighten arousal and orgasm.
   c. is used by cardiac patients to treat heart pain; can heighten arousal and orgasm.
   d. dilates arteries that supply the genital area, thereby producing a feeling of warmth.

10. Which of the following statements concerning priapism is **true**?
    a. It is associated with frequent use of amyl nitrate.
    b. It is a painful condition independent of sexual arousal.
    c. It occurs during the orgasm phase of the sexual response cycle.
    d. It is brought about by the use of aphrodisiacs.

11. Which of the following terms does **not** belong with the others?
    a. pheromones
    b. potassium nitrate
    c. copulins
    d. alpha androstenal

12. This substance may be a true aphrodisiac, at least for rats.
    a. LSD
    b. Benzedrine
    c. yohimbine
    d. L-dopa

13. Drugs used for treating high blood pressure as well as drugs used to treat a variety of emotional disorders also
    a. inhibit sexual behavior.
    b. induce priapism.
    c. are linked with the development of prostate cancer.
    d. increase sexual desire.

14. How does nicotine affect sexual arousal and function?
    a. It promotes relaxation and loosens inhibitions.
    b. It increases testosterone levels in the blood.
    c. It expands the blood vessels thereby enhancing vasocongestive response.
    d. It delays and decreases sexual arousal.

15. The desire stage is one of the significant features of whose sexual response model?
    a. Singer and Singer's
    b. Masters and Johnson's
    c. Kaplan's
    d. Freud's

16. Which of the following is the **best** example of myotonia?
    a. vaginal lubrication
    b. erection of the penis
    c. muscular spasms during orgasm
    d. the formation of the orgasmic platform

17. An example of vasocongestion is
    a. erection of the penis.
    b. vaginal lubrication.
    c. engorgement of the clitoris.
    d. all of the above

18. The labia majora flatten and move away from the vaginal opening during the _____ phase of sexual response.
    a. excitement
    b. plateau
    c. orgasm
    d. resolution

19. If the Cowper's glands produce secretions, this will typically occur in the _____ or _____ stage of sexual response.
    a. desire; plateau
    b. orgasm; plateau
    c. desire; excitement
    d. excitement; plateau

20. Which of the following statements concerning the orgasmic platform is **true**?
    a. It develops during the plateau phase.
    b. It refers to the vaginal expansion that occurs in the inner two-thirds of the vagina.
    c. It is an example of myotonia.
    d. all of the above

21. Which of the following types of orgasm described by the Singers most closely corresponds to the type of orgasmic response described by Masters and Johnson?
    a. vulval
    b. uterine
    c. blended
    d. clitoral

22. The Grafenberg spot may be stimulated by
    a. applying pressure to the mons veneris.
    b. vigorous palpation of the anterior wall of the vagina.
    c. applying pressure to the urethral opening.
    d. gently stroking the clitoris.

23. A recent study of U.S. and Canadian women disclosed that _____ percent of the respondents had experienced fluid release and ejaculation at the point of orgasm.
    a. 20
    b. 40
    c. 60
    d. 80

24. The fluid that some women ejaculate following Grafenberg spot stimulation is chemically similar to
    a. urine.
    b. menstrual fluid.
    c. seminal fluid.
    d. Bartholin's glands secretions.

25. The _____ is when all of the sexual systems return to their nonaroused state.
    a. refractory period
    b. resolution phase
    c. denouement
    d. plateau phase

26. The clitoris is retracted under the hood during the _____ and _____ phases of sexual response.
    a. desire; excitement
    b. excitement; plateau
    c. plateau; orgasm
    d. orgasm; resolution

27. That ejaculation triggers a short-term neurological inhibitory mechanism is **one** explanation for
    a. the male resolution phase.
    b. the male "monthly cycle."
    c. multiple orgasms in men.
    d. the male refractory period.

28. The _____ refers to the period of time immediately after male orgasm when no amount of additional stimulation will result in orgasm.
    a. resolution phase
    b. charge phase
    c. postejaculatory remission period
    d. refractory period

29. In comparing Kinsey's survey to more contemporary surveys, the number of women who experience multiple orgasms during penile-vaginal intercourse
    a. has decreased significantly.
    b. has increased significantly.
    c. has stayed about the same.
    d. Kinsey's survey did not include this information.

30. One explanation for the difference in the number of women who are capable of having multiple orgasms and the number of women who actually experience them is
    a. the source of sexual stimulation.
    b. whether or not the women own vibrators.
    c. the size of her partner's penis.
    d. whether or not the woman's G-spot was stimulated.

31. Vasocongestion is to blood vessels as myotonia is to
    a. muscles.
    b. respiration.
    c. heart rate.
    d. excitement.

Insight and Application

1. Thinking in terms of the five senses listed below, give examples of what you find sexually arousing as well as sexually inhibiting or irritating. You may think in terms of a partner or potential partner (specific visual, olfactory, auditory stimuli related to that person) or in more general terms, or both.

	Sexually Arousing Stimuli	Sexually Irritating Stimuli
Touch		
Vision		
Smell		
Taste		
Hearing		

2. Take some time to think about what your conditions are for good sex—alone or with a partner—from physical, psychological and emotional perspectives. Examples of these might include the environment in which you would most enjoy sex, being free of fears of unwanted pregnancy or of contracting a sexually transmitted disease, specific sexual behaviors or positions you most enjoy, degree of privacy you would like, if you are well-rested or freshly showered, how you feel about your body, the kind of thoughts or fantasies you enjoy prior to sexual interaction, how you are feeling about yourself in general, yourself in relationship to your partner (if you have one), and the degree of trust, affection and commitment in the relationship, etc. Write down your conditions for good sex. How aware have you been of your conditions for good sex in seeking sexual gratification for yourself or with a partner? If you are in a relationship (or reflecting back on past relationships), have you been willing to make your conditions for good sex known to your partner? Have you been willing to discover theirs? If not, why not? Is that something you would like to change?

3. In reflecting on (1) and (2) above, do you think there would be overall sex differences in what men and women find arousing or what their conditions are for good sex? If so, to what might this be attributed?

Matching Answers

1. c	2. i	3. a–d	4. a	5. a	6. b	7. e	8. b
9. b, d	10. f	11. c	12. a	13. h	14. a	15. a, b	16. c, e
17. c, e	18. g	19. d, f, g	20. j	21. a	22. e	23. c	

Multiple Choice Answers

1. c	2. d	3. b	4. d	5. d	6. a	7. c	8. d
9. d	10. b	11. b	12. c	13. a	14. d	15. c	16. c
17. d	18. a	19. d	20. a	21. a	22. b	23. b	24. c
25. b	26. c	27. d	28. d	29. c	30. a	31. a	

vomeronasal system

orchidectomy

antiandrogens

Depo-Provera

hypogonadism

estrogens

cerebral cortex

limbic system

primary erogenous zones

secondary erogenous zones

the medical term for castration	a channel of sensory input whose exclusive task is to detect pheromones
a well-known antiandrogen	drugs that reduce the amount of testosterone in the bloodstream; have been used to treat sex offenders and certain medical conditions
female sex hormones	a state of androgen deprivation that results from certain diseases of the endocrine system
a subcortical brain system composed of several interrelated structures that influences the sexual behavior of humans and other animals	the "grey matter" of the brain that is responsible for higher functions like thinking, feeling, remembering and language abilities
areas of the body other than primary erogenous zones that have become erotically sensitive through learning and experience	areas of the body containing dense concentrations of nerve endings very responsive to tactile pleasuring; e.g., genitals, buttocks, anus, breasts, mouth, armpits, neck, thighs, earlobes, navel, etc.

pheromones

copulins

alpha androstenal

aphrodisiac

yohimbine hydrochloride

anaphrodisiacs

Kaplan's model of
sexual response

Masters and Johnson's
sexual response cycle

refractory period

vasocongestion

pheromones from the vaginal secretions of rhesus monkeys	substances secreted by the body, related to reproductive functions, that produce certain odors
a substance that allegedly arouses sexual desire and increases the capacity for sexual activity	pheromones secreted by pigs; it has also been found in the perspiration of humans
substances that are known to inhibit sexual behavior — such as tranquilizers, opiates, antihypertensives, and nicotine	a crystalline alkaloid derived from the sap of the tropical evergreen yohimbe tree in West Africa that appears to be an aphrodisiac for rats but not for humans
four phases in sexual response for men and women that include excitement, plateau, orgasm and resolution	three stages of sexual response that include desire, excitement and orgasm
the engorgement of blood vessels in particular body parts in response to sexual arousal	in the male resolution phase of Masters and Johnson's sexual response cycle, a recovery stage in which there is a temporary inability to reach orgasm

myotonia

sex flush

orgasmic platform

vulval orgasm

uterine orgasm

blended orgasm

multiple orgasm

a pink or red rash that
appears in the chest
or breasts during
sexual arousal

increased muscle tension
that occurs throughout
the body in response to
sexual arousal

a type of orgasm described
by Singer and Singer that
may be induced by coital
or manual stimulation

the increased engorgement
of the outer third of the
vagina during the plateau
phase of the sexual
response cycle

a type of orgasm described
by Singer and Singer that
is a combination of vulval
and uterine orgasms

a type of orgasm described
by Singer and Singer that
occurs only as a result of
vaginal penetration and is
characterized by specific
breathing patterns

more than one orgasm
experienced within a
short time period

7

Love and the Development of Sexual Relationships

Introduction

Until recently, attempts to define, measure, explain or control the concept of love have remained elusive. However, this chapter presents current information from a variety of psychological, sociobiological, philosophical, cross-cultural and clinical perspectives that enable us to better understand this mysterious and intriguing part of our lives. Specific sections in the text deal with the relationship between love and sex, how to deal with jealousy, the development of intimacy, and maintaining relationship satisfaction over time.

Objectives

After studying this chapter, you should be able to:

1. Explain how Zick Rubin attempted to measure love, including a list and description of the three components of his love scale and what his findings revealed.

2. Describe the characteristics of passionate love, including research on the chemistry of love.

3. Describe the characteristics of companionate love.

4. Explain Sternberg's triangular theory of love.

5. List and describe six styles of loving as proposed by John Lee.

6. Discuss the factors that affect with whom we fall in love.

7. Describe the role self-love plays in the development of intimacy.

8. List and describe each of the following phases of a relationship as it develops and becomes more intimate:
   a. inclusion
   b. response
   c. care
   d. trust
   e. affection
   f. playfulness
   g. genitality

9. Describe the relationship between love and sex and how men and women tend to perceive the connection between the two in different ways. Cite relevant research and compare the views of Albert Ellis, Rollo May and Masters and Johnson on this subject.

10. Discuss strategies for determining personal values and guidelines regarding sexual expression.

11. Define jealousy, and discuss the role it plays in love relationships and how to decrease jealous feelings.

12. Discuss some of the factors that contribute to maintaining relationship satisfaction over time.

13. Describe research findings that clarify whether romantic love is a universal experience.

14. From a cross-cultural perspective, discuss men's and women's preferences in mate selection.

Key Terms and Concepts

"Flash cards" listing key terms and concepts on one side and their corresponding definitions and explanations on the other side are provided at the end of the chapter.

Chapter Overview With Fill-Ins

After reading each of the major sections in the chapter, check your retention by **mentally** filling in each of the blanks in the corresponding sections below. Cover the answers in the margin as you go along, and write the answers in the space provided only when you are doing your final review.

What is Love?

Zick Rubin

love scale
attachment
intimacy

Love is very difficult to define. One of the more ambitious attempts to measure love was undertaken by psychologist _____ _____, who developed a 13-item measurement device that he called a _____ _____. As measured by Rubin's scale, love has three components: _____, caring and _____.

Types of Love

philia
Passionate

Companionate

Love between friends, known to the Ancient Greeks as _____, involves concern for the other's well-being. _____ love (also known as romantic love or infatuation) is characterized by intense emotional and sexual desire. _____ love is characterized by affection and deep attachment that is based on extensive familiarity with the loved one.

triangular
commitment
patterns
six

pragmatic

Robert Sternberg has proposed a _____ theory of love that has three components: passion, intimacy and _____. These exist in different _____ and to varying degrees in different relationships. John Lee's theory suggests _____ different styles of loving: romantic, game-playing, possessive, companionate, altruistic and _____.

Falling in Love: Why and With Whom?

proximity
similarity
interests

Physical; attractive-
ness; early

One factor that affects why people fall in love with whom they do is _____, or physical nearness of that individual. Another factor is _____ in social class, religious orientation, educational background, etc. Commonality of _____ is another reason why people become involved with the partners they do. _____ _____ also plays a dominant role in drawing lovers together, especially in the _____ stages of a relationship.

The Development of Intimacy

self-love
respect

Satisfying intimacy within a relationship begins with _____-_____, which has been defined as a genuine interest, concern and _____ for ourselves.

inclusion

response
care
trust
affection
playfulness

genitality

The different phases of a relationship are: _____, when one person extends the invitation to relate to another; _____, the nature of which will determine whether a relationship begins; _____, or the genuine concern for another's welfare; _____, a feeling that is essential to the ongoing development of a relationship; _____, or feelings of warmth and attachment; _____, which is characterized by delight, exhilaration, and expansive laughter that is expressed in the relationship; and _____, when the couple agrees to express feelings through genital sex.

Issues in Loving Relationships

women
men

A number of surveys indicate that _____ link love and sex to a greater extent than _____ do.

love; affection

Other studies suggest a shift toward a greater emphasis on _____ and _____ in both sexes.

love

Albert Ellis, a psychotherapist and author of *Sex Without Guilt*, concluded that sex without _____ can be quite satisfying, although sex with love is probably more so.

intimacy
passion

Rollo May believes that the contemporary preoccupation with technique and performance, and the de-emphasis of _____ has resulted in a lack of sexual enjoyment and _____ for many people.

value

The first step in integrating sex into your life in a meaningful way is to consider what you _____ in life and relationships before initiating a sexual involvement with another.

enhance

You can also ask yourself if your decision to engage in a sexual relationship will _____ your positive feelings about yourself and the other person.

attractive; intimacy

physical contact

You may decide to be sexually involved, but you may not want to do that right away. You can indicate that you find the other person _____, that you desire greater sexual _____, but that you want to progress slowly. Being specific about the kind of _____ _____ you desire at a given point in time can minimize confusion and help to reassure the other person.

envy
attractiveness
fame
acknowledge
deny

A *Psychology Today* survey indicated we are likely to be jealous of people who have qualities we _____. In general, women were more envious of _____ and popularity while men were more envious of wealth and _____. In another study, it was found that women are more likely to _____ jealous feelings and men are more likely to _____ them.

selective ignoring

Respondents to a recent survey on jealousy described three strategies used to attempt to cope with it: self-reliance, positive comparison and self-bolstering, and _____ _____.

Maintaining Relationship Satisfaction

best friend

inclusion

A study of 300 happily married couples revealed that the most frequently named reason for an enduring and happy marriage was seeing one's partner as one's _____ _____.

Maintaining positive _____ and response experiences contributes to the continued satisfaction of committed couples.

sexual

routine

For some people, maintaining _____ excitement in their relationship is a high priority. However, some people find sexual _____ a comfort and a source of security.

Matching

Match the theorists below with the appropriate descriptions or quotations. Note that each theorist may be used once, more than once, or not at all, but choose only **one** answer for each blank.

a. Zick Rubin
b. Erich Fromm
c. Robert Sternberg
d. John Allen Lee
e. Albert Ellis

f. William Masters
g. Rollo May
h. Jankowiak and Fischer
i. Erik Erikson
j. David Buss

_____1. his three components of love include intimacy, passion and commitment

_____2. describes the game-playing love style as one that is characteristic of people who like to "play the field"

_____3. concluded that sex without love can be quite satisfying

_____4. believes that there is too much focus on technique and performance at the expense of sexual enjoyment and passion

_____5. "romantic love is a delicious art form but not a durable one"

_____6. conducted research to determine to what extent romantic love is a human universal

_____7. "the Victorian person sought to have love without falling into sex; the modern person seeks to have sex without falling into love"

_____8. attempted to measure love by developing a device called a love scale

_____9. defines fatuous love as typical of the whirlwind courtship

_____10. a human development scholar; believes that positive self-feelings are a basis for a satisfying relationship.

_____11. his three components of love include attachment, caring and intimacy

_____12. said that people who aren't capable of love shouldn't be denied sex

_____13. suggested that union with another person is the deepest human need

_____14. conducted a cross-cultural study on sex differences in partner preferences

Short Answer

1. List and describe the three components of Rubin's love scale. (Obj. #1)

2. According to research, what behavior was observed in "strong lovers" as opposed to "weak lovers?" (Obj. #1)

3. List at least four characteristics of passionate love. (Obj. #2)

4. To what has recent research attributed the "high" of being in love? (Obj. #2)

5. Describe the various aspects of companionate love. (Obj. #3)

6. According to a *Psychology Today* survey on love and romance, what were the three **most** important ingredients of love? (Obj. #3)

7. List the three components of Sternberg's theory of love. (Obj. #4)

8. List and describe the eight love patterns that Sternberg outlines. (Obj. #4)

9. List and briefly describe Lee's six different styles of loving. (Obj. #5)

10. List four factors that influence why people fall in love with whom they do. (Obj. #6)

11. Briefly discuss the concept of self-love and the role it plays in the development of intimacy. (Obj. #7)

12. List and briefly describe the seven phases of a relationship. (Obj. #8a–g)

13. Briefly summarize recent research studies on how men and women view the relationship between love and sex, and how that has changed over time. (Obj. #9)

14. Compare Albert Ellis', Rollo May's and Masters and Johnson's views on love and sex. (Obj. #9)

15. What are some ways in which you can clarify your values in relation to a specific decision regarding sexual activity? (Obj. #10)

16. Describe the steps you can take to let a person know that you are not ready for sex yet. (Obj. #10)

17. Describe some effective ways to deal with rejection. (Obj. #10)

18. According to a *Psychology Today* survey, what three traits were found in people who were prone to jealousy? (Obj. #11)

19. In what ways do men and women tend to respond to jealousy differently? (Obj. #11)

20. Briefly describe three suggestions Walster and Walster offer to people who want to minimize their jealous feelings. (Obj. #11)

21. List three strategies that survey respondents used to cope with jealousy. (Obj. #11)

22. What does the research say regarding the reasons why happily-married couples are able to remain that way over time? (Obj. #12)

23. List at least six suggestions that the authors offer for couples who wish to maintain sexual excitement in their relationships. (Obj. #12)

24. When Jankowiak and Fischer studied the prevalence of romantic love in 166 societies, what did they find? (Obj. #13)

25. What did David Buss' cross-cultural study on mate preferences reveal? (Obj. #14)

Multiple Choice

Select the best alternative. Check your answers with the answer key at the end of the chapter.

1. Which of the following is **not** one of the components of Rubin's love scale?
   a. attachment
   b. inclusion
   c. intimacy
   d. caring

2. Love that involves concern for the other's well-being is
   a. ludus.
   b. eros.
   c. philia.
   d. passionate love.

3. Generalized physiological arousal is one characteristic of
    a. philia.
    b. companionate love.
    c. storge.
    d. passionate love.

4. Another word for companionate love is
    a. agape.
    b. storge.
    c. ludus.
    d. mania.

5. According to authors Liebowitz and Walsh, the "high" or euphoria characteristic of
    passionate love is **best** explained by
    a. recognizing qualities in our lovers that we experienced with our parents when we
        were children.
    b. pheromones.
    c. the cognition that our feelings of attraction to someone are being reciprocated.
    d. surging levels of brain chemicals.

6. Passion, commitment and intimacy are all components of _____ theory of love.
    a. Sternberg's
    b. Rubin's
    c. Lee's
    d. Erikson's

7. Ted and Tamara have been married for a long time and are committed to staying together
    to raise their two children, despite the lack of passion and intimacy they experience
    together. Sternberg would characterize this type of love experience as
    a. companionate love.
    b. nonlove.
    c. consummate love.
    d. empty love.

8. The tendency to fall in love with people who live nearby and are seen frequently is said to
    be the factor of
    a. equidistance.
    b. similarity.
    c. proximity.
    d. habituation.

9. Self-love refers to
    a. selfishness.
    b. lack of consideration for others.
    c. the first component of Rubin's love scale.
    d. respect for ourselves.

10. The first phase of an intimate relationship is
    a. inclusion.
    b. trust.
    c. symbiosis.
    d. caring.

11. The **best** example of the response phase of a relationship is
    a. saying "hello" to someone.
    b. asking someone to dance.
    c. riding on the swings in the playground with your partner.
    d. trying to understand your partner's point of view.

12. Which of the following is an example of inclusion-response?
    a. having sex at least three times a week
    b. demonstrating caring behaviors for your partner that make him/her feel loved
    c. riding a roller coaster together
    d. avoiding routine sex

13. _____ is the phase of a relationship in which there is genuine concern for the other person's welfare.
    a. Inclusion
    b. Care
    c. Affection
    d. Response

14. The affection phase of a relationship is characterized by
    a. feelings of warmth and attachment.
    b. feelings of exhilaration and abandon.
    c. genital contact.
    d. a gesture of inclusion.

15. Which of the following statements concerning love and sex is **true**?
    a. A *Parade* magazine survey found that over half of the men and women surveyed reported that they found it difficult to have sex without love.
    b. According to student surveys in the authors' classes, roughly an equal number of men and women indicated that love is a necessary component of sexual relationships.
    c. A recent study found that the majority of men and women had their first intercourse experience with someone with whom they were in love.
    d. all of the above

16. Albert Ellis has suggested that
    a. sex should take place within the context of a marital relationship.
    b. sex should take place within the context of a love relationship.
    c. sex between individuals who are not in love should be socially acceptable.
    d. sex without love tends to be more satisfying than sex with love because there are fewer demands placed on the relationship.

17. Which of the following individuals has suggested that the contemporary focus on technique and performance has resulted in a lack of sexual enjoyment and passion for people?
    a. Albert Ellis
    b. Rollo May
    c. Zick Rubin
    d. Alfred Kinsey

18. If you would like to better understand the role that sex and relationships play in your life, you should ask yourself which of the following questions?
    a. "When do I want to get married?"
    b. "Should I have sex on the first date or wait for a while?"
    c. "Where do my sexual values come from — family, friends, etc.?"
    d. "Is my partner more sexually experienced than I am?"

19. A *Psychology Today* survey indicated that, in general, women were more envious of
    a. attractiveness and popularity.
    b. wealth and fame.
    c. social position and emotional security.
    d. attractiveness and wealth.

20. One of the traits possessed by people prone to jealousy is
    a. being distrustful of others.
    b. having low self-esteem.
    c. the tendency to repress feelings.
    d. a pessimistic outlook on life in general.

21. In general, women are more likely than men to _____ jealous feelings.
    a. project
    b. deny
    c. rationalize
    d. acknowledge

22. One strategy that was described to cope with jealousy was _____, which involves containing any expression of jealousy.
    a. selective ignoring
    b. self-reliance
    c. introjection
    d. self-bolstering

23. Which of the following would a man be **most** likely to do in response to jealous feelings?
    a. secretly search through his lover's belongings
    b. question his lover about a past romance
    c. blame himself for not being as attractive or successful as the other guy
    d. get angry at his girlfriend for wearing sexually provocative clothing

24. In the survey of 300 happily married couples, which reason was cited **most** frequently for the success of their marriages?
    a. I want the relationship to succeed.
    b. Our sexual intimacy is the best it has ever been.
    c. My spouse is my best friend.
    d. We agree on aims and goals.

25. Which of the following is the **best** suggestion for maintaining sexual excitement in a relationship?
    a. flirting with someone at a party to make your partner just a little jealous
    b. having sex on a regular basis (2–3 times a week)
    c. making "dates" with each other
    d. being naked together more often

26. Two anthropologists, Jankowiak and Fischer, found that romantic love existed in 147 out of the 166 societies they studied. They speculated that the reason it didn't exist in all societies was that
    a. the societies were generally unsophisticated than the majority.
    b. the societies had no leisure time compared to the majority.
    c. the pragmatic values of the societies didn't allow for something as indulgent as romantic love.
    d. their research methods were flawed.

27. The explanation that Buss provides regarding why men and women select the mates they do is best described as _____ in nature.
    a. psychological
    b. sociobiological
    c. psychological
    d. biological

Insight and Application

Styles of Loving

Recent research indicates that there are six main styles of loving. The following material combines the work of three sociologists — John Alan Lee, Tom Lasswell, and Marcia Lasswell, with the research of psychologist Martin Rosenman, and explores the implications of these styles of loving. The six basic lovestyles are: Friendship, Giving, Possessive, Practical, Game-Playing, and Erotic.

You can determine your own concept of love by taking the fifty-item test below. Scoring the test shows you your position on each of the six lovestyles. After you take the test, read the description for each style of loving, bearing in mind that a person can score high in more than one lovestyle.

The Styles of Loving Test

In responding to the items below, when it is appropriate think of your most significant peer love relationships. If you cannot decide which has been the most significant, think of your most recent significant love relationship. If you wish you may think of your ideal love relationship whether you have actually experienced it or not. Answer *all* of the following items either true or false.

1. I believe that "love at first sight" is possible.

2. I did not realize that I was in love until I actually had been for some time.

3. When things aren't going right with us, my stomach gets upset.

4. From a practical point of view, I must consider what a person is going to become in life before I commit myself to loving him/her.

5. You cannot have love unless you have first had *caring* for a while.

6. It's always a good idea to keep your lover a little uncertain about how committed you are to him/her.

7. The first time we kissed or rubbed cheeks, I felt a definite genital response (lubrication, erection).

8. I still have good friendships with almost everyone with whom I have ever been involved in a love relationship.

9. It makes good sense to plan your life carefully before you choose a lover.

10. When my love affairs break up, I get so depressed that I have even thought of suicide.

11. Sometimes I get so excited about being in love that I can't sleep.

12. I try to use my own strength to help my lover through difficult times, even when he/she is behaving foolishly.

13. I would rather suffer myself than let my lover suffer.

14. Part of the fun of being in love is testing one's skill at keeping it going and getting what one wants from it at the same time.

15. As far as my lovers go, what they don't know about me doesn't hurt them.

16. It is best to love someone with a similar background.

17. We kissed each other soon after we met because we both wanted to.

18. When my lover doesn't pay attention to me, I feel sick all over.

19. I cannot be happy unless I place my lover's happiness before my own.

20. Usually the first thing that attracts my attention to a person is his/her pleasing physical appearance.

21. The best kind of love grows out of a long friendship.

22. When I am in love, I have trouble concentrating on anything else.

23. At the first touch of his/her hand, I knew that love was a real possibility.

24. When I break up with someone, I go out of my way to see that he/she is O.K.

25. I cannot relax if I suspect that he/she is with someone else.

26. I have at least once had to plan carefully to keep two of my lovers from finding out about each other.

27. I can get over love affairs pretty easily and quickly.

28. A main consideration in choosing a lover is how he/she reflects on my family.

29. The best part of love is living together, building a home together, and rearing children together.

30. I am usually willing to sacrifice my own wishes to let my lover achieve his/hers.

31. A main consideration in choosing a partner is whether or not he/she will be a good parent.

32. Kissing, cuddling, and sex shouldn't be rushed into; they will happen naturally when one's intimacy has grown enough.

33. I enjoy flirting with attractive people.

34. My lover would get upset if she/he knew some of the things I've done with other people.

35. Before I ever fell in love, I had a pretty clear physical picture of what my true love would be like.

36. If my lover had a baby by someone else, I would want to raise it, love it and care for it as if it were my own.

37. It is hard to say exactly when we fell in love.

38. I couldn't truly love anyone I would not be willing to marry.

39. Even though I don't want to be jealous, I can't help it when he/she pays attention to someone else.

40. I would rather break up with my lover than to stand in his/her way.

41. I like the idea of me and my lover having the same kinds of clothes, hats, bicycles, cars, etc.

42. I wouldn't date anyone that I wouldn't want to fall in love with.

43. At least once when I thought a love affair was all over, I saw him/her again and knew I couldn't realistically see him/her without loving him/her.

44. Whatever I own is my lover's to use as he/she chooses.

45. If my lover ignores me for a while, I sometimes do really stupid things to try to get his/her attention back.

46. It's fun to see whether I can get someone to go out with me even if I don't want to get involved with that person.

47. A main consideration in choosing a mate is how he/she will reflect on one's career.

48. When my lover doesn't see me or call for a while, I assume he/she has a good reason.

49. Before getting very involved with anyone, I try to figure out how compatible his/her hereditary background is with mine in case we ever have children.

50. The best love relationships are the ones that last the longest.

Scoring

- Score only "True" answers.
- Your friendship love score is the number of "True" answers to questions 2, 5, 8, 21, 29, 32, 37, 50.
- Your giving love score is the number of "True" answers to questions 12, 13, 19, 24, 30, 36, 40, 44, 48.
- Your possessive love score is the number of "Trueî answers to questions 3, 10, 11, 18, 22, 25, 39, 43, 45.
- Your practical love score is the number of "True" answers to questions 4, 9, 16, 28, 31, 38, 42, 47, 49.
- Your game-playing love score is the number of "True" answers to questions 6, 14, 15, 26, 27, 33, 34, 46.
- Your erotic love score is the number of "True" answers to questions 1, 7, 17, 20, 23, 35, 41.

	Love Score	Percentile
Friendship	_____	_____
Giving	_____	_____
Possessive	_____	_____
Practical	_____	_____
Game-Playing	_____	_____
Erotic	_____	_____

To get the correct percentile, use the following table for each love score:

Percentiles for Each of the Styles of Loving

		Friendship	Giving	Possessive	Practical	Game-Playing	Erotic
	0	1	1	3	4	1	1
	1	5	2	11	12	6	2
	2	16	8	28	26	14	29
	3	33	25	38	48	26	52
LOVE	4	56	47	53	70	34	74
SCORE	5	78	56	64	83	59	91
	6	88	71	80	91	80	98
	7	95	91	91	97	95	99
	8	99	97	96	99	99	
	9		99	99			

Interpreting the Test

Your percentile score for each style of loving tells you how you compare with other people who have taken the test. In other words, a percentile score of 78 on a lovestyle would indicate that your were higher on that lovestyle than 78 percent of the people. A percentile score of 50 on another scale would place you in the middle. A percentile score of 5 would indicate that 95 percent of the people were higher than you on that scale

Different relationships bring out different lovestyles. You might be interested in retaking the test using a different relationship as the basis.

(Thomas E. Lasswell and Marcia E Lasswell, "I Love You But I'm Not In Love With You", *Journal of Marital and Family Therapy, 2*, No. 3 (1976), pp. 222–24. Reprinted by permission.)

STYLES OF LOVING

Friendship Love

Sharing, mutual understanding, respect, compassion, and concern characterize friendship lovers. As good friends, they feel comfortable with each other and assume that their relationship will be permanent. They enjoy the security, the naturalness, the comfortableness of their love.

Friendship love usually develops gradually. Sexual intimacy often comes late in the relationship, emerging from the already existing verbal intimacy. And many friendship lovers do not realize they are in love until they have been for some time.

This lovestyle shows less preoccupation with the beloved than do the other lovestyles. Mostly absent are intense emotions, either painful or ecstatic. Taking a less romantic attitude, the intimates may forget or minimize the importance of birthdays, anniversaries, and other significant occasions.

Stability, rather than impulsiveness, permeates the relationship — the comfort of the home environment, the power of patience and loyalty, the endurance of brother-sister type love. Even if these lovers break up or move on, they try to maintain contact, and they usually have good friendships with their former intimates. This lovestyle is supportive and undemanding, allowing each partner time to pursue hobbies, platonic friendships, and professional interests. With the passage of time, shared and discussed activities enhance mutual understanding and the friendship grows.

Pitfalls. Some observers would find the predictability, security stability, and quiet homelife of this type of love to be lacking in excitement. Compared to the possessive, game-playing, and erotic types of love, friendship love is uneventful.

Giving Love

As the name implies, giving lovers are giving and forgiving.

Placing the happiness and best interests of their intimates ahead of their own, they are patient, understanding, and supportive. They have a sense of duty and obligation not only to the beloved but also to other people and to society in general. They are dependable and will come through in a crisis. Giving lovers are compassionate, altruistic, committed, loyal, and patient.

Giving lovers gradually develop, rather than fall into, love. They seek an ideal love relationship rather than an ideal type of person. Giving lovers try to perceive and accept the needs of the intimate and derive more pleasure from giving than from receiving. They have the ability to allow the partner to do what he/she needs to do and will go so far as to tolerate the partner's participation in activities that are incompatible with their own values. The giving lover will even consider giving up the intimate if that will be to the intimate's benefit, even though there will be personal pain felt as a result of the loss. The giving lover does not want to stand in the intimate's way and understands the old saying that "it is better to have loved and lost than never to have loved at all."

Pitfalls. Too much giving of any kind can become irritating rather than special. A relationship is likely to become boring if one partner excessively puts the needs and wants of the other ahead of his/her own. This is especially true in the sexual area, where at least some self-interest is needed. If one partner is so concerned with giving that she/he becomes a spectator rather than a true participant, sex can lose its excitement.

Possessive Love

Possessive lovers view jealousy as an integral part of being in love, and make statements such as "I am jealous because I love you so much" or "If you loved me, you would be more jealous." Obsessed with love, they require attention and affection and togetherness.

The possessive lover requires much time with his intimate and cannot tolerate times apart. Even brief separations elicit frequent phone calls.

Preoccupied with thoughts of the intimate, the possessive lover showers him/her with attention. Operating on the assumption that true love is not easy, he is upset over little slights, is elated by dramatic moments of coming together, and has a need to create problems when none exist. The possessive lover feels that this important love must be constantly tested, and emotional agitation is a small price to pay when experiencing deep love.

Pitfalls. Although many people like to possess an intimate completely, or feel security in being possessed, the jealousy, clinging, and forced togetherness of possessive love inevitably create problems. A possessive lover will eventually become burdensome to a more self-sufficient partner.

Practical Love

Practical lovers plan their lives, relying more on logical thoughts than on feelings. They realistically evaluate their own assets, appraise their "market value," and try to obtain the best possible deal in a partner. The practical lover, when involved with the right person, will be dependable and loving and will be committed to the mutual solution of any problems that might arise.

In a sense, this is shopping-list love; the person decides what particular assets he or she wants and then attempts to find a suitable partner. Practical lovers choose a partner for their planned lifestyle, commit themselves to finding a commonsense, practical solution to everyday problems, and accept a less idealistic view of love with fewer unrealistic expectations. Not surprisingly, they usually have stable relationships.

A practical lover will not select a mate who deviates too far from the ideal pattern.

Pitfalls. Problems will occur if one of the partners can no longer meet the needs of the other, or if one partner decides to pursue different life objectives which are unacceptable to the other. Practical lovers will at first attempt to find a rational solution to the incompatibility and will often consider professional help. If they cannot come up with an acceptable solution, they may plan a separation or a divorce based upon practical considerations — such as when the partner completes college or when a certain goal is reached or when the children grow older.

Game-Playing Love

Game-playing lovers try to minimize dependency and commitment. The game, when properly played, controls involvement and prevents the participants from being hurt. Partners best suited for this lovestyle are undemanding and self-sufficient.

By having two or more partners at the same time, the game-playing lover can lessen commitment, increase excitement, and have someone in reserve so that he or she can quickly move on if problems arise. Variety and good times are the goal, and as much emphasis is placed on playing the game as on winning the prize.

Placing emphasis on quantity, game-players are good at meeting people and are not too selective in their choice of partners. The philosophy is that if you're not with the one you love, then love the one you're with. Love is a game with much fun while it lasts. Game-players thrive on excitement and challenge.

Pitfalls. Although game-playing lovers try to avoid involvement and commitment, one partner may lose the feeling of detachment and fall into the well. Becoming overly involved is likely to result in problems. The game is no longer fun, and unless both participants are willing to modify the rules, the game is abruptly terminated. A particularly awkward, though not infrequent, situation occurs when one partner is a possessive lover.

Game-players, at times, feel guilty about their lovestyle. Many of them view game-playing as a fun stage to pass through, rather than as a permanent lifestyle.

Erotic Love

Erotic lovers search for their preconceived physical ideal. They emphasize quality rather than quantity, believe in the possibility of love at first sight, and become excited and energized when they finally find love. The closer the partner comes to the ideal — body build, face hair, height, skin, fragrance, voice, intellect, personality — the more the enchantment.

Sex and deep personal sharing usually come early because once the potential ideal person appears, the erotic lover wants to plunge into the relationship.

Commitment at first is intense, with a desire to discuss experiences ranging from day-to-day activities to past lovers to childhood memories. Erotic lovers enter into a monogamous relationship, experiment with sexual techniques, and search for new ways to please each other. Erotic love, like a fire on which most of the available logs have been piled, burns at first with great intensity — but like the fire, the intensity is destined to diminish.

Pitfalls. Erotic love, with its intensity of emotions, has many peaks and valleys. The powerful attraction of the first several weeks provides the exhilaration of being on a high mountain, but coming down is inevitable. Successful erotic lovers appreciate what they have and are willing to settle for less than the highest peak. Other erotic lovers, unable to sustain the initial excitement and unwilling to tolerate lower levels of passion, move on and often enter into a series of intense monogamous relationships.

COMPATIBLE COMBINATIONS

In general, intimates with the same style of loving are compatible. An exception might be possessive lovers who, propelled by jealousy and restrained by holding on too tightly, have a roller-coaster type of relationship. The most stable and enduring relationships occur between friendship lovers, between giving lovers, and between practical lovers, in the above order. Game-players get along best with other game-players, but the emphasis is on fun together while it lasts, rather than on making future plans. Erotics, despite the ecstasy of the first few months, will fare best if they accept the inevitable lessening of the romance and if they supplement their erotic style with an additional lovestyle.

Intimates with different lovestyles can also form compatible combinations. The possibilities are listed below:

- Friendship — with Giving or Practical

- Giving — with all types except Game-Playing

- Possessive — with Giving, and under the right circumstances with Practical or Erotic, or to a lesser extent with Friendship

- Practical — with Giving or Friendship and, under the right circumstances, with all the other types

- Game-Playing — best with Game-Playing, but under the right circumstances, with Practical

- Erotic — under the right circumstances with Friendship, Giving, Practical, or Possessive, if that person meets erotic ideals

When analyzing compatibilities, remember that a person's pattern in all six of the lovestyles has great importance. To look only at the highest score would be oversimplifying the complicated way in which a person loves.

(Martin Rosenman, *Loving Styles: A Guide for Increasing Intimacy* (NY: Prentice-Hall, 1979), pp. 6–24. Adapted with permission of the author.)

Insight and Application Questions

1. Based on your knowledge, experience, and what you have observed and read, how would you define love? If you wanted to measure love, what behaviors, in addition to the ones discussed in the text, do you think would be important to observe?

2. If you have been in love, **why** do you think you were? What led you to fall in love with the particular person(s) you did? How do your answers compare to what is in the text?

3. Have you even been jealous? **Why** do you think you were? How did you deal with the situation? How do your answers compare to the discussion in the text?

4. What is the connection between love and sex for you? What knowledge and/or experiences have contributed to shaping your values on this subject?

5. In light of the discussion in the text, do you have sex and/or relationships on **your** terms? How, if at all, could you improve in this area?

6. What kinds of thoughts do you say to yourself regarding the possibility or the reality of being rejected? How do your fears of rejection restrict or inhibit the number and quality of relationships you have, if at all? How might you alter your perception of rejection in order to allow yourself to comfortably take more risks in this area?

7. If self-love is the foundation for a satisfying intimate relationship, how do you assess the degree and quality of your own self-love? Give specific examples of how you demonstrate interest, concern, and respect for yourself. How might you improve in this area, if at all?

Matching Answers

1. c	2. d	3. e	4. g	5. b	6. h	7. g	8. a
9. c	10. i	11. a	12. e	13. b	14. j		

Multiple Choice Answers

1. b	2. c	3. d	4. b	5. d	6. a	7. d	8. c
9. d	10. a	11. d	12. b	13. b	14. a	15. a	16. c
17. b	18. c	19. a	20. b	21. d	22. b	23. d	24. c
25. c	26. d	27. b					

Rubin's love scale	attachment
caring	intimacy
philia	passionate love
companionate love	genitality
Sternberg's triangular theory of love	nonlove

a component of Rubin's love scale that refers to a person's desire for the physical presence and emotional support of the other person	a 13-item measurement device designed by Zick Rubin that attempted to measure a couple's level of attachment, caring and intimacy
a component of Rubin's love scale that refers to the desire for close, confidential communication with the other	a component of Rubin's love scale that refers to an individual's concern for the other's well-being
romantic love or infatuation, characterized by intense feelings of tenderness, elation, anxiety, sexual desire and ecstasy	love between friends, known to the ancient Greeks as philia
sexual feelings in an intimate relationship that culminate in genital sex	characterized by a friendly affection and a deep attachment that is based on extensive familiarity with the loved one
the absence of Sternberg's three components of love; what we feel in casual relationships	a theoretical framework for conceptualizing what people experience when they report being in love; includes the components of passion, intimacy, and commitment

friendship

infatuation

empty love

companionate love

fatuous love

romantic love

consummate love

Lee's styles of loving

reciprocity

self-love

what we experience when just the passion component of Sternberg's theory of love is present	what we experience when just the intimacy component of Sternberg's theory of love is present
the presence of Sternberg's love components of intimacy and commitment but without passion; often characteristic of happy couples who have been together for a long time	the presence of Sternberg's love component of commitment without passion and intimacy; often characteristic of a long-term, static relationship
the presence of Sternberg's love components of passion and intimacy but without commitment	the presence of Sternberg's love components of passion and commitment but without intimacy; often characteristic of whirlwind courtships
a theory that describes six different styles of loving that include romantic, game-playing, possessive, companionate, altruistic and pragmatic love styles	when all three components of Sternberg's theory of love are present: passion, intimacy, and commitment
genuine interest, concern and respect for ourselves	the notion that when we receive expressions of liking and loving we tend to respond in similar ways

inclusion	**response**
care	**trust**
affection	**playfulness**

how a person responds to a gesture of inclusion, the nature of which will determine future contact	the first step a person takes in meeting another; e.g., eye contact, a smile, or a greeting
a belief that each partner in a relationship will act consistently in ways that promote the relationship's growth and stability, and that affirm each partner	a genuine concern for another's welfare
a phase in the development of intimacy where each person exhibits delight, exhilaration and laughter in the presence of the other	characterized by feelings of warmth and attachment, it elicits a desire to be physically close to another; usually expressed by holding hands, sitting close, hugs and caresses

8

Communication in Sexual Behavior

Introduction

Being able to talk easily and comfortably about our bodies and our sexuality is an important aspect of developing sexual intimacy with a partner. This chapter opens with a discussion on why sexual communication is difficult and goes on to elaborate on strategies used to initiate sexual interaction with a partner. The heart of the chapter focuses on specific communication techniques that couples can use, and a number of examples are provided in order to illustrate the application of these techniques.

Objectives

After studying this chapter, you should be able to:

1. Define mutual empathy and explain how it relates to effective sexual communication.

2. List and describe at least three reasons why sexual communication is difficult, and note the difference between clinical terminology and street language.

3. Discuss three strategies that may be helpful to begin talking about sex.

4. Identify and describe at least six characteristics of effective listening and feedback.

5. List and expand upon four different strategies that could be used to discover what is pleasurable to your partner.

6. Enumerate and describe three aspects of communication to consider in learning to make sexual requests.

7. Discuss seven aspects of communication to consider in order to give criticism effectively.

8. Describe four strategies to consider in order to receive criticism effectively.

9. Outline a three-step approach that can be used to effectively turn down offers for sexual involvement.

10. Discuss the effects of sending mixed messages and explain how to respond if receiving them.

11. Articulate four aspects of nonverbal communication that play an important part in the process of communication.

12. Enumerate and discuss several strategies for dealing with an impasse that may occur in sexual communication.

13. Discuss some of the ways in which men and women tend to communicate differently.

Key Terms and Concepts

"Flash cards" listing key terms and concepts on one side and their corresponding definitions and explanations on the other side are provided at the end of the chapter.

Chapter Overview With Fill-Ins

After reading each of the major sections in the chapter, check your retention by **mentally** filling in each of the blanks in the corresponding sections below. Cover the answers in the margin as you go along, and write the answers in the space provided only when you are doing your final review.

The Importance of Communication

mutual
empathy

The basis for effective sexual communication is _____ _____ — the underlying knowledge that each partner in the relationship cares for the other and knows the care is reciprocated.

Some Reasons Why Sexual Communication is Difficult

socialization

language
self-exposure

There are several important reasons why sexual communication is difficult. One reason has to do with our _____, which often contributes to negative attitudes, shame, or embarrassment about sexual matters. A second reason relates to the lack of a suitable _____ of sex. Finally, difficulties in sexual communication for some people may be rooted in fears of too much _____-_____; by talking, people place themselves in a position vulnerable to judgment, criticism and even rejection.

Talking: Getting Started

talking
about talking

discussing

histories

The authors suggest three ways to "break the ice:" _____ _____ _____, or in other words, discussing why sexual communication is difficult for you and what your fears are in bringing up a sexual topic with your partner; reading and _____ a variety of books and articles on sexual topics that may provide the stimulus for personal conversations; and sharing sexual _____.

Listening and Feedback

passive

eye contact

feedback

supporting

empathy

unconditional pos-
itive regard

paraphrasing

There are a number of traits that characterize good listening skills. One skill is being an active vs. a _____ listener. Another skill, maintaining _____ _____, is one of the most vital aspects of good verbal communication. Providing _____ is another listening skill that helps to clarify how you have perceived your partner's comments and also indicates that you are actively listening. Because communicating about sexual matters can make a person feel quite vulnerable, _____ our partner's communication efforts when they do talk can help foster mutual _____ as well as encourage them to continue to communicate openly and candidly with us. The concept of _____ _____ _____ means conveying to our partners the sense that we will continue to value and care for them regardless of what they do or say. A final listening skill, _____, prevents miscommunication from occurring as it clarifies discrepancies between the communicator's intent and the listener's interpretation.

Discovering Your Partner's Needs

questions; yes or no

open-ended

self-disclosure

Comparing notes

giving permission

One of the most obvious ways to learn about our partner's needs is to simply ask _____. You may ask _____ _____ _____, either/or, or _____-_____ questions, depending on the effect you are trying to achieve. In addition to asking questions, the technique of _____-_____, or sharing your feelings regarding a particular topic, may often encourage your partner to reciprocate.

_____ _____ is a very natural way to discover our partner's preferences in food, music, entertainment, etc.; it can also be a way to discover our partner's sexual preferences as well. Finally, a technique called _____ _____ is a way of encouraging and reassuring our partners to talk about specific feelings or needs.

Learning to Make Requests

responsibility

specific

I

Learning to ask for what you want is an integral part of sexual communication, and to begin with, it is important to take _____ for your own pleasure. In asking for what you want, it is important to make your requests _____, which will maximize the possibility of your partner understanding and following through on your request. In addition, using "_____" language brings the desired response more often than a general statement does.

Giving Criticism

motivation

caring

place

praise

backsliding

small

why

behavior
character; I
you
one

There are several strategies to keep in mind in order to give criticism effectively. For one, be aware of your _____ in criticizing your partner. The strategies offered in this section will be effective only if your motivation is based on a _____ desire to make your relationship better. A second consideration in delivering criticism is to choose the right time and _____. It is also a good idea to temper the criticism with _____, or to focus on some positive aspect of your partner or the relationship in expressing your concerns. Keep in mind that _____, or reverting back to old patterns and behaviors, is natural and predictable, and people typically don't alter these patterns overnight. So it is important to nurture _____ steps toward changes in hopes of ultimately getting what you want instead of criticizing what has not changed. Avoid asking "_____" questions; these are usually thinly veiled attempts to criticize or attack our partners instead of taking responsibility for how we are feeling and what we want. Express anger appropriately by focusing on the _____ as opposed to the _____ of your partner. Use "_____" statements as opposed to _____ statements. Finally, limit your criticism to _____ complaint per discussion.

Receiving Criticism

empathizing
paraphrasing

acknowledge
clarifying

feelings

changes

This section describes four different ways in which you can respond to criticism. To begin with, _____ with your partner and _____ the criticism is one way to make certain you understand exactly what your partner's concerns are. Secondly, you can, if appropriate, _____ the criticism and find something with which you can agree. Asking _____ questions is also helpful, especially if your partner's criticism is a bit vague. You can also express your _____ in regard to the criticism rather than letting these emotions dictate your response. Finally, an excellent closure to receiving criticism is to focus on future _____ that the two of you can make in order to improve the situation.

Saying No

three
appreciation; vali-
date;
alternative

verbal

One approach for saying no to invitations for intimate involvements includes _____ distinct phases: Step 1: express _____ for the invitation, and if you want, _____ the value of the other person; Step 2: say no in a clear, unequivocal fashion; and Step 3: offer an _____, if appropriate.

Another aspect to consider in saying no is to avoid inconsistencies between _____ messages and subsequent actions either in your behavior or in that of your partner's.

Nonverbal Sexual Communication

facial
interpersonal

Components of nonverbal communication that we should be aware of in communicating sexually with our partner are: _____ expression, _____ distance, touching, and making and hearing sounds.

Impasses

validate
break
change
counseling

If your discussion with your partner results in an impasse, there are several options that might be helpful: try to see things from your partner's perspective; _____ your partner's position; take a _____ from each other for a while; schedule another time to talk; grant your partner the right not to _____; or seek professional _____.

Matching

Match each term below with the appropriate communication. Each letter is used only once.

a. mutual empathy
b. unconditional positive regard
c. "why" question
d. paraphrase
e. either/or question
f. yes/no question
g. open-ended question
h. self-disclosure
i. comparing notes
j. giving permission
k. specific request

_____1. Your partner says "I love how you talk to me when we make love" and you respond: "So you like that sweet talk, huh?"

_____2. "Do you like it when I kiss the back of your arm?"

_____3. "It's a good feeling to trust you and care about you so much, and to know you feel that way about me too."

_____4. "Do you like it when I undress you, or do you prefer to do it yourself?"

_____5. "You know how much I love you, but when you avoid being affectionate or intimate I feel very frustrated."

_____6. "Tell me where you like to be touched."

_____7. "It is difficult for me to talk about my abuse because it is still so painful for me, but each time I do I feel so much better because I feel you really care and understand."

_____8. "I would really like you to be on top this time. I love being able to watch you, and I like how you take control when you're on top."

_____9. "Why don't you ever want to go down on me?"

_____10. "I love it when you touch me very lightly with your nails or fingertips, but it seems like when I do that for you it tickles. Is that right?"

_____11. "Since you've been taking that belly-dancing class, I know you've been shy about practicing in front of me. But I just want you to know that I would **love** it; you're so sensual when you dance that I just love watching you."

Short Answer

1. Define mutual empathy. (Obj. #1)

2. List and describe three reasons why sexual communication is difficult. (Obj. #2)

3. List and describe three strategies for initiating sexual communication. (Obj. #3)

4. What are the characteristics of active listening? (Obj. #4)

5. Define unconditional positive regard. (Obj. #4)

6. Paraphrase the following comment: "It seems like I'm the only one who ever wants to have sex around here." (Obj. #4)

7. What are the advantages and disadvantages of the following types of questions: (Obj. #5)

    a. yes or no

b.   open-ended

c.   either/or

8.   Assume that you are interested in talking to your partner about the possibility of acting out some sexual fantasies together. Provide an example for each of the following types of questions in this situation. (Obj. #5)

a.   yes or no

b.   open-ended

c.   either/or

9.   Describe the use of self-disclosure as a communication technique. (Obj. #5)

10. Give an example of "comparing notes." (Obj. #5)

11. What is meant by "giving permission?" (Obj. #5)

12. What communication strategy eliminates the problem of your partner having to use his or her intuition to figure out what you want? (Obj. #6)

13. Rewrite the following statement using "I" language: "You are always in such a rush to have intercourse." (Obj. #6)

14. List three destructive motives for criticizing a partner. (Obj. #7)

15. At what times or in what situations is delivering criticism inappropriate? (Obj. #7)

16. Rewrite the following complaint tempering the criticism with praise: "Whenever we have sex, it's because I initiate it." (Obj. #7)

17. What is the underlying motive behind a "why" question? (Obj. #7)

18. Distinguish between "I" and "you" statements. Give an example of each. (Obj. #7)

19. Empathize with and/or paraphrase the following criticism: "You never want to experiment with anything new." (Obj. #8)

20. Use the strategy of acknowledgment in response to the following criticism: "You expect me to have sex with you after you have just finished working out?" (Obj. #8)

21. Write a comment that would express your feeling in response to the following criticism: "You never seem to enjoy it very much when we have sex." (Obj. #8)

22. List the three steps that are suggested for saying no to a sexual invitation. (Obj. #9)

23. If your partner is sending you mixed messages, how do the authors suggest that you respond? (Obj. #10)

24. Name four important components of nonverbal sexual communication. (Obj. #11)

25. List six ways that a couple might respond to a communication impasse. (Obj. #12)

26. Briefly discuss some differences in male/female communication according to Deborah Tannen. (Obj. #13)

Multiple Choice

1. Mutual empathy is
    a. caring for someone regardless of what they do or say.
    b. the basis for effective sexual communication.
    c. a suggested technique for "breaking the ice" in sexual conversations.
    d. a technique whereby both partners use "you" statements.

2. A suggested technique for getting started talking about sex is
    a. asking which method of birth control your partner prefers.
    b. seeing an erotic film together.
    c. self-disclosing the nature of any sexually transmitted diseases you have had and asking the other person to do the same.
    d. sharing sexual histories.

3. _____ is when a listener summarizes, in his or her own words, the speaker's message.
    a. Paraphrasing
    b. Validating
    c. Using "I" language
    d. Passive listening.

4. Unconditional positive regard is best described as
    a. continuing to smile and be courteous regardless of the type of criticism being received.
    b. a feeling of being spiritually connected not only to your partner, but to the rest of the world.
    c. caring for your partner as a person regardless of what he or she says or does.
    d. the knowledge that each partner in a relationship cares for the other and knows the care is reciprocated.

5. A (an) _____ question would allow your partner the freedom to share any relevant information or feelings.
    a. yes or no
    b. either/or
    c. open-ended
    d. structured

6. Which of the following does **not** belong with the others?
    a. "What are your feelings about having sex during my menstrual period?"
    b. "What do you enjoy most about our lovemaking?"
    c. "Do you think the kids should see us naked?"
    d. "How do you feel about having sex in the morning?"

7. Sharing fantasies is suggested as one way to
    a. self-disclose.
    b. give permission.
    c. express unconditional positive regard.
    d. deliver criticism.

8. Which of the following is an example of giving permission?
    a. "I had a very traumatic sexual experience about a year ago. Since then I've had a difficult time relaxing and enjoying sex."
    b. "I realize that you're not real comfortable with nudity, but I love to look at your naked body, so anytime your want to practice feeling more comfortable, let me know."
    c. "Do you like making love in unusual places?"
    d. "I have had this fantasy about having sex with you in the bathroom while we're at a party together."

9. Which of the following does **not** belong with the others?
   a. self-disclosure
   b. comparing notes
   c. giving permission
   d. taking responsibility for our own pleasure

10. When you don't expect your partner to read your mind and you are willing to ask for what you want, you are
    a. comparing notes.
    b. taking responsibility for your own pleasure.
    c. giving permission.
    d. expressing unconditional positive regard.

11. Which of the following is a strategy for discovering your partner's needs?
    a. maintaining eye contact
    b. paraphrasing
    c. expressing unconditional positive regard
    d. self-disclosure

12. Requests are **most** likely to be understood and heeded if they
    a. are specific.
    b. are vague, so your partner doesn't feel threatened.
    c. are general, so your conversation remains open-ended.
    d. are made on a regular basis.

13. Which of the following is **not** a suggested technique for learning to make requests?
    a. taking responsibility for your own pleasure
    b. giving permission
    c. using "I" language
    d. making requests specific

14. Delivering criticism will be **most** effective if the motive behind the criticism is to
    a. let your partner know that you have been hurt and are not willing to take it anymore.
    b. bring about a change that will enhance the relationship.
    c. put your partner on the defensive, thereby making him/her more willing to listen to you.
    d. get even with your partner for not paying enough attention to you.

15. Before verbalizing a complaint to your partner, it is a good idea to
    a. rehearse what you want to say, using "you" statements.
    b. frame your complaints in general terms; specific statements will put your partner on the defensive.
    c. list all of your complaints so you do not forget to mention all of them.
    d. be aware of your motivation behind offering the criticism.

16. Which of the following is one of the suggestions for receiving criticism?
    a. ask clarifying questions
    b. focus on future changes you can make
    c. empathize with your partner
    d. all of the above

17. Which of the following is **not** one of the suggested steps for saying no?
    a. Say no in a clear, straightforward manner.
    b. State specific consequences in the event that the person doesn't accept no for an answer.
    c. Express appreciation for the invitation.
    d. Offer an alternative, if appropriate.

18. Which of the following is the **best** example of a mixed message?
    a. Your partner says, "I know it's cold, but I want to make love outside anyway."
    b. Your partner says, "I know I said we could make love tonight, but I'm really tired. How about in the morning?"
    c. Your partner says, "Let's go park somewhere on the way home," and then falls asleep in the car.
    d. None of the above are examples of mixed messages.

19. When we speak of facial expression, touching and sounds, we are referring to the _____ aspects of sexual communication.
    a. nonverbal
    b. verbal
    c. intuitive
    d. interpersonal

20. Tom and Sherry have become frustrated in their communication with one another and have decided to take a break from discussion for a while. They are even considering seeking some counseling. According to the text, they are facing _____ in their communication.
    a. "the wall"
    b. an impasse
    c. a point of no return
    d. a crisis point

Insight and Application

1. Spend some time thinking about your communication skills — with your partner or past partners, friends and family members. How would **you** assess your communication skills — and how do you think the significant other people in your life would assess them? In the space below, list some of the specific models in your life for interpersonal communication — names of parents, teachers, other adults or family members, friends, counselors, clergy, etc. What did you learn from each of these people — both positive and negative — about how to express your thoughts and feelings, deal with conflict, listen and show respect for another person's point of view, give and receive criticism, acknowledge and support someone, etc.?

2. Based on your assessment above, identify and list below some **specific** communication skills you would like to improve — regarding your sexual relationship or just social/emotional relationships in general (all of the skills discussed in this chapter are applicable in nonsexual situations as well).

3. List past, current or future situations in which you would like to implement better communication skills. Based on information in the text, attempt to mentally rehearse these situations using better or different skills than you have used in the past. Then practice aloud, if possible, the way in which you might express yourself in a different way. Finally, role play this scenario with a partner or close friend — allow yourself some "simulated real life" practice. Get feedback from the other person. Offer to role play a situation of theirs if you would like. It will be awkward at first, but you will begin to become conscious of specific behaviors you would like to change, and over time, with practice, you will notice significant improvement.

4. Finally, if you are really serious about improving your skills in this area, take a class or workshop, read a book, see a counselor that specializes in communication skills development. Learning good communication — both verbal and nonverbal — is much like learning a new language, but the benefits will pay off for you many times over in improved relationships in your personal and professional life.

Matching Answers

1. d   2. f   3. a   4. e   5. b   6. g   7. h   8. k
9. c   10. i   11. j

Multiple Choice Answers

1. b   2. d   3. a   4. c   5. c   6. c   7. a   8. b
9. d   10. b   11. d   12. a   13. b   14. b   15. d   16. d
17. b   18. c   19. a   20. b

mutual empathy	passive listening
active listening	unconditional positive regard
paraphrasing	yes or no questions
open-ended questions	either/or questions
self-disclosure	giving permission

staring blankly into space, perhaps mumbling an "uh-huh" now and then while another person is talking	the underlying knowledge that each partner in a relationship cares for the other and knows that the care is reciprocated
conveying to other people that you will continue to value and care about them no matter what they do or say	being actively involved in what another person is saying by attentive body language and facial expressions, asking questions, paraphrasing and reciprocating
a question that requires only a yes or no answer	summarizing, in your own words, the content or the feelings of another person's message
in asking a person a question, offering two alternative responses in the form of an either/or question, e.g. "do you like making love with the lights on or off?"	questions that allow the respondent to elaborate on his or her answer, as opposed to replying either "yes" or "no."
encouraging and reassuring another person that it is okay to talk about specific feelings or wants	sharing some personal information about yourself in hopes that the person with whom you are speaking will do the same

"I" language   **validating**

acknowledging another person's point of view, even if you do not agree with it or have no intention of giving up your own position

taking responsibility by speaking in the first person when expressing feelings and wants as opposed to using "you" statements which tend to be more accusatory and judgmental

9

Sexual Behavior Patterns

Introduction

Sexuality may be expressed in many ways, including decisions to practice celibacy, to engage in erotic dreams and fantasy, masturbation, oral-genital sex, anal stimulation, and coitus. Making references to a variety of research studies as well as personal anecdotes selected from their files, the authors explore the range of options for sexual behavior.

Objectives

After studying this chapter, you should be able to:

1. Explain the significance of the Maltz hierarchy of sexual interactions and briefly describe the six levels of sexual interaction according to this model.

2. Define the two types of celibacy and discuss some of the reasons a person might become celibate.

3. Discuss erotic dreams and fantasy, making specific reference to the following:
   a. how common they are in men and women
   b. what nocturnal orgasm is, and when and in whom it occurs
   c. what research has demonstrated on the content of erotic fantasy
   d. functions that fantasies serve
   e. similarities and differences in the fantasy lives of men and women
   f. research that supports both the positive and negative aspects of sexual fantasy

4. Define masturbation, and discuss the following in regard to it:
   a. traditional and contemporary views of masturbation
   b. reasons why people masturbate
   c. what research has revealed regarding masturbatory patterns throughout the life cycle
   d. differences and similarities between male and female masturbatory patterns and experiences
   e. various self-pleasuring techniques

5. Explain some of the benefits of shared touching, and discuss areas of the body that are especially sensitive to stimulation.

6. Define cunnilingus and fellatio, discuss the origin of negative attitudes toward these sexual behaviors, and cite research that reveals how common oral-genital sex is in recent years.

7. Describe some of the considerations in practicing anal stimulation and cite research indicating how common this sexual practice is.

8. Explain the origin and current status of sodomy laws.

9. Define intromission and discuss considerations in using various coital positions.

10. Summarize how different racial, educational and religious backgrounds may affect a person's experience with oral sex.

Key Terms and Concepts

"Flash cards" listing key terms and concepts on one side and their corresponding definitions and explanations on the other side are provided at the end of the chapter.

Chapter Overview With Fill-Ins

After reading each of the major sections in the chapter, check your retention by **mentally** filling in each of the blanks in the corresponding sections below. Cover the answers in the margin as you go along, and write the answers in the space provided only when you are doing your final review.

Sexual Expression: The Importance of Context and Meaning

context

Maltz
six
destructive

In addition to being familiar with the range of behaviors that are options for sexual expression alone or with a partner, the _____ within which the behaviors occur is important in order for them to be enhancing to the individual and to the relationship. The _____ hierarchy of sexual interactions is a model that describes _____ levels of constructive or _____ sexual expression.

Celibacy

celibate
complete
partial

A physically mature person who does not engage in sexual behavior is said to be _____. There are two types of celibacy: _____ celibacy, in which a person neither masturbates nor has sexual contact with another person; and _____ celibacy, in which a person engages in masturbation but does not have sexual contact with anyone else.

Erotic Dreams and Fantasy

orgasm
Nocturnal
wet dreams

Erotic dreams and occasionally _____ may occur during sleep without a person's conscious direction. _____ orgasm occurs during sleep, commonly referred to as "_____ _____" in men.

masturbation

sexual arousal
gender-role

Erotic fantasies commonly occur during daydreams, _____, or sexual encounters with a partner. Fantasies serve a variety of functions during intercourse, the most common of which is to facilitate _____ _____. Another function of erotic fantasy can be to provide relief from _____-_____ expectations.

frequency

content
intercourse

The similarities between men's and women's fantasy lives include the following areas: 1) the _____ of fantasy is similar for both sexes during daydreams, masturbation, and sexual activity with a partner; 2) both men and women indicate a wide range of fantasy _____; and 3) similar percentages of research subjects fantasize while masturbating about having _____ with a loved one.

genital
emotional; non-
genital
forced

The differences between male and female fantasies include: 1) men's fantasies contain more explicit _____ images; 2) women emphasize _____ feelings and _____ caressing; and 3) almost twice as many women as men fantasize about being _____ to have sex.

heterosexual

Erotic fantasies are generally considered a healthy and helpful aspect of sexuality, although they have also been considered symptomatic of poor _____ relations or other problems.

Masturbation

self-stimulation

Masturbation is used to describe _____-_____ of one's genitals for sexual pleasure. Many of the negative attitudes toward masturbation are rooted in the early Judeo-Christian view

procreation

that _____ was the only legitimate purpose of sexual behavior. Current research has indicated that a greater frequency of dating, kissing, breast and genital touching, and intercourse was found to correlate with a higher likelihood and increased frequency

masturbation

of _____ among college students.

orgasm

People masturbate for a variety of reasons: for the pleasure of arousal and _____; at certain times the pleasure of an autoerotic session may be more satisfying than sex with a partner; it may help people make better decisions about relating sexually to others; it can

interest
shared
self-exploration
sleep

help deal with differences in sexual _____ within a relationship; it can be a _____ experience; it can be a valuable means of _____-_____; and it can be a way to reduce tension and induce _____.

normal

It is _____ for infants to touch their genitals and to respond pleasurably to self-stimulation. During adolescence, the

increases

number of boys who masturbate _____ dramatically. The reasons masturbation is more common among males are

unknown
androgen; toilet

_____, although there is speculation that differences in _____ levels and _____ training as well as social expectations for gender-role stereotyped behavior may be factors.

majority

In adulthood, the _____ of men and women, both married and unmarried, masturbate on occasion.

Shared Touching

maladjusted

A classic study demonstrated that when baby monkeys' and other primates' physical needs were met but they were denied their mothers' touch, they grew up to be extremely _____. The entire body responds to touching, but some specific areas are more

sexual feelings

receptive to _____ _____ than others.

alcohol
variation

In touching the vulva, a lubricant such as K-Y jelly, a lotion without _____, or saliva can be used. There is great _____ from one woman to another in the kind of touches that create arousal.

glans

saliva

anus

In touching male genitals, gentle or firm stroking of the penile shaft and _____, and light touches or tugging on the scrotum may be desired. Some men find that lubrication with lotion or _____ increases pleasure, and some men enjoy manual stimulation or penetration of the _____.

Oral-Genital Stimulation

Cunnilingus; fellatio

women

_____ is oral stimulation of the vulva and _____ is oral stimulation of the penis and scrotum. Both of Kinsey's studies found that, in heterosexual couples, _____ were much less likely to stimulate partners orally than the reverse.

oral-genital

procreation

coitus

urinary

homosexual

The reservations that some people have concerning _____-_____ stimulation stem from several sources. For one, sex for purposes other than _____ has historically been labeled immoral. In fact, sexual behaviors other than _____ are still illegal in many states. Many people perceive the genitals as "dirty" because they are close to the _____ opening and the anus. However, routine hygiene is adequate for cleanliness. Another reason why some people object to oral sex is that they believe it is a _____ act.

Anal Stimulation

homosexual

10

orgasmic

orgasm

Like oral-genital stimulation, anal stimulation may be thought by some to be a _____ act. However, penile penetration of the anus is practiced regularly by about _____ percent of heterosexual couples. Some women report _____ response from anal intercourse, and heterosexual and homosexual men often experience _____ from stimulation during penetration.

vaginal

infections

Heterosexual couples should never have _____ intercourse directly following anal intercourse because bacteria that are normal in the anus often cause _____.

Coitus and Coital Positions

coitus

intromission

orgasm

There is a wide range of positions a couple may choose for penile-vaginal intercourse, or _____. Some couples may find mutual cooperation during _____ (entry of the penis into the vagina) helpful. Coitus can occur with or without _____ for one or both partners.

Short Answer

1. List and briefly describe the six levels of sexual interaction according to Maltz. (Obj. #1)

2. List at least five advantages of celibacy. (Obj. #2)

3. List three disadvantages of celibacy. (Obj. #2)

4. How common is sexual fantasy among men and women? Cite specific statistics. (Obj. #3a)

5. According to some research studies, how does the amount of sexual experience people have affect the amount of sexual fantasizing they do? (Obj. #3a)

6. List four functions that fantasies serve during intercourse. (Obj. #3d)

7. Explain why a certain percentage of men and women fantasize about being forced to have sex. (Obj. #3c)

8. List three similarities in men's and women's fantasy lives. (Obj. #3e)

9.   List two differences between men's and women's fantasies. (Obj. #3e)

10. List the two most common sexual fantasies **during masturbation** for women. Then, list two for men. (Obj. #3c, e)

11. List the two most common sexual fantasies **during intercourse** for men. Then, list two for women. (Obj. #3c, e)

12. How can having sexual fantasies be healthy? (Obj. #3f)

13. Under what circumstances can sexual fantasizing be problematic? (Obj. #3f)

14. From an historical perspective, why has masturbation been perceived as evil and unhealthy? (Obj. #4a)

15. What was Freud's perception regarding masturbation? (Obj. #4a)

16. List eight benefits of masturbation. (Obj. #4b)

17. At what point could masturbation become a problem? (Obj. #4c)

18. What are some factors that may account for why masturbation is more common among males than females? (Obj. #4d)

19. Briefly outline masturbatory patterns in each of the following: (Obj. #4c)

    a.   childhood

    b.   adolescence

    c.   adulthood

20. Compare the incidence of masturbation among Whites, African-Americans and Hispanics. How does educational level relate to incidence of masturbation? (Obj. #4c)

21. What is the most common self-stimulation technique for women? The least common? (Obj. #4e)

22. According to Masters and Johnson, what purposes does touching serve? (Obj. #5)

23. Describe how breast size is related to breast sensitivity. (Obj. #5)

24. List three types of lubrication that can be used during manual stimulation. (Obj. #5)

25. According to Kinsey's research, which was more common — fellatio or cunnilingus? (Obj. #6)

26. List three reasons why people may have negative attitudes toward oral-genital sex. (Obj. #6)

27. Describe the changes in the percentages of people engaging in oral-genital sex from Kinsey's time to the present. (Obj. #6)

28. How do race, education and religion affect experience with oral sex? (Obj. #6)

29. To what sexual behavior(s) does sodomy refer? (Obj. #8)

30. As of 1992, how many states still have sodomy laws on the books? (Obj. #8)

31. Cite statistics indicating how common anal intercourse is. (Obj. #7)

32. What are the health risks associated with anal sex and how can they be reduced? (Obj. #7)

33. What is a good intercourse position during pregnancy? (Obj. #9)

Multiple Choice

Select the best alternative. Check your answers with the answer key at the end of the chapter.

1. John and Rita have just begun a sexual relationship. They both enjoy how creative and uninhibited they are sexually, and their comfort with role flexibility allows them to communicate with each other more freely and to enjoy greater intimacy. According to the Maltz hierarchy of sexual interaction, this couple would probably be at _____ level.
   a. -1; irresponsible interaction
   b. +1; positive role fulfillment
   c. +2; making love
   d. +3; authentic sexual intimacy

2. In partial celibacy, a person
   a. neither masturbates nor has sexual contact with another person.
   b. engages in masturbation but does not have sexual contact with another person.
   c. engages in masturbation and oral sex but not sexual intercourse.
   d. does not masturbate or have sexual contact with another person for at least six months.

3. According to the text, for which of the following reasons would a person be **most likely** to say that he or she was celibate?
   a. He or she has sexual problems and does not want to acknowledge them.
   b. The person is not sexually interested in the other party, so this is a way of extricating himself or herself from the situation.
   c. She or he is newly recovering from drug dependency.
   d. He or she wants to see how the other person will react.

4. The most common fantasy that men have during masturbation is
   a. sex with more than one person of the other sex.
   b. oral sex with stranger.
   c. intercourse with a loved one.
   d. being forced to have sex.

5. According to one study, the highest percentage of men reported which of the following as their fantasy content during intercourse?
   a. oral-genital sex
   b. having others give in to you after resisting
   c. group sex
   d. sex with a former lover

6. According to Kinsey's research, erotic dreams occur for _____ of the males and for _____ of the females.
   a. two-thirds; almost all
   b. two-thirds; two-thirds
   c. almost all; two-thirds
   d. almost all; almost all

7. Which of the following statements concerning sexual fantasy is **true**?
   a. Twice as many women as men fantasize about being forced to have sex.
   b. Many sex therapists encourage their clients to use fantasy as a source of stimulation.
   c. One purpose of fantasy is to relieve boredom.
   d. all of the above

8. Which of the following is **not** a word for masturbation?
   a. autoeroticism
   b. fellatio
   c. self-stimulation
   d. "jerking off"

9. Which of the following **best** describes Reverend Sylvester Graham's view of masturbation?
   a. It does not result in procreation, therefore it is sinful.
   b. Since ejaculation reduces precious vital fluids, masturbation, as well as intercourse, should be avoided.
   c. Masturbation is normal during childhood but could result in "immature" sexual development in adulthood.
   d. Masturbation is how we discover eroticism, so it should be learned and practiced.

10. Which of the following statements is **true**?
    a. Kinsey's research indicated that the number of adolescent boys and girls who masturbated was roughly equal.
    b. Recent statistics indicate that a greater number of adolescent girls engage in masturbation than boys.
    c. Kinsey's research indicated that from age 12–15 the number of boys who masturbated increased dramatically.
    d. all of the above

11. Which of the following statements is **true**?
    a. Women appear to use a greater variety of masturbatory techniques than men.
    b. Some men, and to a greater degree women, enjoy using vibrators for added sexual pleasure.
    c. According to one study, females wanted to spend more time in foreplay and afterplay than men.
    d. all of the above

12. A way to tell if you are "masturbating to excess" is when
    a. it interferes significantly with any aspect of your life.
    b. your hand develops calluses.
    c. you begin to lose your eyesight.
    d. you sleep frequently due to your constant state of relaxation.

13. Which of the following is **not** cited as a reason why masturbation may be more common among men than women?
    a. Young boys receive encouragement to touch themselves during toilet training.
    b. The value of sex for pleasure is more closely related to stereotyped male attitudes toward sexuality.
    c. Men have more androgen than women.
    d. Men become more aroused because they experience more vasocongestion than women.

14. Which of the following individuals would be **least likely** to masturbate?
    a. a single, college educated African-American man
    b. a married, high school educated White woman
    c. a single, high school educated Hispanic woman
    d. a married, college educated African-American man

15. In regard to breast stimulation, which of the following statements is **most** accurate?
    a. Men do not enjoy having their nipples stimulated.
    b. The size of the breasts is not related to how erotically sensitive they are.
    c. Women can become highly aroused by breast stimulation but are unable to achieve orgasm this way without additional clitoral stimulation.
    d. A woman's breasts are usually tender immediately following her menstrual period.

16. _____ is oral stimulation of the penis and scrotum.
    a. Oralingus
    b. Analingus
    c. Fellatio
    d. Cunnilingus

17. Which of the following statements concerning oral-genital sex is **true**?
    a. The risk of contracting AIDS while practicing this behavior is high.
    b. "69" is another term for cunnilingus.
    c. The belief that it is a homosexual act is why some people are opposed to it.
    d. The incidence of oral sex has decreased over the last forty years

18. Sodomy refers to
    a. rear-entry coitus.
    b. oral-genital stimulation.
    c. anal intercourse.
    d. oral-genital stimulation and anal intercourse.

19. Which of the following statements concerning anal intercourse is **true**?
    a. Oral-genital sex is more risky than anal intercourse in terms of AIDS transmission.
    b. Due to the scarcity of nerve endings surrounding the anus, most of the pleasure comes from depth of penetration.
    c. It is practiced regularly by about 20 percent of heterosexual couples.
    d. Hunt's survey found that 25 percent of couples under age 35 practiced it occasionally.

20. *Vitalogy*, an encyclopedia of health and home published in 1918, describes the effects of masturbation as
    a. extremely debilitating, resulting in the hopeless ruin of mind and body.
    b. a potential health hazard if not monitored closely.
    c. inconsequential in terms of physical or mental health.
    d. extremely positive, in that it increases self-awareness and reduces tension.

Insight and Application

1. Before you read this chapter, if you began dating someone to whom you were very attracted who announced that he or she was celibate, how would you have responded? Think in terms of your verbal response as well as what you would say to yourself. Now, taking into account what you have read, would you respond to this same situation any differently? If so, what would the differences be?

2. Do you think your reaction to a person's choice to be celibate would vary depending upon the person's gender? If so, why?

3. Do you engage in sexual fantasy alone and/or with a partner? If so, what functions do your fantasies serve? What is the content of your fantasies during masturbation and/or intercourse? How does this compare to the information presented in the text?

4. What are your feelings regarding masturbation? Is it something you do and enjoy, do and feel somewhat guilty and ashamed of, or choose to not do at all? If you do engage in masturbation, is it something you would acknowledge with your partner or avoid discussing? How does it affect your feelings about yourself and/or your relationship with your partner? What are the reasons you choose to masturbate? Is this something you would do in front of your partner (while your partner held or caressed you) or have your partner do for you? Why or why not? How would you feel if you knew your partner masturbated in addition to being sexually active with you?

5. What are your personal feelings regarding fellatio and cunnilingus? Would you/do you feel comfortable discussing various aspects of these behaviors with your partner (for example: how you feel about genital odors and secretions; your willingness to comfortably give and receive; whether or not you prefer to do this simultaneously, if at all; will the activity culminate in ejaculation for the male partner and if so, is that comfortable/acceptable for the other partner? Will the ejaculate be swallowed or not?) In receiving oral-genital stimulation are you capable of asking specifically for what you want as well as receiving feedback from your partner?

6. One study of college students indicated that men prefer coitus and women prefer foreplay and afterplay. Based on your knowledge and experience, would you agree with this? If so, why do you think this is the case?

7. Although penile-vaginal intercourse is the "main event" of sexual sharing for many couples, that is certainly not the case for everyone. For many individuals, while intercourse may be pleasurable for them, it is not as pleasurable as other activities or it may be difficult to achieve orgasm that way. In addition, individuals with a homosexual orientation, individuals who are physically disabled in some way, or individuals with chronic illnesses or other medical conditions may be unable or unwilling to have intercourse. If you have experienced intercourse, what are your feelings about it? Are you easily aroused and/or orgasmic with intercourse? Is it ever awkward/uncomfortable/painful for you? If so, why? Which coital positions do you prefer? Why? Have you been able to communicate your preferences to your partner? If not, what gets in the way?

Multiple Choice Answers

1. c	2. b	3. c	4. c	5. a	6. c	7. d	8. b
9. b	10. c	11. d	12. a	13. d	14. c	15. b	16. c
17. c	18. d	19. d	20. a				

complete celibacy

partial celibacy

nocturnal orgasm

masturbation

cunnilingus

fellatio

sodomy

intromission

a physically mature person who engages in masturbation but does not have interpersonal sexual contact with another person	a physically mature person who does not masturbate or have sexual contact with another person
self-stimulation of one's genitals for sexual pleasure; autoeroticism is another term for it	orgasm that occurs during sleep; it is experienced by both men and women
oral stimulation of the penis and scrotum	oral stimulation of the vulva
entry of the penis into the vagina	an ill-defined legal category for noncoital genital contacts such as oral-genital and anal intercourse

Homosexuality

Introduction

The chapter begins by introducing Kinsey's continuum of sexual orientation. Specifically, homosexual, bisexual, and heterosexual orientations are discussed, but the focus of the chapter is on homosexuality. Societal attitudes toward homosexuality over time are explored, as well as various theoretical perspectives that have attempted to explain how sexual orientation develops. The range of homosexual lifestyles is also examined, and the chapter concludes with a discussion of some of the social and political issues facing the homosexual population today.

Objectives

After studying this chapter, you should be able to:

1. Define the following terms:
   a. homosexual
   b. gay
   c. lesbian
   d. sexual orientation
   e. bisexual

2. Describe Kinsey's continuum of sexual orientation and discuss how his estimates of the incidence of homosexuality in the general population compare to the findings in the National Health and Social Life Survey.

3. Discuss bisexuality and the problems in defining it, and compare it to other sexual orientations.

4. List and describe four different types of bisexuality.

5. Briefly outline and describe how attitudes toward homosexuality have evolved over time, beginning with Judeo-Christian tradition in the seventh century B.C.

6. List and describe four current positions toward homosexuality represented in contemporary Christianity.

7. Discuss some cross-cultural perspectives on homosexuality, citing specific examples.

8. Define homophobia, discuss various ways in which it may be expressed, and explain how homophobic attitudes can change.

9. Making reference to relevant research, discuss the psychosocial and biological theories regarding how sexual orientation develops.

10. Discuss what research has revealed regarding the following:
    a. homosexual relationships
    b. homosexual family life
    c. sexual behavior among homosexual women
    d. sexual behavior among homosexual men

11. Define "coming out" and describe five different steps that may be involved in that process.

12. Discuss some of the significant events in the gay rights movement, beginning with the 1950s and continuing to the present time.

Key Terms and Concepts

"Flash cards" listing key terms and concepts on one side and their corresponding definitions and explanations on the other side are provided at the end of the chapter.

Chapter Overview With Fill-Ins

After reading each of the major sections in the chapter, check your retention by **mentally** filling in each of the blanks in the corresponding sections below. Cover the answers in the margin as you go along, and write the answers in the space provided only when you are doing your final review.

social

same

A homosexual person is an individual "whose primary erotic, psychological, emotional, and _____ interest is in a member of the _____ sex, even though that interest may not be overtly expressed."

A Continuum of Sexual Orientations

Bisexuality

_____ refers to attraction to both same and other-sex partners.

seven

Alfred Kinsey devised a _____-point continuum in his analysis of sexual orientations in American society. The scale ranges from 0 (exclusive contact with and erotic attraction to the

other

_____ sex) to 6 (exclusive contact with and attraction to

same; equal

the _____ sex). Category 3 represents _____ homosexual and heterosexual attraction and experience.

context

It is the _____, not the contact, that may be most signif-icant in defining bisexuality. Bisexuality can be considered as a

identity

behavior or as an _____, and the two are not always the same. There are several different types of bisexuality: bisexuality as

orientation

a real _____, as a transitory orientation, as a

transitional; denial

_____ orientation, or as homosexual _____.

Societal Attitudes

negatively

procreation

Within the Judeo-Christian tradition, homosexuality has been viewed _____. The pursuit of sexual pleasure outside of the purpose of _____ was viewed as immoral.

four

rejecting-punitive

One theologian has described _____ current positions toward homosexuality: 1) a _____-_____ orientation; 2) the rejecting-nonpunitive position; 3) the qualified

full acceptance

acceptance position; and finally, 4) the _____ _____ position.

sick

contradicts
Psychiatric
mental

The belief that homosexual people are sinners has been replaced to some degree by a belief that they are "_____", and that they can be cured by means of a variety of medical and psychological treatments. Current research _____ this notion. In 1973, the American _____ Association removed homosexuality per se from the category of a _____ disorder.

Homophobia
oneself

education

_____ is defined as irrational fear of homosexuality in others, the fear of homosexual feelings within _____, or self-loathing because of one's homosexuality. Homophobic attitudes can change over time with experience, deliberate thought or _____.

What Determines Sexual Orientation?

Bell

sexual orientation

A variety of theories have attempted to explain the origins of sexual orientation, and although considerable research has been done, there are still no definitive answers regarding how a homosexual orientation is developed. _____ and his colleagues (1981) have done the most comprehensive study to date about the development of _____ _____.

parenting

inability

Some of the theories about the development of a homosexual orientation relate to life incidences, _____ patterns or psychological attributes of the individual. For example, it is sometimes believed that unhappy heterosexual experiences or the _____ to attract partners of the other sex cause a person to become homosexual. Research has demonstrated that this is not the case.

older
caught

school age

Another myth that research has shown to be false is that young men and women become homosexual because they have been seduced by _____ homosexuals. Some people believe that homosexuality can be "_____" from someone else, i.e., a homosexual teacher, etc. In fact, a homosexual orientation appears to be established before _____ _____, and modeling is not a relevant factor.

family

childhood

Another prevalent theory regarding the development of homosexuality has to do with certain patterns in a person's _____ background. Despite the influences of Freud, and later, some of Bieber's data, it has not been clearly established that _____ factors are the critical determinants in the development of a homosexual orientation.

biological

hormone

cause; result

In addition to psychosocial causes, researchers have looked into a number of areas in an effort to establish _____ causes for sexual orientation. Some researchers have speculated that _____ levels in adults may contribute to homosexuality. Even if consistent differences were found in the hormonal patterns of homosexual and heterosexual adults, it would remain unknown whether the differences were a _____ or a _____ of sexual orientation.

prenatal

brain

Some researchers speculate that _____ hormone imbalances can alter the masculine and feminine development of the fetal _____ and that this may contribute to a homosexual orientation.

brains

Recent research reported structural differences in the _____ of homosexual and heterosexual men, supporting a biological explanation for sexual orientation.

genetic

Other research has confirmed the possibility that _____ factors may contribute to the development of male homosexuality.

gender
nonconformity

stereotypic

Bell and his colleagues believe that evidence for a biological predisposition for homosexuality is the strong link between adult homosexuality and _____ _____ as a child. Gender nonconformity is a variable the researchers used that measured the extent to which the research subjects conformed to _____ characteristics of masculinity or femininity during childhood.

biological

In conclusion, research is suggesting that there is a _____ predisposition to exclusive homosexuality, but the causes of sexual orientation in general, and homosexuality specifically, remain speculative at this point.

Lifestyles

stereotypes

While it is true that some homosexual individuals dress and act according to commonly held _____, many do not.

passive

gender-role
homosexual

Some people mistakenly think that homosexual partners always enact the stereotypical active "male" or _____ "female" roles. One study reported that heterosexual couples were likely to adhere more closely to traditional _____-_____ expectations than were _____ couples.

fewer; lesbian

AIDS

hundreds

There are some differences between homosexual men and women in the number of their sexual partners. Lesbians are likely to have had _____ sexual partners, and _____ couples are more likely than male couples to have monogamous relationships. Prior to the _____ epidemic, more homosexual men were often involved in casual sexual encounters, sometimes with _____ of partners.

emotional closeness

Several studies have found that lesbians differ from homosexual men in the extent to which they associate _____ _____ with sex.

multidimensional

Sexual involvement with many partners is not universal among homosexual men. Homosexual relationships are _____ and are not based solely on sex.

marriage

Although _____ between two people of the same sex is not legally recognized by any state, many homosexual couples share significant one-to-one relationships.

parents

heterosexual

parenting
artificial
insemination

carry

Some homosexual individuals or couples become _____ with adopted or foster children, or they have children who were born in previous _____ marriages. Lesbian mothers have been found to be similar to heterosexual mothers in lifestyle, maternal interest, and _____ behavior. Children may also be adopted or conceived by lesbians through _____ _____. A homosexual man who wants to be a father may make a personal agreement with a woman who agrees to _____ his child.

penile-vaginal
manual-genital

Homosexual individuals who are in sexual relationships engage in sexual behaviors similar to those of heterosexual persons with the exception of _____-_____ intercourse. These behaviors include touching, kissing, body contact, _____-_____ stimulation, oral-genital contact and anal stimulation.

penis; dildos

tribadism

There are several misconceptions that exist concerning lesbian sexual expression: 1) that sex between women is unsatisfactory because a _____ is lacking, and 2) that _____ (penis-shaped devices) are used extensively among lesbians. Manual stimulation, oral contact, and rubbing genitals together or against the partner's body (called _____) are included in lesbian sexual behaviors.

Anal intercourse

fellatio
masturbation

_____ _____ is often thought to be the most prevalent sexual behavior between homosexual men. However, the Bell and Weinberg study (1978) found that _____ is the most common mode of expression. Mutual _____ is the next most common and anal intercourse is the least common.

coming out

gay community

There are several steps in the process of _____ _____: self-acknowledgment, self-acceptance, disclosure, telling the family, and involvement in the _____ _____.

The Gay Rights Movement

New York City
Stonewall
resisted

gay rights

The symbolic birth of gay activism occurred in 1969 in _____ _____ _____ when police raided a gay bar, the _____. Police raids in gay bars were common, but this time the people _____ and fought back, and a riot ensued. The Stonewall incident acted as a catalyst for the formation of _____ _____ groups and other activities such as Gay Pride Week.

discrimination

consensual sex

Since the early 1970s, groups have worked to end various kinds of _____ against gay people. The gay rights movement has been primarily concerned with legislation related to _____ _____ and civil rights.

Civil Rights Act

sexual

A major legislative goal of gay rights advocates is an amendment to the 1964 _____ _____ _____ that would broaden it to include "affectional or sexual preference" along with race, creed, color, and sex. This would make it illegal to discriminate in housing, employment, insurance, and public accommodations on the grounds of _____ orientation.

Matching

Match the people below with their ideas or contributions. Note that each person may be used once, more than once, or not at all, but choose only **one** answer for each blank.

a.	Alfred Kinsey	d.	Alan Bell
b.	James B. Nelson	e.	Sigmund Freud
c.	Martin Weinberg	f.	Simon LeVay

_____1.   used the term "homophobia" to describe anti-homosexual attitudes

_____2.   has conducted the most comprehensive study to date regarding the development of sexual orientation

_____3.   his data has been criticized for producing an inflated estimate of the number of homosexual people in our society

_____4.   a theologian who has described four positions on homosexuality that are represented in contemporary Christianity

_____5.   believed that men and women passed through a "homoerotic" phase in the process of establishing a heterosexual orientation

_____6.   devised a seven-point continuum of sexual orientation

_____7.   found structural differences in the brains of homosexual and heterosexual men

_____8.   his subjects were asked in-depth questions regarding childhood, adolescence and sexual practices during four-hour, face-to-face interviews

Short Answer

1.   Define "homosexual." (Obj. #1)

2.   Describe Kinsey's continuum scale of sexual orientation. On what grounds has it been criticized? (Obj. #2)

3.   According to the National Health and Social Life Survey, what percentage of men and women identify themselves as homosexual? (Obj. #2)

4. What factors need to be taken into account in defining bisexuality? (Obj. #3)

5. Comment on the degree of erotic interest that bisexual individuals appear to demonstrate compared to heterosexual or homosexual individuals. (Obj. #3)

6. List and briefly describe the four types of bisexuality. (Obj. #4)

7. Briefly explain how negative attitudes toward homosexuality have evolved, beginning with the reformation movement that began in the seventh century B.C. (Obj. #5)

8. What are some of the treatments people have been subjected to in an attempt to "cure" their homosexuality? (Obj. #5)

9. What action did the American Psychiatric Association take regarding the treatment of homosexuality as a mental illness? (Obj. #5)

10. List and briefly describe four current theological positions on homosexuality. (Obj. #6)

11. In a cross-cultural survey of 190 societies, what percent found homosexuality acceptable for some people or in some situations? (Obj. #7)

12. Cite two cross-cultural examples in which homosexuality was/is considered acceptable. (Obj. #7)

13. List at least three examples of homophobia. (Obj. #8)

14. Can homophobic attitudes be changed? If so, how? (Obj. #8)

15. Cite research that refutes the notion that unhappy heterosexual experiences are what cause a person to be homosexual. (Obj. #9)

16. Cite research that refutes the myth that a young person becomes homosexual because he or she has been seduced by an older homosexual. (Obj. #9)

17. Briefly explain how Freud explained the development of homosexuality. (Obj. #9)

18. What is the current focus of therapy for homosexual clients? (Obj. #9)

19. Compare hormone levels in adult heterosexual and homosexual men. (Obj. #9)

20. Briefly summarize the research on the influence of prenatal hormone levels on sexual orientation. (Obj. #9)

21. What did LeVay find in his study of brain differences in homosexual and heterosexual men? (Obj. #9)

22. Explain how genetic factors may contribute to the development of male homosexuals. (Obj. #9)

23. What is known concerning the relationship between sexual orientation and gender nonconformity? (Obj. #9)

24. Describe the similarities or differences between homosexual men and women in the following areas: (Obj. #10)

    a.   number of sexual partners

    b.   tendency to associate emotional closeness with sex

    c.   likelihood of sharing a household

25. What did one study find was most important in a love relationship, regardless of the couples' sexual orientation? (Obj. #10)

26. Summarize the research that compares the children of lesbian and heterosexual mothers, as well as the parenting behavior of the two groups of women. (Obj. #10)

27. Name three sexual behaviors common among for lesbians. (Obj. #10)

28. List in order of frequency the types of sexual behavior common to male homosexuals. (Obj. #10)

29. List and briefly describe the five steps in the process of "coming out." (Obj. #11)

    a.

b.

c.

d.

e.

30. What is considered to be the symbolic birth of gay activism? (Obj. #12)

31. Summarize the British Wolfenden Report of 1957. (Obj. #12)

32. What issues are the focus for the gay rights movement? (Obj. #12)

Multiple Choice

Select the best alternative. Check your answers with the answer key at the end of the chapter.

1. A homosexual person is best defined as an individual
   a. who has sexual contact with a person of the same sex.
   b. whose gender identity is inconsistent with his or her biological sex.
   c. who is sexually and emotionally attracted to a person of the same sex.
   d. whose primary erotic, psychological and emotional interest is in a person of the same sex.

2. In Kinsey's scale of sexual orientation, the number "3" represents
   a. exclusive homosexual contact and attraction.
   b. exclusive heterosexual contact and attraction.
   c. equal homosexual and heterosexual contact and attraction.
   d. a person who is asexual.

3. The recent *Sex in America* study found that _____ % of women and _____ % percent of men identified themselves as homosexual.
   a. 1.5; 3
   b. 3; 5.5
   c. 4.5; 7
   d. 6; 8.5

4. Bisexual behavior can be a _____, in which a person is changing from one exclusive orientation to another.
   a. transitory orientation
   b. transitional orientation
   c. denial of one's homosexuality
   d. real orientation

5. A woman who earns a living having sex with men for money has fantasized about women since she can remember and has lived with her female lover for the past five years. According to information presented in the text, this woman's sexual orientation would **best** be described as
   a. bisexual as the result of homosexual denial.
   b. transitory bisexual.
   c. transitional bisexual.
   d. true bisexual.

6. Current theological positions toward homosexuality
   a. unconditionally reject homosexuality.
   b. maintain that while homosexuality is a sin, people are unable to change their orientation, so committed homosexual relationships should be accepted.
   c. are fully accepting of homosexuality.
   d. demonstrate a great range of convictions.

7. Influenced by Judeo-Christian tradition, our society has for centuries believed that homosexuality was _____. This view was replaced to a large extent with the belief that homosexuality was _____.
   a. an illness; immoral
   b. immoral; an illness
   c. conditionally acceptable; an illness
   d. an illness; conditionally acceptable

8. Which of the following is an expression of homophobia?
   a. You find out a friend of yours is gay, and so you invest less time in the relationship.
   b. You do not go to a gay bar for fear that someone you know might see you.
   c. You laugh at a "queer" joke.
   d. all of the above

9. Which of the following would be **least** indicative of homophobia?
    a. being outspoken about lesbian and gay rights but making sure everyone knows that you are straight
    b. thinking that if a gay or lesbian person touches you that they are making sexual advances
    c. feeling that a lesbian is just a woman who can't find a man
    d. firing your gardener, who is gay, because you have not been pleased with the quality of his work

10. The cause of lesbianism is
    a. a history of poor sexual relationships with men.
    b. related to an abnormal hormonal imbalance.
    c. the result of faulty parenting.
    d. unknown.

11. Which of the following statements is **true**?
    a. In general, lesbians are less attractive than heterosexual women.
    b. Young men and women often become homosexual because they have been seduced by older homosexuals.
    c. Sexual orientation is not fully established until the onset of puberty, so care should be taken prior to that time to provide children with appropriate heterosexual role models.
    d. none of the above

12. Research comparing levels of sex hormones in adult heterosexual and homosexual males has indicated that
    a. the heterosexual group has consistently higher levels of sex hormones than the homosexual group.
    b. the homosexual group has consistently higher levels of sex hormones than the heterosexual group.
    c. there are no differences between the two groups.
    d. The data have been contradictory.

13. Gender nonconformity rates in childhood are
    a. higher for female homosexuals than heterosexuals.
    b. higher for male homosexuals than heterosexuals.
    c. higher for both male and female homosexuals than heterosexuals.
    d. approximately the same for both homosexuals and heterosexuals.

14. Which of the following statements about the relationship between hormones and the development of homosexuality **best** reflects the current state of knowledge?
    a. Treating male homosexuals with estrogen increases the degree to which they experience gender nonconformity.
    b. Treating male homosexuals with testosterone reduces their sexual desire.
    c. A homosexual orientation causes the fluctuations of hormone levels.
    d. Homosexuality could cause differences in hormone levels and differences in hormone levels could cause homosexuality.

15. Which of the following statements is **false**?
    a. In Bell and Weinberg's study, three-fourths of lesbians and one-half of gay men were in primary relationships.
    b. Heterosexual couples were likely to adhere more closely to traditional gender-role expectations than were homosexual couples.
    c. Lesbian couples are more likely than male couples to have monogamous relationships.
    d. Marriage between two people of the same sex is not legally recognized by any state.

16. Simon LeVay of the Salk Institute found differences in the _____ of the homosexual and heterosexual men he studied.
    a. brains
    b. gonads
    c. hormone levels
    d. childhood sexual and family history

17. In one study, _____ was most important in homosexual male love relationships, and _____ was most important in heterosexual love relationships.
    a. "having a satisfying sexual relationship"; "being able to talk about my most intimate feelings"
    b. "being able to talk about my most intimate feelings"; "being able to talk about my most intimate feelings"
    c. "being able to talk about my most intimate feelings"; "having a satisfying sexual relationship"
    d. "having a satisfying sexual relationship"; "having a satisfying sexual relationship"

18. According to research, the parenting behavior of lesbians
    a. is generally more consistent than that of heterosexual mothers.
    b. is generally less consistent than that of heterosexual mothers.
    c. is similar to that of heterosexual mothers.
    d. The data are inconsistent.

19. The term for rubbing genitals against another person's body is called
    a. sensate focus.
    b. tribadism.
    c. rimming.
    d. body pressing.

20. Which of the following is the **most** prevalent form of sexual behavior between homosexual men?
    a. fellatio
    b. manual stimulation
    c. tribadism
    d. anal intercourse

21. Homosexual sexual expression
    a. is unique to homosexual relationships.
    b. is very similar to heterosexual expression.
    c. is pleasurable, but does not typically result in orgasm.
    d. requires a certain degree of agility that discourages heterosexuals from participating in it.

22. Which of the following statements about men in the Sambia society of New Guinea is **true**?
    a. They experience fellatio with other men but not with their wives.
    b. Once married, heterosexual contact is primary, but homosexual contact continues on an occasional basis.
    c. They believe that drinking the semen of post pubertal boys makes them become better warriors.
    d. With the exception of ceremonial heterosexual contacts, homosexuality is the primary form of sexual expression throughout the life cycle.

Insight and Application

1. In terms of behavior, attraction, fantasy, and self-identity, how would you describe your sexual orientation? Have you ever had difficulty understanding or accepting people with a sexual orientation that differs from your own? If so, why? If, over time, you have noticed a difference in your ability to understand and accept people with different orientations, what factors have contributed to that change?

2. In what ways have you observed homophobia expressed? Give specific examples.

3. If a close friend or family member of yours were to tell "queer" jokes or make other homophobic comments, how would you respond, if at all?

4. From what you have observed, how do you think the AIDS epidemic has affected attitudes toward homosexuality? From a personal standpoint, how has it affected your attitudes and behavior, if at all?

Matching Answers

1. c   2. d   3. a   4. b   5. e   6. a   7. f   8. d

Multiple Choice Answers

1. d   2. c   3. a   4. b   5. b   6. d   7. b   8. d
9. d   10. d   11. d   12. c   13. c   14. d   15. a   16. a
17. b   18. c   19. b   20. a   21. b   22. c

homosexual	gay
lesbian	bisexuality
Kinsey's continuum of sexual orientation	rejecting-punitive orientation
rejecting-nonpunitive orientation	qualified acceptance orientation
full acceptance	homophobia

a common synonym for homosexual	an individual whose primary erotic, psychological, emotional and social interest is in a member of the same sex, even though those interests may not be overtly expressed
attraction to both same — and other — sex partners	a common term for homosexual women
a current theological position which unconditionally rejects homosexuality and bears a punitive attitude toward gay people	Alfred Kinsey's seven-point scale analyzing sexual orientation, ranging from 0 (exclusive heterosexual contact) to 6 (exclusive homosexual contact)
a current theological position maintaining that homo-sexuality is a sin but can't be changed so that gay people who can't refrain from sexual interaction should maintain fully committed relationships	a current theological position that maintains that homo-sexuality is unnatural, but because of God's grace, supports the civil liberties of gay people
irrational fears of homo-sexuality in others or within oneself, or self-loathing because of one's homosexuality	a current theological position that views sexuality as intrinsic to the capacity for human love, and therefore supports loving relationships regardless of the sexual orientation of the partner

gender nonconformity	**tribadism**
coming out	**passing**

rubbing genitals against someone's body or genital area	the extent to which individuals conform to stereotypic characteristics of masculinity or femininity during childhood
a term that is sometimes used to describe maintaining the false image of heterosexuality	acknowledging, accepting and openly expressing one's homosexuality; there are several steps involved in this process

11

Contraception

Introduction

The chapter begins by presenting the historical and social perspectives on contraception. With an emphasis on shared contraceptive responsibility on the part of both men and women, currently available contraceptive methods are discussed, examining the advantages, disadvantages, effectiveness, and safety of each. Finally, new directions in contraception are explored.

Learning Objectives

After studying this chapter, you should be able to:

1. Explain when efforts to control conception first began and list various contraceptive methods that have been used throughout history.

2. From an historical and social perspective, briefly discuss each of the following:
   a. available methods of contraception throughout U.S. history
   b. obstacles to reliable contraceptive availability
   c. key people involved in promoting birth control
   d. key legislation related to contraceptive use

3. List some of the reasons why reliable contraception is a major worldwide concern today for many people in our society as well as what some of the objections are to contraceptive use.

4. Identify some of the ways in which couples can share responsibility for birth control.

5. List and describe several variables that influence the effectiveness of birth control.

6. Compare the effectiveness of various birth control methods in terms of both theoretical and actual use.

7. For each of the following contraceptive methods, describe what it is and how it works, and list the advantages and disadvantages of each:
   a. "outercourse"
   b. oral contraceptives
   c. Norplant
   d. Depo-Provera
   e. "morning-after" pills
   f. condoms
   g. diaphragms
   h. cervical caps
   i. vaginal spermicides
   j. intrauterine devices
   k. methods based on the menstrual cycle
   l. sterilization
   m. other methods such as nursing, withdrawal and douching

8. Discuss some of the future possibilities for contraceptive methods that may be available to men and women.

Key Terms and Concepts

"Flash cards" listing key terms and concepts on one side and their corresponding definitions and explanations on the other side are provided at the end of the chapter.

Chapter Overview With Fill-Ins

After reading each of the major sections in the chapter, check your retention by **mentally** filling in each of the blanks in the corresponding sections below. Cover the answers in the margin as you go along, and write the answers in the space provided only when you are doing your final review.

Historical and Social Perspectives

Margaret Sanger

1960; Griswold
Connecticut

Eisenstadt v. Baird

_____ _____ was the person most instrumental in promoting changes in birth control legislation and availability in the United States. The first birth control pills came on the U.S. market in the year _____. In _____ v. _____, the Supreme Court ruled that states could not prohibit use of contraceptives by married people. Years later, in _____ v. _____, the Supreme Court ruled that unmarried individuals had the legal right to contraception.

physical; over-
population

In recent years, reliable birth control has been seen as desirable for a variety of reasons: people want to be able to plan and limit the size of their families; use of birth control can also contribute to the _____ health of the mother; and _____ is a serious threat to the earth's environment.

religious

Objections to contraception often stem from _____ mandate.

Shared Responsibility

enhance

intercourse
discussing
accompany
expenses

Sharing the responsibility of contraception can _____ a relationship. Ways in which contraceptive responsibility might be shared include: 1) for either partner to initiate a discussion of birth control before having _____ the first time; 2) reading about and _____ various alternatives; 3) for a man to _____ his partner to a medical exam if appropriate; and 4) to share the _____ for the exam and birth control.

Choosing Among Currently Available Methods

effectiveness

outercourse
kissing
masturbation
pregnancy
sexually transmitted
diseases

Some of the most important considerations to be aware of in choosing a birth control method are convenience, safety, expense and _____.

Noncoital forms of sexual intimacy, called "_____", include _____, touching, petting, mutual _____, and oral and anal sex. The voluntary avoidance of coitus offers effective protection from _____, is free from side effects, and reduces the risk of spreading _____ _____ _____ , with the exception of anal intercourse.

Hormone-Based Contraceptives

constant-dose
progestin

There are three basic types of oral contraceptives currently on the market: the _____-_____ combination pill, the multiphasic pill and the _____-only pill. Advantages of oral contraceptives include: convenience; high rate of

effectiveness
mittelschmerz

_____; elimination of _____ (pain at ovulation); reduction of menstrual cramps and premenstrual tension symptoms; treatment of a wide variety of medical problems; reduction of the incidence of rheumatoid arthritis, and of

ovarian

_____ and endometrial cancers; enlargement of the breasts; and improvement of acne. Disadvantages of oral contraceptives can be summarized by the acronym ACHES, which

Chest
Eye

stands for: Abdominal pain; _____ pain; Headaches; _____ problems; or Severe leg pain.

Norplant
progestin
five

_____ consists of six, thin capsules filled with _____ that are implanted under the skin of a woman's upper arm. The capsules prevent conception for _____ years.

injectable
twelve

Depo-Provera is an _____ contraceptive that needs to be given once every _____ weeks.

Morning-after

"_____-_____" pills have been effective in preventing pregnancy if taken within 72 hours following intercourse

uterine

and are presumed to work by affecting the _____ lining so that the developing embryo cannot implant in it.

Barrier Methods

Condoms

_____ are currently the only temporary method of birth control available for men. They can be made of natural skin (sheep

polyurethane

membrane), latex or _____ .

Female

_____ condoms, which were approved for sale in the United States in 1988, resemble regular condoms but are worn

internally

_____ by women.

diaphragm

The _____, a round, soft latex dome with a thin, flexible spring around the rim, is inserted into the vagina with a contra-

cervix

ceptive cream or jelly, and fits around the back of the _____ and underneath and behind the pubic bone. The diaphragm

barrier
sperm

provides a chemical as well as a mechanical _____ to prevent _____ from entering the cervix and uterus.

cervical cap

The _____ _____ is a thimble-shaped cup made of rubber or plastic that fits over the cervix and can be left in

diaphragm;
spermicide

place longer than a _____. It is usually recommended that a _____ be used with the cap.

sponge
film
spermicide

There are several types of vaginal spermicides: foam, suppositories, the contraceptive _____, creams, jellies and vaginal contraceptive _____ (VCF). All of the above contain a _____, or chemical that kills the sperm.

Intrauterine Devices

uterus
os
Copper T

fertilization

pelvic
inflammatory
infertility
insertion
year
uterine
miscarriage

<u>A</u>bdominal
<u>I</u>ncreased

Intrauterine devices, or IUDs, are small plastic objects that are inserted into the _____ through the vaginal canal and cervical _____. Two types of IUDs are currently available: the _____, called the ParaGard, and the Progestasert T. Recent studies have indicated that the copper and the progesterone in IUDs prevent _____. The advantages of the IUD are: it is highly effective, convenient, allows for uninterrupted sexual interaction, and there are no further supplies to be purchased after the initial cost. Disadvantages are: increased risk of _____ _____ disease; fallopian tube problems which can contribute to _____; discomfort, cramping or bleeding during _____; uterine expulsion of the IUD within the first _____ following insertion; perforation of the _____ wall by the IUD; and 50 percent chance of _____ if a woman becomes pregnant. Serious problems associated with the IUD can be summarized by the acronym PAINS, which stands for: <u>P</u>eriod late, no period; _____ pain; _____ temperature, fever, chills; <u>N</u>asty or foul discharge; and <u>S</u>potting, bleeding, and clots.

Methods Based on the Menstrual Cycle

ovulation

rhythm

basal body-
temperature

drops

There are three methods of birth control that are based on the menstrual cycle: the mucus method, also called the _____ method, which is based on the cyclic changes of cervical mucus; the calendar method, also called the _____ method, in which a woman estimates the calendar time during her cycle when she is ovulating and fertile; and the _____-_____ _____ method, in which a woman takes her temperature on a regular basis and is able to determine when she is ovulating because the BBT, immediately prior to ovulation, _____ slightly.

Sterilization

Sterilization

tubal

culpotomy; safer
effective
Vasectomy
vas deferens

vasovasostomy

_____ is the most effective method of birth control except abstinence from coitus, and it is the leading method of birth control in the United States. One method of female sterilization is _____ sterilization, which can be accomplished by a variety of techniques including minilaparotomy, laparoscopy, and _____. In general, male sterilization is _____, considerably less expensive, and as _____ as female sterilization. _____ is a minor surgical procedure that involves cutting and tying the _____ _____, the two sperm carrying ducts. Some men request a _____, a reversal of a vasectomy.

Other Methods

Nursing

ovulation

withdrawal

Douching

_____ a baby delays the return to fertility after childbirth; however, it is not a reliable method because there is no way of knowing when _____ will resume.

The practice of _____ is not very effective as a birth control method for several reasons. _____ is another ineffective method as it may actually help sperm reach the opening of the cervix.

New Directions in Contraception

motility

vaginal ring

RU-486

Research efforts with respect to male contraception concentrate on inhibiting sperm production, _____, or maturation.

A range of techniques are currently under experimentation for women, including progesterone injections; a "_____ _____," which is like a diaphragm that releases hormones and an antiprogesterone substance, _____ .

Matching

Match the birth control methods below with the correct descriptions. Note that each method may be used more than once and there may be more than one answer for each blank.

a. combination pill
b. IUD
c. Norplant
d. diaphragm
e. condom
f. cervical cap

g. ovulation method
h. rhythm method
i. BBT method
j. sterilization
k. progestin-only pill

_____1. should be inserted no longer than six hours prior to intercourse

_____2. available without prescription

_____3. contains synthetic progestin that is released over 5-year period

_____4. may damage cervix

_____5. inhibits ovulation

_____6. should not be used by women with history of PID (pelvic inflammatory disease)

_____7. women learn to monitor changes in vaginal secretions

_____8. reduces the risk of endometrial cancer

_____9. some contain nonoxynol-9

_____10. after removal, fertility resumes within 24 hours

_____11. increased risk of blood clots, heart attacks and liver tumors

_____12. next to the pill, the contraceptive most commonly used by college-age adults

_____13. alters cervical mucus to block sperm

_____14. can be used for postcoital contraception

_____15. should not be left in for longer than 24 hours

_____16. both men and women can use this method

_____17. most commonly used reversible method of birth control in U.S. today

_____18. the copper and progesterone in them prevent fertilization

_____19. a woman keeps a chart of the length of her monthly cycles

_____20. cases of toxic shock syndrome have been associated with using it

_____21. when a yellow or white sticky discharge begins, should use back-up method of birth control

_____22. ovulation is determined by measuring body temperature

_____23. the leading method of birth control around the world today

Short Answer

1. When did efforts to control conception begin? List four methods of birth control used prior to this century. (Obj. #1)

2. What were the Comstock laws? (Obj. #2)

3. What was the purpose of the clinic that Margaret Sanger opened? (Obj. #2e)

4. When did birth control pills first come on the market? (Obj. #2a)

5. Briefly discuss the difference between Griswold v. Connecticut and Eisenstadt v. Baird. (Obj. #2d)

6. According to one study, how did contraceptive use among Catholic and non-Catholic women compare? (Obj. #3)

7. Identify five ways in which couples can practice shared responsibility concerning birth control. (Obj. #4)

8. What characteristics do men and women who do not use birth control have in common? (Obj. #5)

9. List the five most reliable birth control methods. (Obj. #6)

10. Name six behaviors that constitute "outercourse." (Obj. #7a)

11. List three types of oral contraceptives and briefly explain the differences among them. (Obj. #7b)

12. List four advantages of oral contraceptives. (Obj. #7b)

13. Explain the potential side effects associated with the pill using the acronym ACHES. (Obj. #7b)

14. List three serious health problems associated with oral contraceptive use. (Obj. #7b)

15. What is Norplant and for how long is it effective? (Obj. #7c)

16. What is Depo-Provera and for how long is it effective? (Obj. #7d)

17. What do "morning-after" pills consist of? (Obj. #7e)

18. Describe three different condom types and their effects on sexually transmitted diseases. (Obj. #7f)

19. List five considerations to be aware of in using condoms. (Obj. #7f)

20. How does the female condom compare to the male condom in terms of protection against sexually transmitted diseases? (Obj. #7f)

21. How far in advance of intercourse can a diaphragm be inserted? How long should it remain in afterwards? (Obj. #7g)

22. What medical problem has been associated with diaphragms? (Obj. #7g)

23. List the advantages and disadvantages of the cervical cap. (Obj. #7h)

24. What is the most common type of vaginal spermicide? (Obj. #7i)

25. How does the IUD prevent pregnancy? (Obj. #7j)

26. List the disadvantages of using an IUD. (Obj. #7j)

27. List symptoms of potential problems associated with the IUD using the acronym PAINS. (Obj. #7h)

28. Briefly describe how the following methods based on the menstrual cycle work: (Obj. #7k)

    a.   mucus method

    b.   calendar method

    c.   basal body-temperature method

29. In using the ovulation method, at what point should unprotected intercourse be avoided? (Obj. #7k)

30. What does the BBT do immediately prior to ovulation? (Obj. #7k)

31. List and briefly describe three types of tubal sterilization. (Obj. #7l)

32. What happens to a woman's egg production after tubal sterilization? (Obj. #7l)

33. What problems may be associated with vasectomy? (Obj. #7l)

34. Define recanalization. (Obj. #7l)

35. Define vasovasostomy. What factor influences its success? (Obj. #7l)

36. Explain why nursing, withdrawal and douching are not reliable methods of birth control. (Obj. #7m)

37. Briefly describe some new birth control options for men that may be available in the future. (Obj. #8)

38. What is RU-486 and how is it used? (Obj. #8)

Multiple Choice

Select the best alternative. Check your answers with the answer key at the end of the chapter.

1. In 1965, the Supreme Court ruled in _____ that states could not prohibit the use of contraceptives by married people.
   a. Griswold v. Connecticut
   b. Eisenstadt v. Baird
   c. Sanger v. McCormack
   d. Roe v. Wade

2. Sharing responsibility means
   a. asking a partner about birth control before intercourse.
   b. accompanying a partner when a medical exam is needed.
   c. discussing alternatives and choosing the best one.
   d. all of the above

3. Women who are uncomfortable with their sexuality are likely to
   a. insist that their partners wear condoms.
   b. use birth control pills.
   c. take a passive role in contraceptive decision-making.
   d. seek sterilization earlier than other women.

4. Oral sex
   a. is a form of "outercourse."
   b. is a recent phenomenon.
   c. is safe sex, in that you cannot contract or transmit a sexually transmitted disease.
   d. all of the above

5. Which of the following is the **most effective** birth control method in actual, as opposed to theoretical, use?
   a. diaphragm and spermicide
   b. progestin-only birth control pills
   c. Norplant
   d. estrogen-progestin pills

6. The combination pill works by
    a. releasing a constant dose of estrogen and progestin.
    b. releasing a variable dose of estrogen and progestin.
    c. releasing a constant dose of pituitary hormones LH and FSH.
    d. altering the cervical mucus to a thick and tacky consistency.

7. If a woman forgets to take one of her birth control pills, she should
    a. take two pills immediately.
    b. take the missed pill as soon as she remembers it and her next pill at the regular time.
    c. consult her health practitioner.
    d. consider IUD insertion to terminate a possible pregnancy.

8. Birth control pills may do all of the following **except**
    a. reduce menstrual cramps.
    b. decrease acne.
    c. enlarge breasts.
    d. minimize yeast infections

9. Which of the following is **not** a potential risk associated with oral contraceptives?
    a. increased incidence of liver tumors
    b. increased risk of ovarian cancer
    c. increased possibility of heart attacks
    d. increased risk of blood clots

10. ACHES, which is an acronym that is associated with danger signs for birth control users, stands for
    a. abdominal pain, chest pain, heart palpitations, eye problems, and stomach ache.
    b. abdominal pain, chest pain, headaches, eye problems, and severe leg pain.
    c. abdominal pain, chest pain, heavy sweating, eye problems, and side aches.
    d. abdominal pain, chest pain, heavy sweating, ear ache, and slight cramping.

11. Which of the following statements regarding Norplant is **false**?
    a. The capsules are implanted in a woman's upper arm.
    b. The capsules are filled with synthetic progestin.
    c. A woman's ability to become pregnant returns within one month after removal of the capsules.
    d. The most common side effect is menstrual irregularity.

12. There is **less** chance of a condom breaking if
    a. it is kept in a hot, dry place prior to use.
    b. it does not have a reservoir tip.
    c. it is lubricated.
    d. all of the above

13. Sexually transmitted diseases can pass through _____ condoms but not _____ condoms.
    a. latex; natural-skin and polyurethane
    b. natural-skin; latex and polyurethane
    c. natural-skin and polyurethane; latex
    d. polyurethane; natural-skin and latex

14. "Morning-after" pills are presumed to work by affecting the
    a. uterine lining.
    b. cervix.
    c. sperm motility.
    d. ovulation process.

15. A diaphragm should remain in the vagina at least _____ hours following intercourse.
    a. one
    b. two
    c. four
    d. six

16. A woman may need a different diaphragm after
    a. a pregnancy.
    b. reaching menopause.
    c. lengthy workouts.
    d. treatment for sexually transmitted diseases.

17. All of the following may be disadvantages associated with diaphragm use **except**
    a. increased incidence of pelvic inflammatory disease
    b. possible interference with oral sex
    c. poor diaphragm fit
    d. bladder discomfort

18. A _____ is usually recommended when using the cervical cap.
    a. spermicide
    b. lubricating jelly
    c. vaginal douche
    d. condom

19. Which of the following statements concerning the cervical cap is **true**?
    a. It is available at local pharmacies.
    b. It is used in conjunction with spermicide.
    c. It can be left in place indefinitely.
    d. It comes in one size that can accommodate most women.

20. Spermicides containing _____ help protect against HIV transmission and other sexually transmitted diseases.
    a. VCF
    b. nonoxynol-9
    c. K-Y jelly
    d. progestin

21. The _____ may work by slightly irritating and inflaming the uterine lining, thereby resulting in the fertilized ovum not attaching.
    a. cervical cap
    b. diaphragm
    c. IUD
    d. birth control pill

22. The most serious complication related to the IUD is that it increases a woman's chance of
    a. liver tumors.
    b. pelvic inflammatory disease.
    c. hypertension.
    d. ovarian cancer.

23. The calendar method is also called the _____ method.
    a. body-temperature
    b. mucus
    c. rhythm
    d. ovulation

24. Present research indicates that methods based on the menstrual cycle
    a. are more effective than most other methods.
    b. are less effective than most other methods.
    c. are more convenient than most other methods.
    d. have more side effects than most other methods.

25. Female sterilization can be done in several ways. The procedure called _____ involves one or two incisions at the navel and below the public hair line. A lighted instrument is inserted to locate the fallopian tubes.
    a. minilaparotomy
    b. laparoscopy
    c. culpotomy
    d. vasectomy

26. Which of the following statements regarding vasectomy is **false**?
    a. It is not as safe as female sterilization.
    b. It is less expensive than female sterilization.
    c. It is a minor surgical procedure.
    d. It may be associated with an increase in prostate cancer.

27. The success rate of vasovasostomy is dependent upon
    a. the sperm count prior to vasectomy.
    b. how recently the vasectomy was performed.
    c. the thickness of the vas deferens.
    d. the age of the man

28. Which of the following statements regarding RU-486 is **false**?
    a. It is not yet available in the United States.
    b. It prevents implantation of the zygote from occurring.
    c. It appears to be helpful in treating endometriosis.
    d. It is an antiprogeterone substance.

Insight and Application

1. If you are sexually active, how have you assumed total responsibility or shared responsibility for birth control? Give specific examples. What are your feelings about shared responsibility? How do you think our society reinforces or discourages shared responsibility with respect to birth control issues? Give specific examples.

2. How do you feel about presenting contraceptive information to adolescents and children? How thoroughly should the information be presented? Should it be presented in conjunction with other kinds of information on human sexuality? If so, what other topics might be included? What type of format, in your opinion, would be appropriate?

3. Do you think men and women should be able to choose sterilization at any age? For example, should a 22-year-old woman be able to have a tubal sterilization? If so, what types of screening procedures, if any, should be implemented for young adults who seek this type of birth control option?

4. How would you describe your personal comfort level in discussing contraception with a partner or potential partner? Is there anything you would like to change? If so, what is it?

Matching Answers

1. d, f	2. e	3. c	4. f	5. a	6. b	7. g	8. a, k
9. e	10. c	11. a	12. e	13. k	14. a	15. f	16. e, j
17. a, k	18. b	19. h	20. d, f	21. g	22. i	23. j	

Multiple Choice Answers

1. a	2. d	3. c	4. a	5. c	6. a	7. b	8. d
9. b	10. b	11. c	12. c	13. b	14. a	15. d	16. a
17. a	18. a	19. b	20. b	21. c	22. b	23. c	24. b
25. b	26. a	27. a	28. b				

Comstock laws

Griswold v. Connecticut

Eisenstadt v. Baird

"outercourse"

constant-dose
combination pill

multiphasic pill

progestin-only pill

ACHES

Norplant

diaphragm

a 1965 Supreme Court ruling mandating that states could not prohibit the use of contraceptives by married people

laws that Anthony Comstock succeeded in enacting that prohibited the dissemination of contraceptive information by mail on the grounds that this information was obscene

noncoital forms of sexual intimacy such as kissing, touching, petting, mutual masturbation, oral and anal sex

a 1972 Supreme Court ruling that extended the right to privacy to unmarried individuals by decriminalizing the use of contraception by single people

an oral contraceptive designed to reduce total hormone dosage and side effects by providing fluctuations of estrogen and progesterone levels throughout the menstrual cycle

the most commonly used oral contraceptive in the U.S.; contains synthetic estrogen and progestin which are released at constant levels throughout the menstrual cycle

an acronym that summarizes serious problems associated with oral contraceptives: abdominal pain; chest pain; headaches; eye problems; severe leg pain

an oral contraceptive that contains no estrogen and only 0.35 mg of progestin — one third the amount of an average combination pill

a contraceptive device consisting of a latex dome on a flexible spring rim. The diaphragm is inserted into the vagina with contraceptive cream or jelly and covers the cervix.

a contraceptive method in which six thin capsules of synthetic progestin are implanted in a woman's upper arm; provides effective contraception for five years

cervical cap	vaginal spermicides
condom	intrauterine devices
PAINS	mucus method
calendar method	basal body-temperature method (BBT)
female sterilization	vasectomy

chemical substances used in foam, suppositories, the contraceptive sponge, creams and jellies and contraceptive film that are inserted in the vagina prior to intercourse in order to kill sperm	a plastic or rubber thimble-shaped cup that covers the cervix in order to provide a contraceptive barrier to sperm
a small, plastic device that is inserted into the uterus for contraception	a latex or membrane sheath that fits over the penis and is used for protection against unwanted pregnancy and sexually transmitted diseases
a birth control method that is based on determining the time of ovulation by means of the cyclical changes of the cervical mucus	an acronym that summarizes problems associated with the IUD: period late or no period; abdominal pain; increased temperature, fever, chills; nasty discharge; spotting, bleeding, heavy periods
a method of birth control based on temperature changes before and after ovulation	a method of birth control based on abstinence from intercourse during the estimated calendar time of her menstrual cycle when she is ovulating and fertile
a male sterilization procedure that involves removing a section from each vas deferens	the leading method of birth control in the U.S. whereby the fallopian tubes are tied off or clipped by any one of the following methods: minilaparotomy; laparoscopy; or culpotomy

vasovasostomy   **Depo-Provera** an injectable contraceptive that contains progestin and is effective for twelve weeks

surgical reconstruction of the vas deferens after vasectomy

12

Conceiving Children: Process and Choice

Introduction

Choosing whether or not to have a child is a major life decision. This chapter explores some of the factors that may affect that decision, and outlines some of the various options available for becoming a parent. How a woman's health care affects the developing fetus and the processes of pregnancy, birth, and postpartum adjustment are also discussed. The controversial topic of abortion is also explored from historical, social and political perspectives.

Objectives

After studying this chapter, you should be able to:

1. Discuss each of the following in relationship to becoming a parent:
    a. advantages and disadvantages of becoming a parent
    b. how common remaining childless is
    c. how women who voluntarily remain childless feel about the decision
    d. how common adoption is
    e. why people choose to adopt children

2. List several factors that will increase the possibility of conception.

3. Cite statistics that indicate how common infertility is, how successful treatment is, and then describe some of the factors that contribute to both female and male infertility.

4. Explain how problems with fertility may affect a couple's emotional and sexual relationship.

5. List and describe options for conception available to couples with infertility problems.

6. Identify the initial signs of pregnancy a woman may experience and how these may be confirmed.

7. Discuss the incidence of and issues involved in spontaneous abortion (miscarriage).

8. Cite statistics that indicate how common elective abortion is among women from various age groups and discuss the characteristics that women who seek elective abortions have in common.

9. Describe various medical procedures that may be used in having an abortion.

10. Discuss research data related to the following:
    a. effects of first-trimester abortion on subsequent fertility
    b. effects of having two or more abortions
    c. number of women that have abortions who have had a previous abortion
    d. what factors can contribute to repeat abortions

11. Describe how a woman's partner might share the responsibility of an unwanted pregnancy.

12. Make reference to research that addresses the emotional effects of legal abortion on both women and men.

13. Explain why some women may risk an unwanted pregnancy by not using contraceptives reliably.

14. Outline and elaborate upon some of the reasons why elective abortion is such a controversial social and political issue.

15. Compare the beliefs of individuals who hold strong pro-choice values with those individuals who are anti-abortion.

16. Discuss some of the following aspects of a healthy pregnancy:
    a. fetal development
    b. prenatal care
    c. detection of birth defects
    d. pregnancy after age 35

17. Compare the different emotional and physical reactions to pregnancy from both a female and male perspective.

18. Discuss how sexual interaction may be affected during pregnancy.

19. List and describe the three stages in the process of childbirth.

20. Outline and briefly explain some contemporary philosophies regarding childbirth.

21. List and briefly describe three birthplace alternatives and under what circumstances each is appropriate.

22. Discuss the advantages and disadvantages of various medical procedures used during childbirth, making reference to appropriate research studies that support each position.

23. Describe the physical and psychological adjustments that family members experience during the postpartum period.

24. Explain the physiological changes that accompany nursing and list the advantages and disadvantages of it.

25. Describe some of the considerations a couple may need to make in resuming sexual interaction after childbirth.

26. Discuss current techniques that are being used to predetermine the sex of a child, and the impact this has had in various countries in which there is a strong preference for having sons.

27. Define all of the key terms and concepts for this chapter listed in the flash card section at the end of the chapter, being able to integrate them with all relevant material outlined above.

Key Terms and Concepts

"Flash cards" listing key terms and concepts on one side and their corresponding definitions and explanations on the other side are provided at the end of the chapter.

Chapter Overview With Fill-Ins

After reading each of the major sections in the chapter, check your retention by **mentally** filling in each of the blanks in the corresponding sections below. Cover the answers in the margin as you go along, and write the answers in the space provided only when you are doing your final review.

Parenthood as an Option

choice
Pronatalism

In contemporary American society, adults have more _____ about becoming parents. _____, or policies and attitudes that tend to encourage parenthood for all couples, may manifest itself as social pressure to have children or in commonly held

stereotypes

_____ about people, especially women, who choose not to have children.

oneself; worries

Some of the potential advantages of not having children are: more time for _____; no _____ about providing for children's needs; more spontaneous recreational, social, and work patterns; more financial resources; increased ability to pursue

careers; relation-
ships

_____; more time and energy for adult _____; and less stress on the marriage.

love

Many potential advantages of having children which parents cite include: the satisfaction of giving and receiving _____; a positive sense of self-esteem and sense of accomplishment; and the opportunity to discover unknown areas of the self and experience greater meaning and satisfaction in life.

Becoming Pregnant

time
conception
ovulation; mucus

Picking the right _____ for intercourse is important in enhancing the probability of _____. Predicting the time of _____ can be done by using the _____ method, or the body-temperature and calendar methods.

year
fertility

If attempts at impregnation are not successful after one _____, both partners should be medically evaluated for _____ problems.

ovulate

cervical

endometriosis

sexually transmitted
diseases

Female infertility may be attributed to failure to _____. If ovulation and semen quality is satisfactory, tests may be performed on the _____ mucus to see if antibodies are being produced against the partner's sperm. Infections, abnormalities of the reproductive system, scar tissue, and _____ may also contribute to female fertility problems. Another major cause of infertility is tubal scarring from _____ _____ _____.

motility
reproductive

varicocele

Most causes of male infertility are related to abnormalities in sperm number and/or _____. Infectious diseases of the male _____ tract, genital tract infections, STD-caused infections, environmental toxins, smoking, alcohol and drug abuse, the presence of a _____ (a damaged or enlarged vein in the testes or vas deferens), hormone deficiencies, and undescended testes may cause male sterility.

Artificial
insemination

_____ _____ is a procedure to help couples overcome the problems of infertility.

zygote intrafallopian transfer

ova

Various procedures have been developed for a woman or couple who cannot conceive through intercourse or artificial insemination: in vitro fertilization (IVF); the _____ _____ _____ (ZIFT); and the gamete intrafallopian transfer (GIFT). Donated _____ may be used in IVF-GIFT procedures, and in some cases, both donated sperm and ova.

Women who are willing to be artificially inseminated by the male partner of a childless couple, carry the pregnancy, deliver the child, and give the child to the couple for adoption are called

surrogate mothers

_____ _____.

absence
Breast

human chorionic gonadotropin
trophoblast
ten

Usually the first indication of pregnancy is the _____ of the menstrual period at the expected time. _____ tenderness, nausea, and vomiting may also accompany pregnancy in the first weeks or months. The blood, and therefore the urine, of a pregnant woman contains the hormone _____ _____ _____ (HCG), secreted by the _____ cells of the placenta. Tests for HCG have become available that can detect pregnancy as early as _____ days after conception.

Spontaneous and Elective Abortion

spontaneous
abortion
Elective

Various genetic, medical, or hormonal problems may cause _____ _____, or miscarriage, to occur, terminating the pregnancy. A miscarriage is a spontaneous abortion that occurs in the first 20 weeks of pregnancy. _____ abortion involves a decision to terminate a pregnancy by medical procedures.

Suction curettage

90

_____ _____ is an abortion procedure that is used in the early stages of pregnancy (up to 13 weeks). About _____ percent of abortions are done at or before 12 weeks.

dilation

D and E, or _____ and evacuation, is currently the safest and most widely used technique for pregnancy termination between 13 and 21 weeks.

Prostaglandins

uterine

_____ (a type of human hormone) are one of the compounds used to induce termination of second trimester pregnancies. These hormones cause _____ contractions, and the fetus and the placenta are usually expelled within 24 hours.

one; Contraceptive
method

Approximately one-third of abortions are performed for women who have had at least _____ previous abortion. _____ _____ failure is the most frequently cited reason for having an abortion.

trauma

repeat

first

Research indicates that legal abortion does not cause lasting emotional _____. However, women who have _____ abortions experience higher emotional distress in interpersonal relationships than do women having a _____ abortion.

controversial
Laws
Roe v. Wade

Hyde Amendment

low-income

overturn

Elective abortion continues to be a _____ issue in the United States. _____ regulating abortion continue to change. It was not until 1973 in the _____ v. _____ ruling, based on the right to privacy, that the United States Supreme Court legalized a woman's right to decide to terminate her pregnancy before the fetus has reached the age of viability. Four years later, the _____ _____ was passed which prohibited federal Medicaid funds for abortion. Since Medicaid provided funds for the majority of _____- _____ citizens, only middle- and upper-income women were able to continue to obtain medically safe abortions. In 1989, the Supreme Court ruled in favor of three state restrictions on abortion that had been unconstitutional under Roe v. Wade. Although the ruling does not _____ the right to abortion, it does give other state legislatures the right to impose these restrictions.

discussing

In June 1991, the Supreme Court, in its Rust v. Sullivan decision, upheld the legislation barring federally funded clinics from _____ abortion with patients.

71

illegal

opposed

A 1992 survey found that _____ percent believe that abortion should remain legal. Antiabortion groups want to make abortion _____ and to establish the constitutional rights of the unborn fetus. Pro-choice forces support a woman's choice to have an abortion, and they are strongly _____ to antiabortion legislation restricting others' choices.

A Healthy Pregnancy

trimesters
zygote

sex

seven

The nine-month span of pregnancy is customarily divided into three thirteen-week segments called _____. The fertilized ova, called a _____, develops into the multicelled blastocyst that implants on the wall of the uterus about one week after fertilization. By the fourth month, the _____ of the fetus can often be distinguished. By the end of the fifth month, the fetus' weight has increased to one pound and will increase to an average of over _____ pounds at birth.

prenatal care

Components of optimal _____ _____ include good nutrition, general good health, adequate rest, routine health care, exercise, and childbirth education.

placenta

Fetal
alcohol syndrome

Although the _____ (a disk-shaped organ attached to the wall of the uterus) prevents some kinds of bacteria and viruses from passing into the fetal blood system, many can penetrate it, including the AIDS virus. Certain medications, as well as drugs, alcohol, and tobacco are known to be dangerous to the fetus. _____ _____ _____ (FAS) is the leading cause of developmental disabilities and birth defects in the United States.

amniocentesis

chorionic villus

If fetal abnormalities are suspected for some reason, a test called _____ can be performed during the fourteenth to sixteenth week of pregnancy. Another procedure for detecting birth defects is called _____ _____ sampling (CVS).

age; Down syndrome

The rate of fetal defects due to chromosomal abnormalities rises with maternal _____. _____ _____, the most common condition caused by chromosomal abnormality, results in impaired intellectual functioning and various physical defects.

The Experience of Pregnancy

shared

anxiety

taboo

Pregnancy, once seen as predominantly the woman's domain, is now commonly viewed as a _____ experience. Although men are encouraged to be active participants in the pregnancy and birth, they sometimes feel that their feelings of _____, anger, sadness, or fear might upset their partners and therefore are _____.

decline

continued

positions

Most research shows a progressive _____ in sexual interest and activity over the nine months of pregnancy. However, it is now generally accepted that in pregnancies where there are no risk factors, sexual activity and orgasm may be _____ until the onset of labor. Over time, it may be necessary for couples to modify intercourse _____.

Childbirth

contractions

The initial indication of first-stage labor may be regular _____ of the uterus, a "bloody show" (discharge from the mucus plug from the cervix), and rupturing of the amniotic sac ("breaking the bag of waters").

effaced

dilation

cervix

born

placenta

Prior to the first stage of labor, the cervix has _____ (flattened and thinned) and dilated slightly. It is the extent of cervical _____ that defines the phases of first-stage labor. When the _____ is fully dilated, second-stage labor begins and the infant descends farther into the birth canal. The second stage ends when the infant is _____. Third-stage labor lasts from the time of birth until the delivery of the _____ (afterbirth).

childbirth

breathing

prepared childbirth

Parents-to-be often participate in _____ classes that provide thorough information about medical intervention and the process of labor and delivery. The classes also provide training in _____ and relaxation exercises designed to ease the pain of childbirth. Although they are sometimes referred to as "natural" childbirth methods, _____ _____ is a more appropriate label for the Dick-Read, Lamaze and other childbirth approaches.

home

incompatibility

placenta previa

There are several options regarding where childbirth occurs: in hospitals, birth centers, or at _____. Possible complications during childbirth can include premature labor, the infant in other than the head-first position, blood _____ between mother and fetus, toxemia (water retention and high blood pressure are early symptoms), _____ _____ (the placenta positioned over the cervical opening) and multiple births, etc.

heart
cesarean

health care

There are a number of various medical interventions that may be used during childbirth including medications, fetal _____ monitors, forceps, episiotomies and _____ sections. There are advantages and disadvantages of all of these that need to be carefully discussed with the _____ _____ provider before labor begins.

Postpartum

postpartum
adjustment

postpartum
depression

The first several weeks following birth are referred to as the _____ period. It is a time of both physical and psychological _____ for each family member, and is likely to be a time of intensified emotional highs and lows. Many mothers experience _____ _____, which may be due to the sudden emotional, physical, and hormonal changes following delivery.

colostrum
advantages

genitals

Production of breast milk begins about one to three days after delivery, following production of _____ (a yellowish liquid which contains antibodies and protein). Numerous _____ have been cited with respect to breast-feeding: breast milk is a digestible food filled with antibodies, nursing induces uterine contractions, and nursing provides close physical contact. However, some women report oversensitive _____ and breasts, less vaginal lubrication, and reduced energy.

sexual

lochia

intimacy

Physical and psychological readiness for _____ activity are important issues after the delivery. Couples are commonly advised that intercourse can resume after the flow of reddish uterine discharge, called _____, has stopped and after the episiotomy incision or vaginal tears have healed. In addition, the significant changes in daily life that a new baby brings can affect sexual _____.

Matching

Match the terms or phrases below with the appropriate descriptions. Some terms may be used more than once but choose only **one** answer for each blank.

a. endometriosis
b. ZIFT
c. Hyde Amendment
d. third trimester
e. CVS
f. below-normal percentage of body fat
g. IVF
h. first-stage labor
i. varicocele
j. first trimester

k. mumps during adulthood
l. suction curettage
m. prostaglandins
n. GIFT
o. undescended testes
p. Rust v. Sullivan
q. second trimester
r. dilation and evacuation
s. Roe v. Wade
t. FAS

_____1. fertilized egg is placed in the fallopian tube

_____2. most widely used abortion procedure between 13 and 21 weeks

_____3. ruling to make abortion a personal decision

_____4. can cause infertility in women

_____5. fertilized eggs are placed in the uterus

_____6. internal organs begin functioning

_____7. major cause of infertility in men

_____8. ruling that prohibited federally funded clinics from discussing abortion with patients

_____9. most common type of abortion procedure

_____10. a rare cause of male sterility

_____11. sex of fetus can first be distinguished

_____12. skin is protected by vernix caseosa

_____13. sperm and egg are placed in the fallopian tube

_____14. ruling to prohibit federal Medicaid funds for abortion

_____15. used to induce termination of second trimester pregnancies

_____16. leading cause of developmental disabilities and birth defects in U.S.

_____17. can help detect Down syndrome

_____18. nausea and fatigue may occur

_____19. breasts may begin to secrete colostrum

_____20. fetal movements can be seen and felt from outside the abdomen

_____21. "bloody show"

Short Answer

1. What does research reveal regarding the feelings of women who decide not to have children? (Obj. #1c)

2. List four potential advantages of **not** having children. (Obj. #1c)

3. List four potential advantages of having children. (Obj. #1a)

4. How many women in their 40s are childless? (Obj. #1b)

5. Has adoption of older or disabled children increased or decreased? (Obj. #1d)

6. List four methods for determining when ovulation occurs. (Obj. #2)

7. What is the success rate for treating couples with infertility? (Obj. #3)

8. List ten causes of female infertility. (Obj. #3)

9. List five major causes of male infertility. (Obj. #3)

10. What is a rare cause of male sterility? (Obj. #3)

11. Explain how problems with fertility may affect a couple's sexual relationship. (Obj. #4)

12. Briefly describe the following procedures that have been used to help infertile couples: (Obj. #5)

    a. artificial insemination

    b. in vitro fertilization (IVF)

    c. zygote intrafallopian transfer (ZIFT)

    d. gamete intrafallopian transfer (GIFT)

    e. intracytoplasmic sperm injection (ICSA)

13. What laboratory techniques are currently being used to predetermine the sex of the child? (Obj. #26)

14. Name three countries where illegal sex selection abortion of female fetuses is common. (Obj. #26)

15. What is the definition of a miscarriage? When do most occur? What are the symptoms? (Obj. #7)

16. Briefly describe the age, race and marital status of women who most commonly obtain abortions. (Obj. #8)

17. How likely are Catholic women to obtain abortions as compared to non-Catholic women? (Obj. #8)

18. Briefly describe the following abortion procedures and indicate when they are used: (Obj. #9)

    a.   suction curettage

    b.   D and E

    c.   prostaglandin induction

19. What does research reveal regarding the emotional effects of abortion on women? (Obj. #12)

20. List seven reasons why some women might not use contraception reliably. (Obj. #13)

21. Briefly describe the following: (Obj. #14)

    a. Roe v. Wade

    b. Hyde Amendment

    c. Rust v. Sullivan

22. Compare African-Americans' and Whites' attitudes toward legal abortion. (Obj. #15)

23. Contrast some of the beliefs and values of pro-choice and anti-abortion individuals, aside from their beliefs regarding abortion. (Obj. #15)

24. Briefly describe physical changes of the zygote/fetus in each of the following: (Obj. #16a)

    a. first trimester

    b. second trimester

    c. third trimester

25. List eight risks to healthy fetal development. (Obj. #16b)

26. When is CVS or amniocentesis used? (Obj. #16c)

27. Briefly describe some of the problems and benefits of pregnancy with increased maternal age. (Obj. #16d)

28. How do sexual interest and responsiveness change through the course of pregnancy? (Obj. #18)

29. Briefly describe each of the following:

    a. first-stage labor

    b. second-stage labor

    c. third-stage labor

30. What were Grantly Dick-Read's and Bernard Lamaze's ideas about childbirth? (Obj. #20)

31. Briefly explain the advantages and disadvantages of the following birthplace alternatives: (Obj. #21)

    a. hospitals

    b. birthing centers

    c. homes

32. How common is episiotomy as a medical intervention in this country as opposed to others? (Obj. #22)

33. In what situations is a cesarean section recommended? (Obj. #22)

34. List four potential beneficial effects of breast-feeding. (Obj. #24)

35. List five potential disadvantages of breast-feeding. (Obj. #24)

36. Summarize current recommendations regarding when intercourse can resume after childbirth. (Obj. #25)

Multiple Choice

Select the best alternative. Check your answers with the answer key at the end of the chapter.

1. Which of the following was stated in the text as an advantage to having children?
    a. Parenthood can provide a sense of accomplishment.
    b. Studies show that marriages with children are happier and more satisfying than are marriages without children.
    c. Parenthood can reduce the stress on a marriage.
    d. all of the above

2. Which of the following is **false**?
    a. Children who are older or disabled are being placed less frequently in adoptive homes.
    b. Adoption is often very expensive.
    c. Some people adopt because of a concern with overpopulation.
    d. A common reason for adoption is a problem with infertility.

3. Ovulation-predictor tests
    a. measure basal body temperature to indicate the onset of ovulation.
    b. measure androgen levels that determine the onset of ovulation.
    c. determine the onset of ovulation by monitoring the consistency of cervical mucus.
    d. measure the rise in LH prior to ovulation.

4. _____ percent of couples who attempt it become pregnant within three months.
    a. Twenty
    b. Forty
    c. Sixty
    d. Eighty

5. Which of the following may be related to failure to ovulate?
    a. poor nutrition
    b. emotional stress
    c. genetic factors
    d. all of the above

6. Which of the following would be **least** likely to cause female fertility problems?
    a. a cervical mucus plug that contains antibodies against men's sperm
    b. scar tissue in the fallopian tubes
    c. toxemia
    d. endometriosis

7. Which of the following affects male fertility?
    a. nutritional habits
    b. lack of exercise
    c. environmental toxins
    d. excessive exercise

8. A major cause of infertility in men is a damaged or enlarged blood vein in the testes of the vas deferens called
    a. a varicocele.
    b. colostrum.
    c. a vernix caseosa.
    d. a sebaceous cyst.

9. In artificial insemination
   a. the eggs are removed from a woman's ovary and are fertilized in a laboratory dish by her partner's sperm.
   b. the male partner of a childless couple impregnates another woman who carries the baby to term and then lets the couple adopt the baby.
   c. the semen from a woman's partner is introduced into the woman's fallopian tube.
   d. semen from a woman's partner is mechanically introduced into her vagina, cervix or uterus.

10. A method called _____ attempts to facilitate fertilization by placing the ova and sperm directly into the fallopian tube.
   a. ICSA (intracytoplasmic sperm injection)
   b. GIFT (gamete intrafallopian transfer)
   c. ZIFT (zygote intrafallopian transfer)
   d. artificial insemination

11. IVF-GIFT
   a. is expensive.
   b. has high success rates.
   c. is the most frequently used method of alternative conception.
   d. all of the above

12. The blood of a pregnant woman contains
   a. human chorionic gonadotropin.
   b. trophoblast cells.
   c. vernix caseosa.
   d. amniotic fluid.

13. A miscarriage
   a. is also called an induced abortion.
   b. usually occurs in the second trimester of pregnancy.
   c. is usually caused by increased levels of HCG in the blood.
   d. none of the above

14. According to research, Catholic women are
   a. more likely to obtain abortions than other women.
   b. less likely to obtain abortions than other women.
   c. as likely to obtain abortions as other women.
   d. much less likely to obtain abortions than other women.

15. Which of the following is **false**?
   a. Approximately one-third of abortions are performed for women who have had at least one previous abortion.
   b. Contraceptive method failure is a major reason for repeat abortions.
   c. Thalidomide is one of the compounds used to induce termination of second-trimester pregnancy.
   d. D and E is currently the safest and most widely used technique for pregnancy termination between 13 and 21 weeks.

16. Unwanted pregnancies may result from all of the following **except**
   a. a low degree of guilt about sex.
   b. the traditional role of female passivity.
   c. fear of contraceptive side effects.
   d. the high social value placed on pregnancy.

17. The Roe v. Wade ruling
    a. made abortion a personal decision on the part of the individual woman.
    b. prohibited federal Medicaid funds for abortion.
    c. decided in favor of states imposing restrictions on abortion.
    d. overturned the right to abortion.

18. _____ is associated with a pro-choice position.
    a. A college education
    b. A fundamentalist religious affiliation
    c. A disapproving attitude toward government spending
    d. A low-paying job

19. According to research, U.S. senators and representatives who are opposed to legal abortion also tend to
    a. support handgun control.
    b. oppose capital punishment.
    c. have opposed the Vietnam War.
    d. oppose legislation that promotes the health and well-being of families and children.

20. Research regarding race differences in support for legal abortion reveals that _____ have the strongest pro-choice attitudes while _____ have the weakest support for legal abortion.
    a. older White men; older African-American men
    b. older African-American men; older White men
    c. older White women; older African-American women
    d. older African-American women; older White women

21. The multicelled _____ implants in the uterus about one week after fertilization.
    a. varicocele
    b. zygote
    c. chorionic villus
    d. blastocyst

22. The protective, waxy substance that covers the fetus is called the
    a. lochia.
    b. vernix caseosa.
    c. placental encasement.
    d. amniotic lubricant.

23. How do nutrients and oxygen in the mother's bloodstream enter the bloodstream of the infant?
    a. Blood vessels of the mother and infant are directly connected to each other at the placenta.
    b. A major artery of the mother flows directly into the fetus' umbilical cord.
    c. Substances in the mother's bloodstream enter the amniotic fluid and are absorbed through the epidermis of the fetus.
    d. Although the two bloodstreams are not connected, substances pass into the fetus' bloodstream through the cell walls in the placenta.

24. Fetal alcohol syndrome
    a. is the leading cause of developmental disabilities and birth defects in the United States.
    b. is the leading cause of Down Syndrome.
    c. is related to damage to an infant's teeth.
    d. is related to a high incidence of reading disorders.

25. Regarding pregnancy after age 35, which of the following statements is **true**?
    a. Because of increased risks to the fetus and the mother, the number of women deciding to have children after age 35 is decreasing.
    b. Women over 35 experience more anxiety and depression than first-time mothers in their mid-twenties.
    c. Women over 35 may have higher rates of pregnancy and delivery complications.
    d. The ability to become pregnant increases after age 35.

26. Most research demonstrates that
    a. a man's active involvement in childbearing bears little relationship to father-newborn interaction.
    b. a man's active involvement in childbearing is positively related to father-newborn interaction.
    c. fathers are not as nurturant as mothers, in spite of training to promote this quality.
    d. none of the above

27. Which stage of labor is the longest?
    a. the first
    b. the second
    c. the third
    d. All three stages of labor are approximately equivalent in length.

28. The third stage of labor is characterized by
    a. labor lasting approximately 10–16 hours.
    b. an effaced cervix.
    c. the delivery of the placenta.
    d. the "transition" phase.

29. The Lamaze method is also referred to as
    a. the water-birthing technique.
    b. the relaxation method.
    c. prepared childbirth.
    d. all of the above

30. Toxemia
    a. is also called placenta previa.
    b. is characterized by water retention and high blood pressure.
    c. results in anoxia.
    d. results from Rh incompatibility.

31. An episiotomy is
    a. an incision in the abdomen to facilitate a cesarean section.
    b. an emergency procedure performed in birth complications such as breech-fetal presentation.
    c. an incision in the perineum from the vagina toward the anus.
    d. an emergency procedure performed on the umbilical cord.

32. "Postpartum blues" refers to
    a. the discoloration of the genitals after delivery.
    b. the fretful fussing of the infant upon delivery.
    c. the withdrawal and jealousy many new fathers experience.
    d. a period after birth when some mothers cry easily and feel sad.

33. Which of the following was **not** given as an advantage of breast-feeding?
    a. inhibits ovulation, so it can be used as a temporary method of birth control
    b. heightened emotional experience for the mother
    c. induces uterine contractions that help return the uterus to its normal size
    d. provides digestible food source for the infant

Insight and Application

1. Under what circumstances would you use a preconception sex selection technique, if any? Why or why not? If these techniques were readily available, accurate, and inexpensive, do you think many people would use them? If so, what might be the effects of that?

2. If you wanted to have children, but you and/or a partner were infertile, would you consider any of the conception alternatives discussed in the text? Why or why not? If so, which alternative would you consider and why?

3. Do you feel that a man should have the right to demand or deny abortion for his partner? Why or why not?

4. How would you describe your personal values or beliefs on abortion? On what knowledge and/or experience do you base your views? How have your values changed over time, if at all? To what degree are you able to empathize with or understand an opposing view? What has been your personal experience with abortion, either for yourself, your partner, or close friend or family member? How have those experiences (or lack of them) affected you, if at all?

Matching Answers

1. b	2. r	3. s	4. a	5. g	6. j	7. k	8. p
9. l	10. o	11. q	12. d	13. n	14. c	15. m	16. t
17. e	18. j	19. q	20. d	21. h			

Multiple Choice Answers

1. a	2. a	3. d	4. c	5. d	6. c	7. c	8. a
9. d	10. b	11. a	12. a	13. d	14. c	15. c	16. a
17. a	18. a	19. d	20. c	21. d	22. b	23. d	24. a
25. c	26. b	27. a	28. c	29. c	30. b	31. c	32. d
33. a							

pronatalism

retroflexed uterus

varicocele

artificial insemination

in vitro fertilization
(IVF)

zygote intrafallopian transfer
(ZIFT)

gamete intrafallopian transfer
(GIFT)

human chorionic
gonadotropin (HCG)

trophoblast cells

spontaneous abortion
(miscarriage)

a uterus that is tipped backward more than normal	attitudes and policies that encourage parenthood for all couples
a procedure in which semen from a woman's partner is mechanically introduced by a health care practitioner into the woman's vagina, cervix, or uterus	a damaged or enlarged vein in the testes or vas deferens which can be a major cause of infertility in men
the same procedure as in vitro fertilization except that the fertilized egg is placed in the fallopian tube instead of the uterus	a procedure in which the eggs are removed from the ovary and are fertilized in a laboratory dish by her partner's sperm, and later introduced into the woman's uterus.
a hormone that is detectable in the urine of a pregnant woman about a month after conception	similar to in vitro fertilization except that the sperm and ova are placed directly into the fallopian tube
the spontaneous expulsion of the fetus from the uterus in early pregnancy, before it can survive on its own	cells of the placenta that secrete human chorionic gonadotropin (HCG)

elective abortion	**suction curettage**
dilation and evacuation	**prostaglandin induction**
Roe v. Wade	**viability**
Rust v. Sullivan	**zygote**
blastocyst	**vernix caseosa**

a medical procedure for abortion that is used in the early stages of pregnancy (7-13 weeks after the last menstrual period)	a decision to terminate a pregnancy by medical procedures
a medical procedure for pregnancy termination during the second trimester	a medical procedure for pregnancy termination between 13 and 21 weeks
the fetus' ability to survive independently of the woman's body	a 1973 Supreme Court ruling that legalized a woman's right to terminate her pregnancy before the fetus has reached the age of viability
the single cell resulting from the union of sperm and egg cells	a 1991 Supreme Court ruling that upheld legislation barring federally funded clinics from *discussing* abortion with patients
a waxy, protective substance on the fetus' skin	a multicellular descendant of the united sperm and ovum that implants on the wall of the uterus

placenta

fetal alcohol syndrome
(FAS)

amniocentesis

amniotic fluid

chorionic villus sampling
(CVS)

Down syndrome

colostrum

first-stage labor

effacement

second-stage labor

	a disk-shaped organ attached to the uterine wall and connected to the fetus by the umbilical cord. Nutrients, oxygen and waste products pass between mother and fetus through its cell walls
the leading cause of developmental disabilities and birth defects in the United States	
the fluid inside the amniotic sac surrounding the fetus during pregnancy	a procedure in which amniotic fluid is removed from the uterus and tested to determine if certain fetal birth defects exist
a chromosomal abnormality that results in impaired intellectual function and physical defects	a prenatal test that detects some birth defects, such as Down syndrome
the initial stage of childbirth in which regular contractions begin and the cervix dilates	a thin, yellowish fluid secreted by the breasts during late pregnancy and the first few days following delivery
the middle stage of labor, in which the infant descends through the vaginal canal	flattening and thinning of the cervix that occurs before and during childbirth

third-stage labor

afterbirth

prepared childbirth

toxemia

placenta previa

episiotomy

cesarean section

postpartum period

lochia

intracytoplasmic sperm
injection (ICSA)

the placenta and amniotic sac following their expulsion through the vagina after childbirth

the last stage of childbirth, in which the placenta separates from the uterine wall and comes out of the vagina

a dangerous condition during pregnancy, an early symptom of which is high blood pressure

birth following an education process that can involve information, exercises, breathing, and working with a labor coach

an incision in the perineum that is sometimes made during childbirth

a birth complication in which the placenta is between the cervical opening and the infant

the first several weeks following childbirth

a childbirth procedure in which the infant is removed through an incision in the abdomen and uterus

when sperm lack the ability to penetrate the egg, the eggs are removed and each is injected with a sperm and then transplanted in the fallopian tube

a reddish, uterine discharge that occurs following childbirth

Sexuality During Childhood and Adolescence

Introduction

This chapter traces the development of sexuality from infancy through adolescence. Childhood sexual development, physical, social and sexual changes that occur during adolescence, the double standard, incidence and frequency of various types of adolescent sexual behavior, homosexuality, teenage pregnancy and androgynous childrearing are among the topics discussed. The authors also suggest strategies for reducing the teenage pregnancy rate, and address questions regarding the nature and timing of sex education.

Objectives

After studying this chapter, you should be able to:

1. List examples that demonstrate how infants of both sexes are born with the capacity for sexual pleasure and response, and identify the person whose research was instrumental in dispelling the myth that childhood is a time of sexual dormancy.

2. Discuss common features of sexual development that occur during childhood and cite research that supports these various phases.

3. Explain how childhood and adolescent sexuality in Western society compares to that of other cultures.

4. Define puberty and explain what happens during this period of development for males and females.

5. Describe the changes that occur in adolescent friendships during puberty.

6. Discuss the double standard as it affects adolescent social and sexual behavior, and make specific reference to what research suggests regarding the current status of the sexual double standard among adolescents.

7. Describe the incidence and frequency of masturbation among male and female adolescents.

8. Define petting and discuss how common it is among adolescent females and males.

9. Explain how likely ongoing sexual relationships tend to be among adolescents.

10. Discuss why the term "premarital sex" may be misleading and then summarize what the research reveals regarding the following:
    a. incidence of premarital sex among adolescents
    b. the effect of AIDS education on premarital coital rates and teenage behavior

11. Discuss how common same-sex contact may be during adolescence and explain how this may reflect a transitory, experimental phase of sexual development or how it may be indicative of a homosexual orientation.

12. Summarize available research and statistical data regarding various aspects of adolescent pregnancy.

13. Discuss how an adolescent mother's decision to keep her child may affect her education, financial status, and the life of her child.

14. Explain how prevalent contraceptive use is among adolescents and what factors affect contraceptive use on a regular basis.

15. Summarize the results of the comparative study of adolescent pregnancy in six countries, discuss factors that may contribute to the difference in pregnancy rates among them, and discuss the directions this suggests in future education and intervention.

16. Summarize the authors' list of five suggestions for reducing the teenage pregnancy rate.

17. Making reference to relevant research, describe some general guidelines that the authors suggest in talking to your children about sex.

18. Discuss the nature of sex education programs in schools, and what the research says regarding the effects of sex education on behavior.

19. Discuss the benefits of raising children in an androgynous manner.

Key Terms and Concepts

"Flash cards" listing key terms and concepts on one side and their corresponding definitions and explanations on the other side are provided at the end of the chapter.

Chapter Overview With Fill-Ins

After reading each of the major sections in the chapter, check your retention by **mentally** filling in each of the blanks in the corresponding sections below. Cover the answers in the margin as you go along, and write the answers in the space provided only when you are doing your final review.

unexpressed
Alfred Kinsey

The viewpoint that childhood is a time when sexuality remains _____ has been the prevailing belief system in Western societies. The research of _____ _____ has been instrumental in dispelling many of these beliefs.

Sexual Behavior During Childhood

genital

In the first few years of life, many children discover the pleasures of _____ stimulation.

doctor
most

Besides engaging in self-stimulation behavior and shows of affection, prepubertal children often engage in certain forms of play, i.e., playing _____, which may be viewed as sexual in nature. Recent surveys indicate that _____ children participate in some form of sex play with friends or siblings. By the time a child is eight or nine years old there is a tendency for boys and girls to play separately and show their curiosity about sexual matters by asking

questions
homosexual

_____ about reproduction and sexuality. During late childhood some _____ activity is probably common.

Masturbation

_____ is one of the most common sexual expressions during the childhood years. For both sexes, masturbation is the most

orgasm

frequent source of preadolescent _____.

The Physical Changes of Adolescence

adolescence
Puberty
physical

gonadotropins

In Western societies, _____ is the transition between childhood and adulthood. _____ is a term frequently used to describe the period of rapid _____ changes in early adolescence. Secondary sex characteristics, i.e., breasts, deepened voice, facial and pubic hair, result from _____ in the bloodstream.

hormone

menstruation
menarche

Under the influence of _____ stimulation, the internal organs of the male and female undergo further development and the female eventually begins _____. The first menstrual period is called _____.

ejaculation

testosterone

Although boys may experience orgasm throughout childhood, _____ is not possible until the prostate and seminal vesicles begin functioning under the influence of increasing _____ levels.

homosocial

The physical changes experienced by the adolescent may be a source of pride or concern and may contribute to feelings of self-consciousness, which may result in a _____ (relating socially primarily with members of the same sex) pattern.

Sexual Behavior During Adolescence

increases
double standard

decline
conquest

ambivalence

Adolescence is a period when sexual behavior, both self-stimulation and partner-shared, generally _____. In most areas of adolescent sexuality, the male-female _____ _____ prevails, although recent research suggests that the sexual double standard may be on the _____. For males, the focus of sexuality may be sexual _____. For females, the message and expectations are very different; they may learn to appear "sexy" to attract males, yet they often experience _____ about overt sexual behavior.

Masturbation

lower

_____ is an increasingly frequent practice in adolescence. Masturbation frequency rates among females are notably _____ among all age groups, including adolescents.

Petting

coitus

oral

_____ refers to erotic physical contact that may include kissing, holding, touching, manual stimulation , or oral-genital stimulation — but not _____. Perhaps one of the most noteworthy recent changes in the pattern of adolescent petting behaviors involves _____ sex, cunnilingus being reported more frequently than fellatio by adolescents of both sexes.

love

It appears that contemporary adolescents are most likely to be sexually intimate with someone they _____ or to whom they feel emotionally attached.

premarital

noncoital
marriage

Most of the available data on sexual intercourse during adolescence are based upon inquiries about type and frequency of _____ sex (defined as penile-vaginal intercourse). This term is misleading for two reasons: 1) it excludes a broad array of _____ heterosexual and homosexual activities, and 2) it implies that _____ is the ultimate goal.

AIDS

spermicides
needle sharing
multiple

minority

A number of health professionals are concerned that American teenagers are particularly at risk for contracting _____. High-risk adolescent behaviors may include: 1) engaging in intercourse without condoms and _____; using drugs and alcohol; _____ _____ among intravenous drug users; and exposing themselves to _____ partners.

Although homosexuality affects a _____ of adolescents, the homosexual experience can create serious problems for the young person.

Adolescent Pregnancy

one

95

educational
offspring

Of the approximately eleven million unmarried adolescent females who are sexually active, about _____ million become pregnant every year. Over half of these pregnancies result in live births, and of these, _____ percent choose to keep their babies. Many adverse consequences of adolescent pregnancy have been cited, ranging from negative health consequences for the adolescent mother to the negative impact on the adolescent mother's _____ progress, and financial resources. In addition, the _____ of teenage mothers are at a greater risk of having physical, cognitive, and emotional problems than are children of adult mothers.

increase

females; males

There have been several major changes in adolescent coital activities in the last four decades: 1) there has been an _____ in the percentages of young men and women who have experienced premarital intercourse; 2) these increases have been larger for _____ than _____; there are still fewer women than men who experience premarital intercourse.

culture

free
birth-control
inadequate

Many professionals believe that the American _____ contributes greatly to the high rate of adolescent pregnancy. Three other reasons given as possible contributing factors to the high pregnancy rate are: 1) the difficulty the adolescent has in obtaining _____ or low-cost contraceptive services; 2) the adolescents' use of ineffective _____-_____ methods; and 3) _____ sex-education programs in schools and communities.

Sex Education

ask

parents

friends

The authors suggest that we should start telling our children about sex when the child begins to _____ questions.

Most young people prefer that their _____ be the primary source of sex information. Several studies have shown that _____, not parents, are the principal source of sex information for young people in this country.

experimentation
activity
beneficial

Parents may hesitate to discuss sex with their children because they are concerned that such communication may encourage early sexual _____. However, there is no evidence that sex education leads to sexual _____. The majority of the research supports the _____ effects of sexual education and suggests a relationship to responsible sexual behavior.

curriculum

safe

In response to the frequent lack of information from the home and the inaccuracy of much of the information from peers, other social institutions, including some schools, have included sex education as part of the _____. A minority of American schools offer comprehensive sex education programs, and much of the information presented is incomplete; often only "_____" topics, such as reproduction and anatomy, are taught.

Androgynous Child Rearing and Sexuality

Androgyny

detrimental

_____ is a term used to describe flexibility in gender roles. The authors emphasize that strict adherence to stereotypic gender roles has a _____ effect on sexual functioning.

Short Answer

1. List signs of sexual arousal and response in infants and children. (Obj. #1)

2. List six patterns of sexual behavior in prepubertal children. (Obj. #2)

3. Describe the physiological changes during puberty for: (Obj. #4)

   a. males

   b. females

4. What is the relationship of body fat to menarche? Of fertility to menarche? (Obj. #4)

5. At what point do males begin ejaculating with orgasm? (Obj. #4)

6. Define homosocial. (Obj. #5)

7. Briefly comment on childhood and adolescent sexuality in the following cultures: (Obj. #3)

    a. Mangaia

    b. Marquesas Islands

    c. Kwoma society of New Guinea

    d. Chewa of Central Africa

    e. Lepcha of the Himalayas

8. Is the double standard on the increase or decrease among adolescents? (Obj. #6)

9. Citing relevant research, explain some of the gender differences in adolescence with respect to masturbation. (Obj. #7)

10. How has the incidence of oral sex among adolescents changed over time? Which is more common — fellatio or cunnilingus? (Obj. #8)

11. How has sexual intimacy changed in adolescence since Kinsey's time? (Obj. #9)

12. Give two reasons why the term "premarital sex" is misleading. (Obj. #10)

13. Describe the effect of AIDS education on premarital coital rates and sexual behavior among adolescents. (Obj. #10)

14. How might homosexual organizations complicate a homosexual adolescent's situation? (Obj. #11)

15. Cite the following statistics: (Obj. #12)

    a. number of adolescent pregnancies each year

    b. percent of pregnancies that result in elective abortion

    c. percent of pregnancies that result in spontaneous abortion

    d.   percent of pregnancies that result in live births

    e.   percent of live births in which mothers keep their babies

16. List at least three possible negative outcomes of teenage pregnancy. (Obj. #13)

17. According to the study of adolescent pregnancy in six countries, which country had the highest rate? The second highest rate? Which countries had the lowest rate? (Obj. #15)

18. Regarding the comparative study on adolescent pregnancy cited in the text, what are three factors which contribute to high pregnancy rates among American adolescents? (Obj. #15)

19. Briefly outline five suggestions given by the authors to help reduce the teenage pregnancy rate. (Obj. #16)

20. What do the authors suggest in terms of when to tell our children about sex? (Obj. #17)

21. What are three questions a parent might ask a child in order to open a discussion of sexual issues? (Obj. #17)

22. From whom do young people prefer to acquire information about sex? How do most children actually get information about sex? (Obj. #17)

23. How does open parent-child communication about sexual activity affect teenage sexual activity? Use of contraceptives? (Obj. #17, 18)

24. Define the term androgyny and explain the benefits of this approach for human experience. (Obj. #19)

Multiple Choice

Select the best alternative. Check your answers with the answer key at the end of the chapter.

1. Which of the following statements is **false**?
   a. Orgasm has been observed in infants who are several months old.
   b. Vaginal lubrication has been observed in female infants.
   c. Penile erection has been observed in male infants.
   d. The research of Masters and Johnson has been the foundation for our knowledge regarding childhood sexuality.

2. During puberty, the pituitary secretes _____ into the bloodstream.
   a. gonadotropins
   b. hypothalamic hormones
   c. androgen
   d. estrogen

3. Childhood masturbation
   a. is one of the early signs of deviant adult sexual behavior.
   b. is a common form of sexual expression in youth.
   c. is related to a high sex drive in adulthood.
   d. decreases when the child enters school.

4. _____ is a term used to describe the period of rapid physical changes in early adolescence.
   a. Menarche
   b. Maturation
   c. Adolescent transition
   d. Puberty

5. The sequence of events in puberty is
   a. hormone production, appearance of secondary sex characteristics, growth spurt, menarche/ejaculation.
   b. menarche/ejaculation, growth spurt, hormone production, growth of axillary hair.
   c. growth of axillary hair, hormone production, secondary sex characteristics.
   d. hormone production, appearance of secondary sex characteristics, growth of axillary hair, growth spurt.

6. Which of the following statements is **true**?
   a. The onset of puberty is approximately one year earlier for girls than for boys.
   b. Many girls are fertile before experiencing menarche.
   c. Growth of pubic hair is an example of a secondary sex characteristic.
   d. During puberty, the pituitary secretes androgen into the bloodstream.

7. Homosocial behavior refers to
   a. cultivating homosexual relationships as a prelude to "coming out".
   b. social interaction with homosexuals.
   c. relating sexually to the same sex.
   d. relating socially to the same sex.

8. The double standard encourages
   a. males to focus on the sexual conquest.
   b. females to realize their full potential.
   c. females to be sexually aggressive.
   d. males to be sensitive regarding female issues.

9. Recent research suggests that the sexual double standard among American adolescents
   a. is increasing.
   b. has leveled off.
   c. is decreasing.
   d. is no longer an issue.

10. According to several studies, a recent change in adolescent sexual relationships is that
    a. females are more comfortable being promiscuous than in the past.
    b. males are more likely to refrain from having sex until their late teens.
    c. females are more likely to "save themselves" for marriage.
    d. males are more likely to have emotional connections with their partners than in the past.

11. The term "premarital sex" is misleading because
    a. many sexually active people choose not to marry.
    b. it overlooks many homosexual activities.
    c. it excludes a broad array of noncoital heterosexual behaviors.
    d. all of the above

12. With respect to the AIDS virus, teenagers
    a. have decreased their sexual activities in order to minimize contact with the virus.
    b. are conscientiously seeking out information about the disease.
    c. are likely to engage in safer sexual practices in order to protect themselves.
    d. have the information but have not changed their behavior.

13. Which of the following statements is **true**?
    a. Most homosexual individuals openly acknowledge their sexual orientation.
    b. A significant number of heterosexuals have early homosexual experiences.
    c. Homosexual organizations are eager to help adolescent homosexuals.
    d. The majority of homosexual contacts in adolescence are with older adults.

14. Of the approximately 1 million adolescents who become pregnant each year, _____ percent result in live births.
    a. 10
    b. 25
    c. 50
    d. 85

15. Of the adolescent girls who become pregnant, approximately _____ percent have elective abortions.
    a. 10
    b. 20
    c. 40
    d. 60

16. Teenage mothers are likely to
    a. be dependent on welfare services.
    b. continue their education after the birth of their child.
    c. be employed full-time.
    d. provide parenting of the same quality as adult mothers.

17. Offspring of teenage mothers are at a greater risk for
    a. physical problems.
    b. cognitive problems.
    c. emotional problems.
    d. all of the above

18. Which country has a higher proportion of sexually experienced teenagers and a lower pregnancy rate than the United States?
    a. Sweden
    b. the Netherlands
    c. France
    d. England

19. The extensive comparative study of six developed countries including the United States revealed that a lower incidence of adolescent pregnancy is related to
    a. sex education.
    b. available contraception.
    c. the assumption of responsibility for sexual activity.
    d. all of the above

20. In European countries, sex is viewed as
    a. private.
    b. natural.
    c. shameful.
    d. synonymous with procreation.

21. A mother finds her son in the bathtub, playing with his penis. The **most** appropriate response in this situation would probably be for the mother to
    a. gently inform the boy that his behavior is inappropriate.
    b. give him a rubber ducky to play with instead.
    c. acknowledge her understanding that the child's action is pleasurable.
    d. tell her son she will buy him a new toy if he never does that again.

22. The authors' response to the question "When should we start telling our children about sex?" is
    a. when the child is two years old.
    b. when the child begins to ask questions.
    c. when you first notice that the child is masturbating.
    d. when the child first begins to "play doctor" with siblings or neighborhood friends.

23. The principal source of information for young people about sexual matters is
    a. parents.
    b. teachers.
    c. movies.
    d. friends.

24. Which of the following statements is **most** accurate?
    a. Open parent-child communication about sex encourages children to experiment sexually.
    b. Open parent-child communication reduces an adolescent's likelihood to engage in premarital sex.
    c. There is no evidence that sex education leads to sexual activity.

25. An important factor in rearing children in an androgynous fashion is
    a. encouraging play with a variety of toys.
    b. parental modeling of gender-free behaviors.
    c. reinforcing play with opposite-sex children.
    d. all of the above

26. Research has demonstrated that adhering to traditional gender-role behaviors is linked with _____ and _____.
    a. having a greater number of sexual partners; less effective contraceptive use
    b. less sexual experimentation within a relationship; more effective contraception use
    c. reluctance to participate in school sex education programs; more effective contraceptive use
    d. earlier age of sexual activity; less effective contraception

Insight and Application

1. If you were a sexually active single parent, how would you deal with this aspect of your life with your elementary school age children? Adolescent children? Would you allow your partner to spend the night with you? Why or why not? What issues might surface regarding this? What kinds of values or information do you think it would be important to be addressed? Be specific.

2. Brainstorm a list of questions that a child might ask a parent, e.g., "Where do babies come from?" "What is a rubber?" "What is '69'?" "What does 'screwing' mean?" Role play with a friend or partner your responses to these questions. Then brainstorm a list of questions that an adolescent might ask and repeat the process.

3. If you found your eight-year-old child with a neighborhood friend in the process of visually exploring each other's naked bodies, how would you respond? If they were touching each other's bodies, would your response be any different? How would your response vary, if at all, depending upon the sex of your child? Would the age of the other child affect your response? How? Would you tell the friend's parents about the incident? Why or why not?

4. Would you provide birth control information and devices to your teenage children? Why or why not? Would the sex of your child affect the kind of information you would discuss? If so, why?

5. Assume you have a teenage son or daughter who is dating. How would you feel about allowing your child private space or time alone in your home? For example, would you let your daughter or son take a partner into his or her bedroom? With the door closed? Would

you allow them to be home alone in the house while you were gone? Why or why not? How would you deal with or address your teenager's needs for privacy, if at all?

6. Complete the sentences below and then provide a specific example from your own life experiences to elaborate upon what you have written. Reflect upon your answers later. If you would like, you could also have a friend or partner complete the exercise and then discuss/compare your answers.

   a. My major source of sexual information as I was growing up was _____

   Example: _____

   b. As a child, how I learned about my body and my sexuality was _____

   Example: _____

   c. How my family dealt with nudity at home was _____

   Example: _____

   d. Physical affection in my family _____

   Example: _____

   e. The way my family dealt with sexual questions or concerns was _____

   Example: _____

   f. As an adolescent, I learned the most about my body and my sexuality when _____

   _____

   Example: _____

   g. The way I felt about my body and/or physical appearance in general while I was

   growing up was _____

   Example: _____

   h. One thing I liked about my body as I was growing up was _____

   Example: _____

   i. How I found out about masturbation and what my experiences with it were _____

   _____

   Example: _____

j. What I remember regarding sex play as a child _____

Example: _____

k. My first menstruation/ejaculation _____

Example: _____

l. The sense I had of my parents' sexual relationship and/or activity was _____

Example: _____

m. An embarrassing or humiliating sexual experience I had was _____

Example: _____

n. A painful or traumatic sexual experience I had was _____

Example: _____

o. My first sexual intercourse experience (if applicable) was _____

Example: _____

p. What I like about my sexuality today is _____

Example: _____

q. How I feel regarding all of the above and how it relates to who I am sexually today is

_____

Example: _____

r. What I would like to change, if anything, regarding my sexual values, attitudes, or

behavior today is _____

Example: _____

Multiple Choice Answers

1. d	2. a	3. b	4. d	5. a	6. c	7. d	8. a
9. c	10. d	11. d	12. d	13. b	14. c	15. c	16. a
17. d	18. a	19. d	20. b	21. c	22. b	23. d	24. c
25. d	26. d						

puberty

gonadotropins

secondary sexual characteristics

menarche

petting

homosocial

androgyny

pituitary hormones that stimulate activity in the gonads (ovaries and testes)	the stage of life between childhood and adulthood during which the reproductive organs mature
the initial onset of the first menstrual period	the physical sexual characteristics other than genitals that indicate sexual maturity such as body hair, breasts and deepened voice
relating socially, primarily with members of the same sex	erotic physical contact that may include kissing, holding, touching, mutual masturbation or oral-genital stimulation
	flexibility in gender roles

14

Sexuality and the Adult Years

Introduction

As adults, we may experience one or perhaps several different relationship styles ranging from single living, cohabitation, marriage, open marriage, and extramarital involvement to divorce and widowhood. In this chapter, the authors explore these relationship alternatives and discuss the patterns of sexual interaction in each.

Objectives

After studying this chapter, you should be able to:

1. Discuss single living, making specific reference to the following:
    a. what factors account for the increasing number of single people and what forms being single takes
    b. sexual activity among single people as opposed to married people

2. Discuss cohabitation, making specific reference to the following:
    a. social attitudes toward it over time
    b. how prevalent it is in our society
    c. advantages and disadvantages of cohabitation
    d. how cohabitation may affect a subsequent marital relationship

3. Discuss the institution of marriage, making specific reference to the following:
    a. statistically how common it is and what marital trends indicate
    b. the functions it serves
    c. the various forms it takes
    d. changing expectations and marital patterns
    e. factors that contribute to marital satisfaction as well as factors that are indicative of marital discord
    f. sexual behavior patterns within marriage

4. Describe consensual and nonconsensual extramarital relationships, noting the motivations for, the prevalence and the effects of.

5. Discuss divorce, making specific reference to the following:
    a. what divorce statistics reveal
    b. factors that account for high and low divorce rates
    c. adjustments a person must make as the result of a divorce
    d. sexual behavior of divorced people

6. Describe how the ratio of widows to widowers has changed since the turn of the century.

7. Compare and contrast the adjustments of widowhood to those of divorce.

8. Discuss how the types of coital positions used and the frequency of sexual contact in marital relationships varies cross-culturally.

Key Terms and Concepts

"Flash cards" listing key terms and concepts on one side and their corresponding definitions and explanations on the other side are provided at the end of the chapter.

Chapter Overview With Fill-Ins

After reading each of the major sections in the chapter, check your retention by **mentally** filling in each of the blanks in the corresponding sections below. Cover the answers in the margin as you go along, and write the answers in the space provided only when you are doing your final review.

Single Living

alone

later
career
divorce

attitudes

Increasing numbers of people in our society live _____. Several factors contribute to this trend: people marrying at a _____ age; more people who never marry; more women putting _____ objectives ahead of marriage; an increase in the number of cohabiting couples; rising _____ rates; a greater emphasis on advanced education; more women who no longer depend upon marriage for economic reasons; and changes in societal _____ toward the single lifestyle.

sexually

long-term

Although lifestyles and levels of sexual activity vary widely, just as they do among married people, some studies have shown that singles are just as likely to be _____ active as their married counterparts. Although single living is becoming more acceptable in our society, the majority of people still choose to enter into a _____-_____ relationship with a partner.

Cohabitation

cohabitation

question
birth-control

AIDS
cohabitation

Recently, there has been a dramatic increase in _____ (living together in a sexual relationship without being married). This increase in cohabitation has been attributed to the growing inclination of young people to _____ traditional mores, increased availability and variety of _____-_____ methods, some sense of protection from the risks associated with _____, and an increasing number of people who view _____ as an end in itself, not just as a precursor to marriage.

informality

legal
roles
divorce

The advantages of living together include: the _____ of living together because of mutual desire, not as the result of a binding _____ contract; less pressure to take on the demanding _____ of husband and wife; and less stigma of failure than is associated with _____ in the event that the relationship is unsatisfactory.

cohabitation

marital

There is some evidence that _____ has no demonstrable effect on subsequent marriage, positive or negative. Other research has indicated that cohabitors have a higher rate of _____ discord than their noncohabiting counterparts.

Marriage

monogamy
polygyny
polyandry

Although marriage is an institution that is found in virtually every society, there is diversity in its form among different cultures, ranging from _____ (one man and one woman) to _____ (one man and several women) and _____ (one woman and several men).

ideal

emotional

decreased

In our society, a large discrepancy exists between the American marriage _____ and actual marriage practices. Today, most people expect more from marriage as they seek fulfillment for their social, _____, financial, and sexual needs. At the same time, our society's supportive network for marriages has _____, making the ideal difficult to attain at best and often unrealistic.

flexible

positive
physical

In Klagsbrun's study, couples married 15 years or more were asked to describe the characteristics of a healthy marriage. The results indicated that spending focused time together, sharing values, and being _____ were associated with positive marital experiences. Other studies provide strong support for the importance of _____ communication, high levels of _____ intimacy, shared leisure time, and perceptions of emotional closeness and mutual empathy.

marital
defensiveness
contempt; stone-
walling

Several recent studies have revealed effective tools for predicting _____ success. Facial expressions of disgust, fear, and misery; _____ on the part of both partners; wife's verbal expressions of _____; and husband's "_____" were all related to a decline in marital dissatisfaction.

PREPARE
80

A premarital inventory called _____ has predicted, with about _____ percent accuracy, couples who divorced from those who were happily married.

50

Since _____ percent or more of all first marriages in the United States will end in separation or divorce, premarital counseling might be advisable.

Kinsey

intercourse
enjoy
frequency

mutuality
active

Compared to the people in _____'s research groups, American married women and men appear to engage in sexual _____ more often, experience a wider repertoire of sexual behaviors, and _____ sexual interaction more. A landmark study found that _____ of marital sexual interaction was strongly associated with sexual satisfaction. In addition, _____ in initiating sex, female orgasm, women taking an _____ role in sexual sharing, and good communication were positively correlated with sexual pleasure.

expectations
attractiveness

There are a number of factors which may interfere with marital sexual enjoyment: new role _____, reduced independence, less motivation to maintain personal _____, busy lifestyle, children, and boredom.

Extramarital Relationships

extramarital
nonconsensual

A term for sexual interaction by a married person with someone other than his or her spouse is called an _____ relationship. In _____ extramarital sex, the married person does not have the consent of his or her spouse. The reasons for having an affair are diverse, and the incidence is difficult to

reluctant

estimate since many people are _____ to acknowledge this kind of behavior. The effects of extramarital sex on a marriage may

vary

_____.

Consensual
supportive

_____ extramarital relationships occur in marriages where both partners are informed about and are _____ of sexual involvements outside the primary marriage bond. An

open

_____ marriage maintains that couples willingly allow each other intimate emotional relationships, with or without sexual sharing, with members of either sex without compromising their

primary

_____ relationship.

Swinging

_____ refers to a form of consensual extramarital sex that a married couple shares. In this case, the husband and the wife participate in extramarital sex simultaneously and in the same

location

_____.

Divorce

half

Current estimates suggest that _____ or more of all first marriages will end in divorce. Although the proportion of marriages ending in divorce has increased steadily since the 1950s, recent statistics reveal that the divorce rate has begun to level off and even

decline

_____.

no-
fault
stigma
increased

Speculation on factors responsible for the high divorce rate in America frequently mention the ease of obtaining _____-_____ divorces, the reduction of the social _____ attached to divorce, increasing expectations for marital and sexual fulfillment, the _____ economic independence of women, a greater abundance of wealth, and a "me

attitude
communication
incompatibility

first" _____. A recent study of divorced people cited _____ difficulties as the most frequent complaint, followed by unhappiness and _____.

education

Research has also revealed that age at marriage and level of _____ may be related to the decision to divorce.

dies

Adjusting to divorce is a difficult process and is often compared to the sense of loss a person feels when a loved one _____. Despite the problems newly single people encounter in establishing non marital sexual expression, a majority of divorced individuals become

first

sexually active within the _____ year of the breakup of their marriage.

four

Approximately _____ out of five divorced persons remarry. Many report that the second marriage is better than the first, but

second
divorce

evidence suggests that _____ marriages are more likely to end _____ than first marriages.

Widowhood

later
man
six
different
intense

Widowhood usually occurs _____ in life and, in most cases, it is the _____ who dies first. The ratio of widows to widowers is currently almost _____ to one. The postmarital adjustment of widowhood is _____ in some ways from that of divorce; the grief may be more _____ and the quality of the emotional bond to the deceased mate is often high.

Short Answer

1. List eight factors which contribute to the increasing number of single adults. (Obj. #1a)

2. Compare the sexual activity of single people to that of married people. (Obj. #1b)

3. What is serial monogamy? (Obj. #1a, b)

4. List four reasons that might explain the dramatic increase in cohabitation in recent years. (Obj. #2a, b)

5. List five advantages of cohabitation. (Obj. #2c)

6. Discuss three disadvantages of cohabitation. (Obj. #2c)

7. What do studies indicate with respect to cohabitation and subsequent marital satisfaction and success? (Obj. #2d)

8. How common is the institution of marriage from a cross-cultural perspective and what functions does marriage serve? (Obj. #3a, b)

9. Compare the practices of monogamy, polygyny, and polyandry. (Obj. #3c)

10. Explain how expectations for marriage have changed in our society. (Obj. #3d)

11. Describe how our society's supportive network for marriage has decreased. (Obj. #3d)

12. List three traits that Klagsbrun found to be associated with successful marriages. (Obj. #3e)

13. Based on additional research, list other characteristics associated with marital satisfaction. (Obj. #3e)

14. List four interaction patterns that Gottman found were predictive of marital dissatisfaction. (Obj. #3e)

15. List three different marriage styles that Gottman identified, and briefly describe the advantages and disadvantages of each style. (Obj. #3e)

16. What is the ratio of positive to negative interactions that are predictive of marital satisfaction according to Gottman? (Obj. #3e)

17. Describe PREPARE. (Obj. #3e)

18. What percent of all first marriages will end in divorce? (Obj. #5a)

19. In what way has sexual behavior within a marriage changed since Kinsey's research? Cite specific examples. (Obj. #3f)

20. According to various researchers, what factors are associated with marital sexual satisfaction? (Obj. #3e, f)

21. If favored coital positions vary from culture to culture, what might that be reflective of? (Obj. #8)

22. Briefly describe the range of the coital frequency from a cross-cultural perspective. (Obj. #8)

23. What factors may interfere with marital sexual enjoyment? (Obj. #3f)

24. List six reasons why someone might engage in nonconsensual extramarital sexual activity. (Obj. #4)

25. How common are extramarital affairs? (Obj. #4)

26. Briefly discuss how an extramarital affair may affect a marriage. (Obj. #4)

27. Explain George and Nena O'Neill's concept of open marriage. (Obj. #4)

28. What is another term for comarital sex, and how common is it? (Obj. #4)

29. When was swinging most popular? (Obj. #4)

30. Describe the changes in the divorce rate since the 1950s and especially what is happening most recently. (Obj. #5a)

31. List six reasons that have been suggested for high divorce rates. (Obj. #5b)

32. According to Cleek and Pearson, what were the three most frequently cited reasons for divorce? (Obj. #5b, 3e)

33. Briefly describe how age at marriage may be associated with the decision to divorce. (Obj. #5b)

34. Briefly describe how level of education may be associated with the decision to divorce. What is an exception to this? (Obj. #5b)

35. According to Helen Fisher, when are people naturally inclined to leave a relationship? Why? (Obj. #5b)

36. Compare the sexual activity and behavior of married men and women to divorced men and women. (Obj. #5d, 3f)

37. What percentage of divorced persons remarry? (Obj. #5a)

38. Why are second marriages more likely to end in divorce than first marriages? (Obj. #5a, b)

39. How has the incidence of widowhood changed from 1900 to 1990? (Obj. #6)

40. What are some of the adjustments widowed people can expect to make? (Obj. #7)

Multiple Choice

Select the best alternative. Check your answers with the answer key at the end of the chapter.

1. Many singles report
   a. high levels of sexual activity.
   b. practicing serial monogamy.
   c. concurrent sexual involvement with many partners.
   d. all of the above

2. Which of the following is **not** a factor contributing to the increase in the number of single adults?
   a. rising divorce rates
   b. people marrying at a later age
   c. more women dropping out of college
   d. a greater number of couples cohabiting

3. Studies of cohabitation show that
   a. marriage is usually the initial goal at the time a couple enters into a cohabitation relationship.
   b. an increasing number of couples do not believe that an eventual marriage commitment is necessary to begin cohabiting.
   c. most cohabitors are college students who benefit economically from the arrangement.
   d. most cohabitors experience similar role expectations as married couples.

4. Which of the following **best** summarizes current research on the on the impact of cohabitation on a subsequent marriage?
   a. Couples who had lived together were just as likely to divorce as those who did not.
   b. There were no differences between cohabitors and noncohabitors regarding relationship stability and sexual satisfaction.
   c. Couples who cohabited prior to marriage were at higher risk of subsequent marital disruption.
   d. Various research studies have reported all of the above.

5. Theorists who propose that living together will have an overall negative impact on marriage suggest that
   a. the immorality of the arrangement will eventually corrode the relationship.
   b. couples who have lived together may treat a marital commitment as casually as a cohabitation arrangement and therefore may terminate a relationship more easily.
   c. our society needs more structure, higher values, and increased commitment rather than temporary, loosely defined relationships.
   d. children learn what they live.

6. Polyandry is a form of marriage between
   a. one woman and several men.
   b. one man and several women.
   c. one woman and one man.
   d. several men and several women.

7. Marriage in our society has typically served all of the following functions **except**
   a. defining inheritance rights to family property.
   b. regulating sexual behavior.
   c. providing for social and emotional support.
   d. providing for more gender role flexibility.

8. According to Klagsbrun, which has been found to be associated with successful marriages?
   a. having children
   b. living a reasonable distance from parents and in-laws
   c. prior cohabitation
   d. spending focused time together

9. In Gottman's study of marital interaction patterns, which of the following was **not** cited as a behavior predictive of marital discord?
   a. making excuses and denying responsibility for disagreements
   b. verbal expressions of contempt
   c. "stonewalling"
   d. whining and complaining

10. A premarital inventory called _____ predicted couples who would get divorced from those who were happily married with about _____ percent accuracy.
    a. PREPARE; 50
    b. Premarital Success Inventory; 65
    c. PREPARE; 80
    d. Premarital Success Inventory; 90

11. Frequency of marital sexual interaction is associated with
    a. age at marriage.
    b. sexual satisfaction.
    c. socioeconomic class.
    d. prior sexual experiences.

12. Nonconsensual extramarital sex means that
    a. both partners engage in sexual relationships outside of their marriage, and they are aware of it but do not talk about it.
    b. a married person engages in an outside sexual relationship without the consent of his or her spouse.
    c. extramarital sex is an occasional, not a habitual practice.
    d. an individual is having a long-term affair as opposed to a one-night stand.

13. Swinging appeared to be **most** popular
    a. in the 1940s and early 1950s.
    b. in the 1950s and early 1960s.
    c. in the 1960s and early 1970s.
    d. in the 1970s and early 1980s.

14. According to Gottman's research, which of the following is **most important** in terms of maintaining marital satisfaction?
    a. being sexually compatible
    b. having similar financial goals and values
    c. maintaining a five to one ratio of positive to negative interactions in the relationship
    d. being able to avoid frequent arguments and talk things out calmly and rationally

15. Research indicates that _____ may be associated with getting a divorce.
    a. having children
    b. monogamy
    c. having a one-career family
    d. getting married at an early age

16. Which of the following is **false**?
    a. Coitus is the most common form of adult sexual activity in all societies.
    b. Most married couples around the world engage in coitus between two and five times a week.
    c. Most societies have more restrictive norms pertaining to premarital sex than to extramarital sex.
    d. With few exceptions, men around the world are allowed greater access to extramarital coitus then women are.

17. The divorce rate in 1993 was one divorce for every _____ marriages.
    a. two
    b. three
    c. four
    d. five

18. Which of the following was **not** given as a reason for the high divorce rates in the United States?
    a. the liberalization of the divorce laws
    b. the reduction of social stigma attached to divorce
    c. a greater abundance of wealth
    d. increasing influence of organized religion

19. Approximately _____ of divorced persons remarry.
    a. 25 percent
    b. 50 percent
    c. 75 percent
    d. 95 percent

20. According to anthropologist Helen Fisher, the reason that humans have a natural inclination to want to end a relationship after four years is
    a. because they naturally crave sexual variety, and most relationships are sexually stagnant after four years.
    b. because they are biologically driven to mate with as many people as possible.
    c. because that is approximately enough time for a child to be weaned from total dependence.
    d. by that time, the qualities that initially attracted them to their partners are now a source of irritation and frustration.

21. With respect to widowhood, a sense of _____ is **not** typical, but strong feelings of _____ are.
    a. relief; anger
    b. failure; relief
    c. anger; grief
    d. grief; relief

22. Which of the following statements regarding widowhood is **false**?
    a. In most marriages, it is the man who dies first.
    b. The ratio of widows to widowers has been slowly decreasing since the early 1900s.
    c. About half of widowed men remarry.
    d. About one-quarter of widowed women remarry.

Insight and Application

1. What is your current lifestyle and/or relationship style? How do the benefits and problems you experience with this lifestyle compare to what you have read in the text? Would you choose a different relationship style if you could? Why?

2. Assume that you and a significant other have decided to cohabit and/or get married. List at least twelve aspects of your relationship that you think would be important to discuss before you made that commitment. In addition to the topics themselves, what specific aspects or dimensions of each of those topics do you think would be important to explore?

3. From your observations and experience, what factors contribute to a successful relationship? When you see people that appear to be dissatisfied or unhappy in their relationships, what seem to be the factors associated with the distress? What might you do in the future to maximize your own relationship satisfaction?

4. Have you ever experienced a nonconsensual extramarital relationship? What were your reasons for becoming involved with a person outside of your primary relationship? Would you do it again? What effect did that have on your primary relationship, if any? To your knowledge, has your partner ever engaged in a nonconsensual extramarital relationship? If your partner did, how would that affect you and the relationship?

Multiple Choice Answers

1. d	2. c	3. b	4. d	5. b	6. a	7. d	8. d
9. d	10. c	11. b	12. b	13. d	14. c	15. d	16. c
17. a	18. d	19. c	20. c	21. c	22. b		
25. d	26. b						

cohabitation	**serial monogamy**
monogamy	**polygyny**
polyandry	**extramarital relationship**
nonconsensual extramarital sex	**consensual extramarital relationship**
open marriage	**swinging**

a single person who has a
succession of sexually
exclusive relationships

living together
in a sexual relationship
without being married

marriage between one man
and several women

marriage between one man
and one woman

sexual interaction
experienced by a married
person with someone other
than her or his spouse

marriage between one
woman and several men

a sexual and/or emotional
relationship that occurs
outside the marriage bond
with the consent of
one's spouse

engaging in an outside
sexual relationship without
the consent (or presumably
knowledge) of his
or her spouse

the exchange of
marital partners
for sexual interaction

a marriage in which spouses,
with each other's permission,
have intimate relationships
with other people as well as
the marital partner

15

Sexuality and Aging

Introduction

The chapter begins with an exploration of the reasons why our society associates aging with sexlessness. Subsequent discussion focuses on the physiosexual changes that occur in men and women as they grow older, and how these changes can affect sexual expression. Finally, various patterns in relationship styles as people age are explored.

Objectives

After studying this chapter, you should be able to:

1. Discuss some of the reasons why aging in our society is frequently associated with sexlessness.

2. Explain how the double standard relates to male and female sexual expression throughout the aging process.

3. Describe how the relatives of nursing home residents and the staff members of these facilities often deal with the sexual feelings and behavior of older people.

4. Discuss three factors that affect sexual activity in later years.

5. Describe some of the options for sexual expression as people grow older, citing specific research studies that support these views.

6. Describe the physiosexual changes that occur in women as they age.

7. Define hormone-replacement therapy and explain its advantages and potential risks.

8 Explain the various changes that occur throughout the sexual response cycle as women grow older.

9 Describe the physiosexual changes that occur in men as they age.

10. Explain the various changes that occur throughout the sexual response cycle as men grow older.

11. Discuss how the aging process affects the prostate gland in men and what treatment options are available for various prostate problems.

12. Describe the nature of sexual expression and relationships in the later years.

13. Explain why people tend to become more androgynous as they age.

14. Describe some characteristics of sexuality and aging in other cultures.

Key Terms and Concepts

"Flash cards" listing key terms and concepts on one side and their corresponding definitions and explanations on the other side are provided at the end of the chapter.

Chapter Overview With Fill-Ins

After reading each of the major sections in the chapter, check your retention by **mentally** filling in each of the blanks in the corresponding sections below. Cover the answers in the margin as you go along, and write the answers in the space provided only when you are doing your final review.

Sexuality in the Later Years: Myth Versus Reality

sexlessness
procreation
youth

acceptable

There are several reasons why aging in our society is often associated with _____: American culture is still influenced by the philosophy that equates sex with _____; there is a disproportionate focus on _____ and the assumption that love, sex, and romance belong exclusively to young people; and there is also an unspoken assumption that it is not _____ for older people to have sexual needs.

double standard

women

menopause

men

The _____ _____ that affects male and female sexual expression during adolescence and adulthood continues into old age, having an especially negative effect on _____. Despite the fact that women's erotic and orgasmic capabilities continue after _____, women are often considered to be past their "sexual prime" relatively early in their life. In contrast, the physical and sexual attractiveness of _____ is often considered to be enhanced by the aging process.

Nursing homes

antisexual
medications

Gray Panthers

_____ _____ have been criticized for their insensitivity to the human rights of aged individuals, and in this case, especially _____ prejudice and practices. Because it is often assumed that older people are not sexual, _____ are sometimes prescribed without consideration of their effects on sexuality. Concerned individuals, progressive nursing home personnel and organizations such as the _____ _____, as well as others, are beginning to have some effect on restrictive practices in nursing homes.

sexual; regularity

Three factors affect sexual activity in later years: 1) a person's _____ activity levels in early adulthood; 2) _____ of sexual expression; and 3) health and illness.

fantasize
approved

Research indicates that a majority of men and women ages 80 to 102 _____ about sex. Another study found that more older people _____ of masturbation than engaged in it.

Physiosexual Changes and Sexual Response: Older Women

climacteric

The term _____ refers to the physiological changes that occur during the transition period from fertility to infertility.

Menopause

_____, one of the events of the female climacteric, refers to the cessation of menstruation. Some women may experience few physical symptoms other than cessation of menstruation, but for many women menopause brings a range of symptoms that are

estrogen
hot flashes

caused by the decline in _____ and may include disturbances in sleep patterns, "_____ _____ ", dizziness, difficulties with balance, diminished pleasure from

touch

_____, itchy or burning skin, sensitivity to clothing or touch, numbness or tingling in the hands and feet, severe headaches, short-term memory loss, difficulty in concentrating, depression, and

anxiety

increased _____.

Hormone replacement

_____ _____ therapy (HRT) involves taking supplemental estrogen and progesterone to compensate for the decrease in natural hormone production that occurs during the

climacteric
risks

_____. HRT has a number of benefits as well as potential _____.

sexual activity

Alternatives to HRT include continued frequent _____ _____, which helps maintain vaginal lubrication, use of

vaginal lubricants

_____ _____, physical exercise, good nutrition and food supplements.

vaginal lubrication

During the excitement phase of sexual response, _____ _____ begins more slowly and the amount of lubrication is reduced. This and other changes can result in painful intercourse, and some women also have reported decreased sexual desire and

clitoris

sensitivity of the _____.

plateau

During the _____ phase, the formation of the orgasmic platform and uterine elevation occur to a somewhat lesser degree.

Contractions
Orgasm

_____ during orgasm continue to occur, although the number is typically reduced. _____ appears to be an important part of sexual activity to older women.

Resolution

_____ phase usually occurs more rapidly in postmenopausal women.

Physiosexual Changes and Sexual Response: Older Men

testosterone

Physiosexual changes that occur as a man grows older are to a large degree related to decreased production of _____. With aging, a man may notice that the size and firmness of his

testicles
sperm

_____ diminishes somewhat, and although there is a gradual decrease in _____ production, many men retain their fertility well into old age.

physical stimulation

During excitement phase, a man may take longer to get an erection and more direct _____ _____ may be required.

myotonia	During plateau phase, men may not experience as much _____ as when they were younger, and complete penile erection is frequently not obtained until just prior to
orgasm	_____ .
orgasm	During the _____ phase, men may experience a decline in orgasmic intensity. The number of contractions may be reduced and
seminal fluid	the _____ _____ is usually less copious and somewhat thinner in consistency.
rapidly	Resolution typically occurs more _____ in older men, while
refractory	the _____ period usually lengthens.
prostatitis	Inflammation of the prostate gland, a condition known as _____ , is a problem that becomes more common as men get older. As men grow older, the prostate gland tends to
increase	_____ in size, a condition known as benign
prostatic hyper-trophy	_____ _____ . It is not uncommon for aging men to develop benign or malignant tumors of the prostate. Prostate cancer is usually treated by removing the entire gland (called
prostatectomy	_____) or administering female sex hormones.

Sexuality and Relationships in the Later Years

sexuality	Many older adults remain interested in _____ .
married	Being _____ is no guarantee of a satisfying sexual relationship for any number of reasons. On the other hand, the opportunities for sexual expression in a relationship often
increase	_____ , as pressures from work, raising children, etc. are minimized and more time is available for sharing with a partner.
heterosexual	The limited research available suggests that gay men and lesbians may be better prepared for dealing with the adjustments of aging than _____ men and women.
Intimacy	_____ becomes more important in later years. Some people
frequent	may have more _____ sexual encounters, and for others,
genital	_____ sexual activity may become less important than the more affectionate aspects of sexual sharing. One survey found that while sexual frequency declines, enjoyment of sex sometimes
increases	_____ with age.
androgyny	Development toward _____ in personal, interpersonal, and sexual styles occurs for many people in later life.

Short Answer

1. List two reasons why aging in our society is often associated with sexlessness. (Obj. #1)

2. Describe the double standard as it affects male and female sexual expression in later years. (Obj. #2)

3. According to one research study, compare the aspects of sexuality that contribute to a general feeling of well-being among older men and women. (Obj. #2)

4. How does Susan Sontag suggest that women approach their later years? (Obj. #2)

5. Briefly characterize the nature of sexual expression among older individuals who live in Abkhasia, a particular region of the Soviet Union. (Obj. #14)

6. List three factors that affect sexual activity in later years. (Obj. #4)

7. List at least four nursing home practices which negatively affect the sexual expression of their elderly residents. (Obj. #3)

8. What changes are beginning to take place in nursing homes as the result of efforts made by the Gray Panthers and other organizations? (Obj. #3)

9.   What percentage of older men and women fantasize about sex? (Obj. #5)

10. What percentage of older people approve of masturbation? (Obj. #5)

11. Describe the incidence of masturbation among older men and women (Obj. #5)

12. From a biological standpoint, what happens during menopause? (Obj. #6)

13. List at least five possible symptoms of menopause. (Obj. #6)

14. Why do "hot flashes" occur? (Obj. #6)

15. List at least eight benefits of HRT. (Obj. #7)

16. The incidence of endometrial cancer has been associated with the use of what hormone? How has that problem been alleviated? (Obj. #7)

17. Discuss some of the health risks of HRT. For whom is its use **not** appropriate? (Obj. #7)

18. What are some alternatives to HRT? (Obj. #7)

19. Briefly outline the physiological changes that occur in men and women as they age in each of the following stages of the sexual response cycle: (Obj. #8, 10)

Stage	**Females**	**Males**
Excitement phase		
Plateau phase		
Orgasm phase		
Resolution phase		

20. What is prostatitis? From what conditions does it usually result? (Obj. #11)

21. What are the symptoms of prostatitis? (Obj. #11)

22. If prostatitis is the result of a bacterial infection, how is it treated? (Obj. #11)

23. How is prostate cancer usually treated? What problems may result? (Obj. #11)

24. According to one study, what techniques did respondents use to enhance their sexual enjoyment? (Obj. #12)

25. How do homosexual men and women cope with the adjustments of aging compared to heterosexual men and women? (Obj. #12)

26. What may contribute to men and women's tendency to be more androgynous as they age? (Obj. #13)

Multiple Choice

Select the best alternative. Check your answers with the answer key at the end of the chapter.

1. Aging in our society is often associated with sexlessness because
   a. many people still equate sex with procreation.
   b. due to decreases in hormonal output over time, the majority of older people lose interest in sex.
   c. as people age, they become more androgynous and therefore less sexual.
   d. all of the above

2. Use of the expression "dirty old man" reflects the fact that
   a. when old men are interested in sex it is usually because they are pedophiles.
   b. there is a cultural bias against sex in old age.
   c. it is acceptable for older women to be interested in sex, but that is not the case for men.
   d. older people are generally not interested in sex.

3. Which of the following statements concerning the double standard is **true**?
   a. It does not negatively affect sexual expression in men and women until later in life.
   b. It affects women more negatively than men, especially in old age.
   c. The 1972 film "Harold and Maude," in which a 60-year-old woman and a 20-year-old man have a love affair, is a good example of the double standard of aging.
   d. all of the above

4. Which of the following statements is **true**?
   a. Aspects of sexuality that contribute to a general feeling of well-being among older men and women are generally the same.
   b. Susan Sontag has encouraged women to maintain their youthful looks by eating well and exercising regularly.
   c. Nursing homes in our country are extremely progressive in terms of how they respect and respond to the rights of older people.
   d. During menopause, the pituitary continues to secrete follicle-stimulating hormone.

5. The climacteric refers to
   a. the point at which the peak level of estrogen is produced during a woman's menstrual cycle.
   b. the cessation of menstruation.
   c. the physiological changes that occur during the transition period from fertility to infertility.
   d. the orgasm phase of the sexual response cycle.

6. Which of the following statements concerning menopause is **true**?
   a. It occurs around 65 years of age.
   b. Ovarian estrogen output increases.
   c. Symptoms of menopause are usually quite severe.
   d. The most acute menopause symptoms occur in the two years prior and two years following the last menstrual period.

7. Which of the following is **not** a physiosexual change in the aging female?
   a. cessation of uterine contractions and orgasm
   b. decreased vaginal lubrication
   c. decrease in length and width of the vagina
   d. decrease in the number of orgasmic contractions

8. A woman's life expectancy has _____ since the fourteenth century.
   a. decreased
   b. more than doubled
   c. more than tripled
   d. stayed the same

9. Daily doses of vitamin E can
   a. increase vaginal lubrication.
   b. improve vaginal elasticity.
   c. alleviate the discomfort of "hot flashes".
   d. increase the potential of multiple orgasms.

10. One of the benefits of taking estrogen is
    a. weight loss.
    b. protection against abnormal bone loss.
    c. increase in sexual desire.
    d. protection against endometrial cancer

11. HRT refers to
    a. hormonal reactivation treatment.
    b. hysteroreconstructive therapy.
    c. hormonal rage tempo.
    d. hormonal replacement therapy.

12. Which of the following groups of women cannot take HRT?
    a. women with estrogen-dependent breast cancer
    b. women with liver impairment
    c. women with high blood pressure
    d. women with osteoporosis

13. Testosterone production in men reaches a peak near age _____ and then steadily declines, leveling off at the age of _____.
    a. 15; 30
    b. 20; 40
    c. 20; 60
    d. 30; 60

14. As a man ages, what changes might he observe in his seminal fluid?
    a. greater amount
    b. thicker in consistency
    c. slightly different odor
    d. none of the above

15. One of the changes that typically occurs in the _____ phase of the sexual response cycle in the aging male is that more stimulation may be required in order to achieve an erection.
    a. excitement
    b. plateau
    c. orgasm
    d. resolution

16. The condition called prostatitis refers to
    a. cancer of the prostate.
    b. inflammation of the prostate.
    c. retrograde prostatic secretions.
    d. prostate atrophy.

17. Which of the following is a symptom of prostatitis?
    a. a cloudy discharge from the penis
    b. backache
    c. pain in the pelvic area
    d. all of the above

18. The prostate gland tends to enlarge as men grow older, resulting in a condition called
    a. benign prostatic hypertrophy.
    b. malignant prostatic atrophy.
    c. hyperprostatic atrophy.
    d. prostatic tumescence.

19. Which of the following statements concerning treatment for prostate cancer is **false**?
    a. Treatment involves removal of the prostate gland.
    b. Treatment involves use of female sex hormones.
    c. Treatment may result in erectile difficulties.
    d. none of the above

20. Which of the following statements is **false**?
    a. According to one survey, over fifty percent of older men and women fantasized about sex.
    b. On one survey reported that more older people approved of masturbation than engaged in it.
    c. A greater percentage of older men reported masturbating than women.
    d. One survey indicated that approximately 25% of older men and women provided oral stimulation to their partners.

21. According to the text, a man may interpret his partner's reduced vaginal lubrication as
    a. symptoms of osteoporosis.
    b. a sign of vaginal atrophy.
    c. an indication that she is less aroused by him.
    d. a sign of an oncoming "hot flash".

22. Surveys of the sexual activity of older people found that
    a. the men stress quantity instead of quality.
    b. the frequency of genital activity may increase or decrease, but overall sexual satisfaction remains stable or increases.
    c. homosexual men reported a marked decrease in sexual satisfaction.
    d. only a relatively small percentage of older men and women engaged in fantasy.

23. According to Masters and Johnson, _____ seems to be the crucial factor in maintaining satisfactory sexual functioning in later years.
    a. making consistent efforts to introduce variety into the sexual relationship
    b. exercising on a daily basis
    c. regularity of sexual expression throughout the adult years
    d. keeping abreast of current literature in the field of human sexuality

24. In Abkhasia, the Caucasus region of the Soviet Union,
    a. most couples remain sexually active beyond the age of 70.
    b. aging individuals are ascribed a high social status.
    c. retirement does not exist.
    d. all of the above

Insight and Application

1. Reflect on television programs you watch, movies you attend, books and magazines you read, and people you observe in your daily life, and cite specific examples of how the double standard of aging is reinforced and supported, as well as challenged or discouraged.

2. If you were responsible for establishing and implementing educational and/or entertainment programs on sexuality, as well as guidelines for sexual behavior in a nursing home, how would you go about it? Cite specific examples.

3. What kinds of opportunities and challenges do you expect as you grow older, especially in the area of sexual development? Think of your parents and/or grandparents, and imagine how you would like your life in general, or your sexual experiences in particular, to be different or similar to theirs.

4. List attitudes and behaviors of your own that have discriminated against older people, especially in regard to their sexuality. In studying this chapter, has your knowledge base changed in any way that would alter these assumptions or behaviors? Give specific examples.

Multiple Choice Answers

1. a	2. b	3. b	4. d	5. c	6. d	7. a	8. b
9. c	10. b	11. d	12. a	13. c	14. d	15. a	16. b
17. d	18. a	19. d	20. d	21. c	22. b	23. c	24. d

climacteric	**menopause**
"hot flashes"	**hormone replacement therapy (HRT)**
osteoporosis	**myotonia**
prostatitis	**benign prostatic hypertrophy**
prostatectomy	

cessation of menstruation due to the aging process or surgical removal of the ovaries	physiological changes that occur during the transition period from fertility to infertility in both sexes
the use of supplemental hormones during and after menopause	a common symptom associated with menopause whereby the fluctuating levels of hormones rapidly dilate the blood vessels, causing a woman to feel a momentary rush of heat
muscle tension	abnormal bone loss
the tendency of the prostate gland to enlarge as men age, which puts pressure on the urethra, thereby decreasing urine flow	inflammation of the prostate gland
	surgical removal of the prostate

16

The Nature and Origin of Sexual Difficulties

Introduction

The authors begin with a discussion of the organic, cultural, individual and relationship influences that may negatively affect sexual expression. From that point, they go on to explore a range of desire, excitement, and orgasm phase sexual difficulties that men and women experience. Some of the factors that contribute to painful intercourse in women and men are also presented.

Objectives

After studying this chapter, you should be able to:

1. Discuss how common various sexual problems are among men and women.

2. Explain how each of the following may contribute to sexual difficulties:
   a. organic factors
   b. cultural influences
   c. individual factors
   d. relationship factors

3. Distinguish between generalized and situational sexual problems.

4. Describe each of the following desire phase difficulties and some of the factors that may contribute to or be associated with each:
   a. hypoactive sexual desire
   b. dissatisfaction with frequency of sexual activity
   c. sexual aversion disorder

5. Define each of the following excitement phase difficulties and discuss some of the factors that might contribute to or be associated with each:
   a. female sexual arousal disorder
   b. male erectile disorder

6. Define each of the following orgasm phase difficulties and discuss some of the factors that might contribute to or be associated with each:
   a. female orgasm disorder
   b. male orgasm disorder
   c. premature ejaculation
   d. faking orgasms

7. Discuss some of the reasons why men and women may experience dyspareunia.

8. Define vaginismus, and explain how common it is and under what circumstances it may occur.

Key Terms and Concepts

"Flash cards" listing key terms and concepts on one side and their corresponding definitions and explanations on the other side are provided at the end of the chapter.

Chapter Overview With Fill-Ins

After reading each of the major sections in the chapter, check your retention by **mentally** filling in each of the blanks in the corresponding sections below. Cover the answers in the margin as you go along, and write the answers in the space provided only when you are doing your final review.

Origins of Sexual Difficulties

positive

common

Some research has indicated that many happily married couples experience sexual problems but feel very _____ about their sexual relations. Research indicates that sexual problems are quite _____.

relationship

Some of the general causes of sexual difficulties can be described under four different categories: organic factors, cultural influences, individual and _____ factors.

neurological

recreational

Any irregularities in the vascular, endocrine and _____ systems can contribute to sexual problems. Medications, surgeries, illnesses and "_____" drugs can interfere with sexual interest and response.

childhood learning

double standard

penile-vaginal

Performance

There are several cultural influences that may contribute to sexual problems people experience. Negative _____ _____ may result in guilt, discomfort, anxiety, or embarrassment concerning sexuality that may affect our sexual functioning as we mature. Although the rigidity of the _____ _____ appears to be lessening somewhat, the notion that women should be sexually passive while men should be ultimately responsible for sexual interaction still lingers, often creating discomfort, frustration, and resentment in sexual relations between men and women. The cultural notion that sex equals _____-_____ intercourse has placed a disproportionate emphasis on coitus while at the same time minimizing the enjoyment of relating sexually in a variety of other ways. _____ anxiety is another cultural influence that can block natural sexual arousal and release.

self-concept

assault

Individual factors that may affect sexual expression include: the sexual knowledge and attitudes people acquire about sex; an individual's _____-_____; emotional difficulties such as anxiety or depression; childhood sexual abuse and adult sexual _____.

communication

orientation

A variety of relationship factors can also affect sexual satisfaction. In addition to a myriad of relationship issues, ineffective _____, fear of pregnancy or sexually transmitted diseases, and discrepancies between sexual _____ and the partner to whom one is actually relating may all contribute to potential difficulties in sexual expression.

lifelong

generalized

situational

A specific sexual difficulty can be of _____ duration or be acquired by a certain time. A person may experience the problems in all situations with all partners (_____) or only in specific situations or with specific partners (_____).

Desire Phase Difficulties

Hypoactive sexual _____ _____ _____, or lack of "sexual
desire appetite," is a common problem experienced by both men and women.
rare Generalized, lifelong HSD is _____; more commonly,
people experience HSD at specific times in their lives or in particular
situations _____.

discrepancies Another type of desire phase difficulty is when sexual partners may
have _____ in their preferences for amount, type, and
timing of sexual activities.

sexual aversion When low desire includes a fear of sex and a strong desire to avoid
sexual situations, it is considered _____ _____.

Excitement Phase Difficulties

Vaginal lubrication _____ _____ is a woman's first physiological
response to sexual arousal. When women do not lubricate, it may be
biological attributed to a variety of _____, psychological or
situational factors.

erectile Problems with male _____ disorder can be classified into
lifelong two broad types: men with _____ erectile disorder, who
penetration have never maintained _____ with a partner throughout
acquired their entire lives; and men with _____ erectile disorder,
who have had erections with partners in the past but who are no
longer able to do so in current situations.

Orgasm Phase Difficulties

The word that is commonly used now to refer to absence of orgasm in
anorgasmia women is _____. A woman who has _____,
generalized lifelong anorgasmia has never experienced orgasm by masturbation
Situational or with a partner. _____ anorgasmia refers to a woman
who experiences orgasm rarely, or in some situations but not in
others.

5; 10 Approximately ____ to ____ percent of adult women have
generalized, lifelong anorgasmia. Several surveys indicate that the
manual-clitoral absence of routine orgasm during coitus without additional
_____-_____ stimulation is a common pattern for
women.

Male orgasmic _____ _____ disorder refers to the inability of a
man to ejaculate during sexual activity.

A common orgasm difficulty that men experience is
premature _____ ejaculation.

Faking   _____ orgasms — pretending to experience orgasms
                         without actually doing so — is typically discussed in reference to
                         women, although a smaller percentage of men do this as well.
                         Reasons given by women for faking orgasm include: to avoid
communication   disappointing their partners, poor _____, limited
                         knowledge of sexual techniques, a need for partner approval, little
                         hope of changing the partner's behavior, an attempt to hide a
                         deteriorating relationship, or to protect a partner's ego.

Dyspareunia

Dyspareunia   _____ is the medical term for painful intercourse, which
                         occurs most commonly in women but which men may experience this
                         as well.

                         Men may experience painful intercourse if they are uncircumcised
foreskin; smegma   and the _____ is too tight, if _____ accumulates
Peyronie's   underneath the foreskin, or if they have _____ disease, a
                         condition where fibrous tissue and calcium deposits develop in the
                         space above and between the cavernous bodies of the penis. In
                         addition, infections of the urethra, bladder, prostate gland, or
seminal vesicles   _____ _____ may induce burning, itching, or
                         pain during or after ejaculation.

                         For women, discomfort at the vaginal opening or inside the vaginal
lubrication   walls is usually due to inadequate arousal and _____.
hormones   Physiological conditions such as insufficient _____ may
                         also reduce lubrication. Other causes of painful intercourse include:
vaginal   _____ infections; contraceptive foams, creams, or jellies;
                         allergic reactions to condoms or diaphragms; an intact
hymen   _____; or scar tissue at the vaginal opening.
Vulvar vestibulitis   _____ _____ syndrome results in severe pain
                         at the entrance of the vagina. Another source of pain may be the
glans   clitoral _____, especially if smegma collects underneath
                         the clitoral hood. Pain deep in the pelvis during coitus may be due to
ovaries   the jarring of the _____ or stretching of the
uterine   _____ ligaments. Another source of deep pelvic pain is
endometriosis   _____, a condition in which tissue that normally grows on
                         the walls of the uterus implants on various parts of the abdominal
                         cavity. Other causes of dyspareunia include infections in the uterus,
gonorrhea   _____, and torn uterine ligaments.

Vaginismus   _____ is characterized by strong involuntary muscle
                         contractions in the outer third of the vagina. The contractions may be
penis   so strong that attempts to insert a _____ into the vagina
                         are very painful. The incidence of vaginismus is believed to be very
low   _____.

Matching

Match the terms below with the appropriate descriptions. Note that some terms may be used more than once but choose only **one** answer for each.

a.	HSD	h.	lubrication inhibition
b.	male erectile disorder	i.	Peyronie's disease
c.	premature ejaculation	j.	male orgasmic disorder
d.	sexual aversion	k.	vulvar vestibulitis
e.	anorgasmia	l.	endometriosis
f.	faking orgasms	m.	vaginismus
g.	dyspareunia		

_____1.   Approximately 5–10 percent of women experience this problem.

_____2.   the most common sexual problem men experience

_____3.   One study indicated that 66 percent of women and 33 percent of men have had this experience.

_____4.   may experience nausea, diarrhea, dizziness as a result of this

_____5.   may occur as the result of low estrogen levels

_____6.   Twenty-five percent of the authors' male students say this is an ongoing problem.

_____7.   Eighty percent of the cases involve organic impairment.

_____8.   lack of sexual appetite

_____9.   This problem may be decreasing in incidence due to available self-help books.

_____10. Eight percent of men experience this problem

_____11. don't fantasize or initiate sex but may be sexually responsive

_____12. may be a result of prolonged intercourse

_____13. This problem is a conscious decision

_____14. the medical term for painful intercourse

_____15. Birth control pills are sometimes prescribed to control this condition.

_____16. can result in curvature of the penis

_____17. severe pain at vaginal entrance

_____18. Two percent of women experience this.

Short Answer

1. According to the National Health and Social Life survey, what is the most common sexual problem that men reported having? (Obj. #1)

2. According to the National Health and Social Life survey, what is the most common sexual problem that women reported having? (Obj. #1)

3. What types of illnesses or medical conditions may affect sexual functioning? (Obj. #2a)

4. What kinds of medications may cause sexual problems? (Obj. #2a)

5. To what kinds of sexual problems might drug and alcohol abuse contribute? (Obj. #2a)

6. With what sexual problems has cigarette smoking been associated? (Obj. #2a)

7. What are some negative childhood experiences that may later lead to sexual difficulties? (Obj. #2b)

8. List expectations regarding women's sexual functioning which are a result of the double standard. (Obj. #2b)

9. List sexual expectations that men experience as a result of the double standard. (Obj. #2b)

10. What is meant by "a narrow definition of sexuality"? (Obj. #2b)

11. List and briefly describe four individual factors that affect sexual expression. (Obj. #2c)

12. List the kinds of relationship problems which may be associated with HSD. (Obj. #2d)

13. List and briefly describe four relationship factors that may affect sexual expression. (Obj. #2d)

14. What are the terms used to describe how sexual problems may vary in duration and focus? (Obj. #3)

15. Define HSD. Can people who have HSD experience excitement and/or orgasm? (Obj. #4a)

16. What common pattern emerges when sexual partners have differences in their preferences for amount, type, and timing of sexual activities? (Obj. #4b)

17. List some of the physiological symptoms that people with sexual aversion might experience. (Obj. #4c)

18. List at least five situations in which women might experience lubrication inhibition. (Obj. #5a)

19. Why is the use of the word "impotence" discouraged in reference to male erectile disorder? (Obj. #5b)

20. List and briefly describe two types of male erectile disorder. (Obj. #5)

21. What percentage of erectile disorder cases involve some degree of organic impairment? (Obj. #5b)

22. What are the effects of lowered levels of nitric oxide? (Obj. #5b)

23. List and describe two different types of anorgasmia. (Obj. #6a)

24. What percentage of women experience generalized, lifelong anorgasmia? Why does the number of women who experience this problem seem to be decreasing? (Obj. #6a)

25. Cite research to indicate how commonly women experience orgasm during coitus without additional manual-clitoral stimulation. (Obj. #6a)

26. List some reasons why women may not have orgasm during intercourse. (Obj. #6a)

27. What percentage of men experience ejaculatory inhibition? (Obj. #6b)

28. How long does intercourse last for the average American couple? Considering this, how is premature ejaculation defined? (Obj. #6c)

29. Cite evidence that indicates how common premature ejaculation is. (Obj. #6c)

30. What percentage of women and what percentage of men have faked orgasm? (Obj. #6d)

31. List four conditions that may cause painful intercourse in men. (Obj. #7)

32. What is Peyronie's disease? (Obj. #7)

33. List at least six factors that might account for pain at the vaginal opening or inside the vaginal walls. (Obj. #7)

34. List three possible causes of deep pelvic pain during intercourse. (Obj. #7)

35. Define vaginismus. How common is it? (Obj. #8)

Multiple Choice

Select the best alternative. Check your answers with the answer key at the end of the chapter.

1. Which of the following statements is **false**?
   a. Research indicates that many happily married couples who experience sexual problems still feel positively about their marriages.
   b. Premature ejaculation is the sexual problem most commonly reported by men.
   c. A *Parade Magazine* survey reported that 16% of men and women had sexual problems.
   d. According to several studies, anorgasmia is the sexual problem that is most commonly reported by women.

2. _____ is the problem most likely to have an organic component.
   a. Erectile inhibition
   b. Anorgasmia
   c. Ejaculatory inhibition
   d. Vaginismus

3. Which of the following is **not** a cultural factor that might contribute to sexual difficulties?
   a. the double standard
   b. a narrow definition of sexuality
   c. negative childhood learning
   d. emotional difficulties

4. A person who is diagnosed as having generalized, lifelong HSD
   a. did not exhibit sexual curiosity as a child and, as an adult, does not fantasize or demonstrate interest in being sexually involved.
   b. has masturbated since childhood but has no interest in being sexually involved as an adult.
   c. did not exhibit sexual curiosity as a child, but is now sexually active yet unable to experience orgasm.
   d. is sexually interested and responsive with a lover but exhibits no interest in being sexually involved with a spouse.

5. Which one of the following statements concerning HSD is **false**?
   a. Generalized, lifelong HSD is a fairly common sexual problem.
   b. Certain medications may be associated with HSD.
   c. HSD would be an adaptive response to a partner who is verbally or physically abusive.
   d. A person with HSD can experience excitement and/or orgasm.

6. One researcher found that the more rigidly orthodox that married members of _____ churches were, the less sexual interest, response, frequency and pleasure they reported in marital sex.
   a. Jewish
   b. Protestant
   c. Catholic
   d. Jewish, Protestant and Catholic

7. A man who experiences sexual aversion
   a. may exhibit physiological symptoms such as sweating and trembling.
   b. will probably desire sex more frequently than his partner.
   c. probably enjoys fantasizing about sex even though he has difficulty responding sexually when he is with a woman.
   d. usually has problems with ejaculatory inhibition.

8. A woman exhibits little interest in initiating and participating in sex with her partner, although when she does have sex, she becomes aroused and is orgasmic. Her sexual problem would **best** be described as
   a. female sexual arousal disorder.
   b. hypoactive sexual desire.
   c. situational anorgasmia.
   d. delayed sexual response.

9. In which of the following situations is diminished lubrication normal?
   a. breast-feeding
   b. following menopause
   c. during prolonged intercourse
   d. all of the above

10. Erection of the penis is equivalent to _____ in women.
    a. sex flush
    b. vaginal lubrication
    c. orgasmic response
    d. sexual desire

11. Which of the following comes from the Latin and means "without power"?
    a. frigidity
    b. impotence
    c. erectile inhibition
    d. sine pudendum

12. A man is unable to have an erection in his sexual encounters with his partner, but that does not bother him and it is acceptable to her as long as he brings her to orgasm in other ways. What the authors would have to say regarding this is that
    a. the man is impotent.
    b. the man has acquired erectile inhibition.
    c. the man suffers from hypoactive sexual desire.
    d. neither the man nor his partner have a problem, since they are satisfied with the situation.

13. Which of the following would be **least** likely to contribute to erectile difficulties?
    a. hormonal disorders
    b. surgeries performed in the pelvic area
    c. severe diabetes
    d. elevated levels of nitric oxide

14. Which of the following statements concerning anorgasmia is **false**?
    a. Individuals with this problem may still maintain sexual desire.
    b. Women may feel highly disappointed or distressed by this condition.
    c. The incidence of generalized, lifelong anorgasmia is decreasing.
    d. Men do not experience anorgasmia.

15. According to Hite's research, how many women have orgasms during intercourse without additional manual-clitoral stimulation?
    a. 80 percent
    b. 50 percent
    c. 30 percent
    d. 10 percent

16. Which of the following statements is **true**?
    a. Causes of anorgasmia are typically physiological in origin.
    b. Approximately 30 percent of adult women in the United States have generalized, lifelong anorgasmia.
    c. A woman with situational anorgasmia experiences orgasm in some situations but not in others.
    d. The number of women with generalized, lifelong anorgasmia is increasing slightly.

17. Men who have never been able to experience intravaginal ejaculation would be diagnosed as having
    a. generalized, lifelong ejaculatory inhibition.
    b. situational, acquired ejaculatory inhibition.
    c. partial ejaculation.
    d. retrograde ejaculation.

18. Based on data available regarding the general public, as well as what male student's in the authors' human sexuality classes have reported, over _____ percent of men have experienced premature ejaculation as an ongoing problem.
    a. 5-10
    b. 15-20
    c. 25-30
    d. 40-50

19. Dyspareunia is
    a. experienced by men.
    b. experienced by women.
    c. experienced equally by both women and men.
    d. experienced by both sexes but most commonly by women

20. A condition in which tissue that normally grows on the walls of the uterus implants on various parts of the abdominal cavity is called
    a. Peyronie's disease.
    b. endometriosis.
    c. vulvar vestibulitis syndrome.
    d. ectopic adhesions.

21. Which of the following statements is **true**?
    a. Jarring of the ovaries during intercourse may cause pain at the vaginal opening.
    b. Vaginismus is a fairly common problem that women experience.
    c. Vulvar vestibulitis syndrome results in deep pelvic pain.
    d. Vaginismus may be associated with a homosexual orientation.

22. One source of painful intercourse that can result in curvature of the penis is
    a. phimosis.
    b. priapism.
    c. Peyronie's disease.
    d. nocturnal penile tumescence.

Insight and Application

1. Have you, a partner, or someone close to you ever experienced a sexual problem? If so, what values and information contributed to your understanding of the problem at the time? Based on what you know now, how would you have perceived or dealt with the problem differently?

2. Think in terms of your own childhood learning, the double standard, the cultural notion that "real sex" equals intercourse, and the goal-oriented nature of sexual expression in our society today. To what extent have these cultural influences affected your sexuality? Give specific examples. Are there any aspects of this with which you are dissatisfied? If so, how might you change them?

3. How would you assess your sexual knowledge and attitudes, as well as your self-concept in terms of how it affects your sexual expression? Are there areas that you would like to change or improve? If so, how might you go about doing that?

4. Describe your worst sexual experience — alone or with someone. "Worst" could be painful, traumatic, embarrassing, humiliating. Knowing what you know now — about sexual problems, sexual functioning, sexual communication, etc. — how could the trauma of that experience be minimized if you could do it over? Give specific details and examples.

Matching Answers

1. e	2. c	3. f	4. d	5. h	6. c	7. b	8. a
9. e	10. j	11. a	12. h	13. f	14. g	15. l	16. i
17. k	18. m						

Multiple Choice Answers

1. d	2. a	3. d	4. a	5. a	6. d	7. a	8. b
9. d	10. b	11. b	12. d	13. d	14. d	15. c	16. c
17. a	18. c	19. d	20. b	21. d	22. c		

hypoactive sexual desire (HSD)	**sexual aversion disorder**
impotence	**male erectile disorder**
frigidity	**female orgasm disorder (anorgasmia)**
male orgasmic disorder	**premature ejaculation**
faking orgasms	**dyspareunia**

extreme and irrational fear
of sexual activity

a sexual difficulty involving
lack of interest in sexual
fantasy and activity

---

a sexual difficulty whereby
a man's penis does not
become erect in response
to sexual stimulation

the term often applied to
male erection difficulty;
literally means
"without power"

---

a sexual difficulty involving
the absence of orgasm
in women

an imprecise and pejorative
term traditionally used to
describe a variety of female
sexual problems

---

the inability of a man to
ejaculate during sexual
activity, usually intercourse

the inability of a man to
ejaculate during sexual
activity, usually intercourse

---

pain or discomfort
during intercourse

a sexual difficulty whereby
a person pretends to
experience orgasm during
sexual interaction

Peyronie's disease

vulvar vestibulitis syndrome

endometriosis

vaginismus

female sexual
arousal disorder

a condition that can result in severe pain at the entrance of the vagina	abnormal fibrous tissue and calcium deposits in the penis which may result in pain or discomfort during intercourse
a sexual difficulty in which a woman experiences involuntary spasmodic contractions of the muscles of the outer third of the vagina	a condition in which tissue that normally grows on the walls of the uterus implants on various parts of the abdominal cavity
	a woman's persistent inability to attain or maintain the vaginal lubrication-swelling response

17

Sex Therapy and Enhancement

Introduction

For many people, what "sex therapy" involves is often largely unknown or misunderstood. This chapter demystifies the process by providing specific information on exactly what sex therapy entails and by describing in detail various strategies that individuals and couples may use to cope with a range of sexual difficulties. Guidelines for selecting a therapist are outlined at the end of the chapter.

Objectives

After studying this chapter, you should be able to:

1. Discuss each of the following and how they can improve body awareness and enhance a relationship with a partner:
    a. self-awareness
    b. communication
    c. sensate focus
    d. masturbation with a partner present

2. Explain some of the procedures involved for women who are learning to become orgasmic, both alone and with a partner.

3. Describe what treatment procedures are available for dealing with vaginismus and what research has indicated regarding the success rate in treating this problem.

4. Outline at least six specific strategies used to cope with premature ejaculation.

5. Describe various treatment alternatives that are available for men who experience erectile difficulties and how successful they typically are.

6. Outline some of the strategies used to treat men who experience ejaculatory disorder.

7. Discuss some of the dynamics and specific treatment strategies involved in dealing with people who experience hypoactive sexual desire.

8. List and describe the four levels of treatment involved in the PLISSIT model of sex therapy.

9. Discuss the following in regard to seeking help for sexual difficulties:
    a. how sessions with a therapist might be structured
    b. various therapy options that are available
    c. criteria to consider in selecting a therapist
    d. the professional background and training of people who practice sex therapy

Key Terms and Concepts

"Flash cards" listing key terms and concepts on one side and their corresponding definitions and explanations on the other side are provided at the end of the chapter.

Chapter Overview With Fill-Ins

After reading each of the major sections in the chapter, check your retention by **mentally** filling in each of the blanks in the corresponding sections below. Cover the answers in the margin as you go along, and write the answers in the space provided only when you are doing your final review.

Basics of Sexual Enhancement and Sex Therapy

four

Permission
Suggestions

behavioral

interpretations

psychosexual
systems

postmodern

The PLISSIT model of sex therapy specifies _____ levels of treatment; each successive level provides increasingly in-depth therapy. PLISSIT is an acronym for _____, Limited Information, Specific _____, and Intensive Therapy.

Treatment that combines _____ techniques with the development of insight into unconscious conflicts is an important development in the sex therapy field. In insight-oriented therapy, the therapist provides _____ and reflection to help clients gain awareness and understanding of the unconscious feelings and thoughts that have been contributing to their sexual problems. Helen Singer Kaplan calls this _____ therapy. In contrast to psychosexual therapy, _____ therapy is based on the concept that the identified problems serve important current functions in the relationship. Integration of all of the above is called _____ sex therapy.

Seeking Professional Assistance

professional
alone

Sex Educators

doctor

sex therapy

cost

Although some people with sexual problems improve over time without therapy, you may decide to seek _____ help. You may wish to see a therapist _____ or with your partner. To locate a therapist, you might ask your sexuality course instructor or health care practitioner for referrals. Also, the American Association of _____ _____, Counselors, and Therapists (AASECT) can send you the names of therapists in your area who have applied and qualified for AASECT certification. Your _____ or friends may know therapists whom they might recommend. In selecting a therapist, such considerations as specific background and training in _____ _____, your goals, the therapists' approach, your comfort level with the therapist, and _____ of therapy sessions are all important considerations to take into account.

awareness	There are several procedures for improving _____ of your body and of activities that provide the most pleasurable
self-awareness	stimulation. Exercises that increase _____- _____ help us to better understand our sexual feelings and needs and how our bodies respond, which in turn makes us
Masturbation	better able to share these feelings with a partner. _____ exercises are an effective way to learn about and experience sexual response. One of the primary benefits of sex therapy is that couples
communication	often develop more effective _____ skills. Masters and Johnson developed a series of touching experiences called
sensate focus	_____ _____ that can be extremely helpful in reducing the anxiety caused by goal orientation and increasing
masturbation	communication and closeness. Finally, _____ in the presence of a partner may be a way for couples to let each other
touching	know what kind of _____ they find arousing.

Specific Suggestions for Women

orgasmic	Women who wish to learn to become _____ may do so by
counseling	seeking individual or group _____, or by reading books such as *Becoming Orgasmic: A Sexual and Personal Growth Program for Women* by Julia Heiman and Joseph LoPiccolo.
	The next series of exercises focuses on interaction with a
partner	_____, beginning with sensate focus experiences and
genital	moving on to mutual _____ exploration, manual stimulation of the woman's genitals, female-initiated intercourse
bridge maneuver	with woman on top, etc. The use of the _____ _____ is suggested for women who wish to try experiencing orgasm during intercourse without direct clitoral stimulation.
pelvic	Treatment for vaginismus usually begins during a _____
spasm	exam with the physician demonstrating the vaginal _____ reaction to the couple. After a series of at-home relaxation and self-
fingertip	awareness exercises , a woman learns to insert a _____ (or a small dilator) into her vagina. As she becomes more relaxed and comfortable, she eventually inserts her whole finger, then two fingers, and then three fingers, etc. Eventually the woman's
partner	_____ becomes involved in the exercises, until the woman is able to experience penile-vaginal containment and, finally, thrusting with intercourse.

Specific Suggestions for Men

	There are several approaches for learning better ejaculatory control.
ejaculate	A man can _____ more frequently; continue sexual interaction after the first rapid ejaculation; alter intercourse position
muscle	so there is minimal _____ tension, which is associated with
communicate	a rapid sexual response cycle; _____ with his partner in
alternatives	order to prolong coitus; and consider _____ to sexual sharing other than intercourse.

stop-start

James Semans, a urologist, developed the _____-_____ technique for controlling premature ejaculation, which is the focus of many sex therapy programs for delaying

squeeze

ejaculation. The _____ technique, while not as commonly used, can still be effective.

anxiety

With the exception of problems that are organic in origin, _____ is the major stumbling block to erectile response. For this reason, all behaviorally-focused approaches to dealing with

reducing

erectile inhibition concentrate on _____ anxiety. These are

sensate focus

usually _____ _____ experiences, and initially it is suggested to not touch genitals and emphasize instead the

sensual

_____ pleasure of touching and being touched.

medical

Some men who have impaired erectile functioning as the result of a _____ problems adjust well to the absence of erection by emphasizing and enjoying other ways of sexual sharing. If illness or injury leave a man permanently unable to have erections, there are several medical treatments available: microsurgical procedures to

vascular; injections

repair _____ problems in the penis; penile _____ of medications that dilate blood vessels and cause erection; and

papaverine
Yohimbine

vasoactive medications such as _____ that increase blood flow into the penis. _____, a drug occasionally prescribed for hypotension, helps induce erection in some cases. Devices that

blood

suction _____ into the penis and hold it there during intercourse have also been developed.

penile prosthesis

Another option is a surgically implanted _____ _____. There are two basic types available: one is a pair of

semirigid
inflatable

_____ rods placed inside the cavernous bodies of the penis, and the second type is an _____ device that enables the penis to be either flaccid or erect.

ejaculatory disorder

A behavioral approach is generally used in the treatment of _____ _____, in addition to psychotherapy aimed at reducing resentment in the relationship when that plays a role in the problem.

Treatment for Hypoactive Sexual Desire

complicated
self-stimulation

Many therapists consider desire problems the most _____ to treat. Various aspects of treatment involve encouraging erotic responses through _____-_____ and arousing fantasies; reducing anxiety with

sensate focus

appropriate information and _____ _____ exercises; improving communication; increasing skill in initiation and refusal of sexual activity; and expanding one's repertoire of

activities

affectionate and sexual _____.

Short Answer

1. List the four procedures that provide the basis for much of sex therapy. (Obj. #1a–d)

2. According to Schnarch, what does the ability to experience an "eyes-open" orgasm indicate? (Obj. #1b)

3. Describe sensate focus. What is its purpose? (Obj. #1c)

4. What are the benefits of masturbating with a partner present? (Obj. #1d)

5. Describe the "sexological exam" exercise. What is its purpose? (Obj. #2)

6. For what is the back-to-chest position used? (Obj. #2)

7. What is the bridge maneuver? When is it used? (Obj. #2)

8. Briefly describe the treatment program for women with vaginismus. (Obj. #3)

9. How successful is the treatment for vaginismus? (Obj. #3)

10. List six strategies that men can use when they want to delay ejaculation. (Obj. #4)

11. Compare and contrast the stop-start and squeeze techniques. Which is more commonly used? (Obj. #4)

12. What is the major focus of treatment programs that deal with male erectile disorder? (Obj. #5)

13. What medical treatments are available for men who are permanently unable to have erections? (Obj. #5)

14. What is papaverine and how does it work? What are some of its drawbacks? (Obj. #5)

15. What does yohimbine do? (Obj. #5)

16. List three surgical treatments that are used for dealing with erectile problems. (Obj. #5)

17. What approach is used in treating ejaculatory disorder? (Obj. #6)

18. What emotion of a man's may contribute to ejaculatory disorder? (Obj. #6)

19. Describe the important aspects of a treatment program to reduce ejaculatory disorder. (Obj. #6)

20. How difficult is HSD to treat compared to other sexual problems? (Obj. #7)

21. What relationship problems are frequently associated with HSD? (Obj. #7)

22. List and briefly describe the four levels of the PLISSIT model of sex therapy. (Obj. #8)

23. Distinguish psychosexual therapy, systems therapy and postmodern therapy. (Obj. #9)

24. What considerations might you want to take into account in selecting a therapist? (Obj. #9c)

25. List four of the most common types of professional training therapists have. (Obj. #9d)

Multiple Choice

Select the best alternative. Check your answers with the answer key at the end of the chapter.

1. Which of the following is **not** one of the basic sex therapy procedures described in the text?
   a. self-awareness exercises
   b. sensate focus
   c. masturbation exercises
   d. the bridge maneuver

2. Schnarch believes that _____ indicates that a couple has a high level of self-expression and sexual intimacy in their relationship.
   a. frequency of sexual interaction
   b. the ability to experience an "eyes-open" orgasm
   c. simultaneous orgasm
   d. demonstrating effective conflict resolution skills

3. Masters and Johnson labeled this technique and use it as a basic step in the treatment of many sexual problems.
   a. stop-start technique
   b. squeeze technique
   c. sensate focus
   d. bridge maneuver

4. Which of the following would be **most helpful** for women learning to experience orgasm with her partner, and for premature ejaculation and erectile difficulties?
   a. using the first two steps of the PLISSIT model
   b. practicing self-awareness exercises
   c. using the stop-start technique
   d. masturbating with a partner present

5. Which of the following statements concerning genital sensate focus is **true**?
   a. The back-to-chest position is recommended when a woman is experiencing genital stimulation by her partner.
   b. Having orgasm during initial sessions is discouraged.
   c. The use of lotion or oil is suggested to increase sensation.
   d. all of the above

6. The bridge maneuver involves
   a. nondemand genital pleasuring.
   b. oral clitoral stimulation in order to achieve orgasm.
   c. manual clitoral stimulation during coitus, followed by pelvic movements.
   d. using a modified rear-entry position to increase sensation for the male.

7. Which of the following is **not** part of the treatment program for vaginismus?
   a. pelvic exam by physician
   b. the bridge maneuver
   c. insertion of fingers or dilators into vagina
   d. relaxation and self-awareness exercises

8. The stop-start technique
   a. is not as commonly used as the squeeze technique.
   b. has been used successfully in the treatment of ejaculatory disorder.
   c. was developed by a urologist named James Semans.
   d. all of the above

9. The _____ refers to a technique whereby a man's partner applies pressure to the glans of the penis in order to delay ejaculation.
   a. stop-start technique
   b. squeeze technique
   c. bridge maneuver
   d. Kegel exercise

10. Which of the following would be **most likely** to delay ejaculation?
    a. woman-above intercourse position
    b. man-above intercourse position
    c. having orgasms infrequently
    d. increased muscle tension during intercourse

11. Which of the following is **not** part of the therapy program for dealing with erectile inhibition?
    a. sensate focus
    b. vaginal penetration as soon as the man is able to sustain an erection
    c. nondemand pleasuring
    d. vaginal penetration in the woman-above position

12. _____ causes erection when injected into the corpus cavernosa of the penis.
    a. Cantharides (Spanish fly)
    b. Papaverine
    c. Testostin
    d. Penerect

13. Transitory numbness of the glans of the penis as well as prolonged erection are possible side effects of taking
    a. yohimbine.
    b. cantharides (Spanish fly).
    c. anaprox.
    d. papaverine.

14. One disadvantage of the penile prosthesis in which two rods are placed inside the cavernous bodies of the penis is
    a. retrograde ejaculation.
    b. an increased number of "partial" orgasms.
    c. that the penis is always semierect.
    d. all of the above

15. Brad and Michelle are seeing a sex therapist for the erectile difficulties Brad is experiencing. Prior to the final intercourse phase of treatment, their therapist will probably advise them to
    a. practice sensate focus exercises until erections are frequent.
    b. practice stimulating, stopping, and then restimulating to experience return of the erection.
    c. focus on mutual pleasure and sensuality rather than worrying about intercourse goals.
    d. all of the above

16. Which of the following statements concerning ejaculatory disorder is **false**?
    a. Treatment for this difficulty usually begins with sensate focus.
    b. This problem is experienced exclusively by heterosexual men.
    c. The success rate in treating this problem is fairly high.
    d. Therapy to reduce resentment toward partner may be part of the treatment.

17. Which of the following statements concerning HSD is **true**?
    a. It is a fairly uncomplicated problem to treat.
    b. Treatment consists of a straightforward behavior modification program.
    c. The dysfunctional partner is typically the focus of treatment and is seen on a one-to-one basis until the problem is resolved.
    d. A power imbalance in the relationship may contribute to HSD.

18. Regarding the selection of a therapist, which of the following statements is **true**?
    a. Most sex therapy is done on an individual basis, as opposed to working with couples.
    b. It is preferable to work with a same-sex therapist.
    c. A basic criterion to use is the amount and type of training a therapist has had.
    d. all of the above

19. Rita and Sebastian are seeing a sex therapist in which their treatment involves participating in behavioral exercises at home, reflecting on the unconscious thought and feelings that might underlie their problems and becoming aware of the function that their sexual problems have served in their relationship. This type of therapy is called
    a. physchosexual therapy.
    b. insight-oriented therapy.
    c. systems therapy.
    d. postmodern therapy.

20. PLISSIT is an acronym for
    a. permission, limited intensity, self-stimulation, and intensive therapy.
    b. playtime, limited interference, sensual sharing, and intimate time.
    c. permission, limited information, specific suggestions, and intensive therapy.
    d. plenty of individuals see sex exams as inherently threatening.

21. Helping clients to appreciate their unique patterns of sexual desire and expression is part of the _____ level of treatment.
    a. permission
    b. limited information
    c. increased self-esteem
    d. intensive therapy

22. Riccardo and Estelle are seeing a sex therapist. Part of the program involves doing sensate focus exercises at home. According to the PLISSIT model, what level of treatment is this?
    a. permission
    b. limited information
    c. specific suggestions
    d. self-stimulation

Insight and Application

1. Assume that you were having difficulty with one of the sexual problems discussed in this chapter. What specific steps would you take to deal with this problem? Would you seek professional assistance? Why or why not?

2. There are various suggestions and exercises presented in this chapter to enhance sexual sharing for men and women, alone or with a partner. Which of the exercises or suggestions, if any, would you be **least** comfortable attempting? Why?

3. Assume that you are a man who, as the result of a injury, is no longer able to have erections. Would you consider getting a penile prosthesis? Why or why not?

Multiple Choice Answers

1. d	2. b	3. c	4. d	5. d	6. c	7. b	8. c
9. b	10. a	11. b	12. b	13. d	14. c	15. d	16. b
17. d	18. c	19. d	20. c	21. a	22. c		

PLISSIT

psychosexual therapy

systems therapy

sensate focus

bridge maneuver

stop-start technique

squeeze technique

postmodern sex therapy

EMDR
(Eye Movement Desensitization
and Reprocessing)

treatment designed to help clients gain awareness of their unconscious thoughts and feelings that contribute to their sexual problems	a model of sex therapy that specifies four levels of treatment: Permission; Limited Information; Specific Suggestions; and Intensive Therapy
a series of touching and communication exercises developed by Masters and Johnson, used to enhance sexual pleasure and to reduce performance pressure	treatment that focuses on interactions within a couple's relationship and on the functions of the sexual problems in the relationship
a treatment technique for premature ejaculation, consisting of stimulating the man's penis to the point of impending orgasm and then stopping until the pre-ejaculatory sensations subside	a technique used to help women experience orgasm during intercourse
the integration of systems, psychosocial and behavioral approaches in treating sexual problems	a treatment technique for premature ejaculation, whereby pressure is applied to the frenum and top side of a man's penis until the man loses the urge to ejaculate
	a therapy technique that appears to stimulate rapid information and emotional processing in the brain, similar to that which occurs during REM sleep

18

Chronic Illness, Disability, and Sexual Adjustment

Introduction

In our society, we encounter a constant barrage of popular media images that suggests that the only people who are sexual are those who are young, beautiful, healthy, and able-bodied. But as the authors have reiterated throughout the text, sexual feelings and expression are an integral part of all of us, regardless of our age, physical appearance, or level of functioning — mentally or physically. This chapter outlines some of the common chronic illnesses and disabilities that people face and includes suggestions for coping with and enhancing sexual interaction in these situations.

Objectives

After studying this chapter, you should be able to:

1. Cite statistics indicating how likely it is that people will confront chronic illness or disability.

2. Discuss some common stereotypes regarding the sexual nature and capacity of people with chronic illnesses and disabilities.

3. Discuss what current studies reveal regarding how patient sexuality is dealt with in medical and institutional settings.

4. Describe each of the following illnesses, discuss how they may affect sexual functioning, and explain what adjustments can be made, if any, to maximize sexual pleasure and function.
   a. multiple sclerosis
   b. diabetes
   c. heart attack
   d. cerebrovascular accidents
   e. arthritis
   f. cancer

5. Describe each of the following disabilities, discuss how they may affect sexual responsiveness, and explain what adjustments can be made, if any, to maximize sexual pleasure and function:
   a. spinal-cord injury
   b. cerebral palsy
   c. blindness and deafness
   d. mental disabilities

6. Discuss various coping and enhancement strategies that can be used in dealing with some of the illnesses and disabilities described above.

Key Terms and Concepts

"Flash cards" listing key terms and concepts on one side and their corresponding definitions and explanations on the other side are provided at the end of the chapter.

Chapter Overview With Fill-Ins

After reading each of the major sections in the chapter, check your retention by **mentally** filling in each of the blanks in the corresponding sections below. Cover the answers in the margin as you go along, and write the answers in the space provided only when you are doing your final review.

Stereotypes About Sexuality, Chronic Illness, and Disability

disabilities

young

mentally

child-like

limitations

pregnancy

Most people with chronic illnesses and _____ must confront the myths that are prevalent in our culture concerning their sexual nature and abilities. For one, there is the common notion that the only people who are sexual are _____ and beautiful. This stereotype is particularly damaging to physically or _____ disabled people. In addition, people whose illnesses and disabilities require depending on others for care are often seen as _____, rather than as individuals interested in age-appropriate sexuality. There are also incorrect assumptions that are made about sexual _____ that certain medical problems present. However, as the authors stress throughout the text, sexuality is an integral part of our being — regardless of whether erection, intercourse, orgasm, or _____ can occur and despite crutches, braces, or wheelchairs.

Chronic Illnesses

brain; spinal cord

sensation

half

Multiple sclerosis (MS) is a neurological disease of the _____ and _____ _____ in which damage occurs to the myelin sheath that covers nerve fibers; vision, _____, and voluntary movement are affected. Most MS patients experience changes in their sexual functioning and at least _____ have had sexual problems.

pancreas
erectile

adolescence

orgasm

Diabetes is an inherited disease that occurs when the _____ fails to secrete insulin. It is a disease of the endocrine system and a leading cause of _____ problems. Research indicates that women who develop diabetes in _____ report few sexual difficulties. However, women whose diabetes begins in adulthood are likely to have problems with sexual desire, lubrication, and _____.

anxiety

exercise

Sexual problems following a heart attack are common and usually due to _____, misinformation, and feeling stigmatized by the illness rather than to organic causes. Research measuring cardiac effects in men during masturbation, noncoital stimulation, and intercourse found that cardiac expenditure was equivalent to light to moderate _____.

strokes

negative
arousal

Cerebrovascular accidents (CVA), commonly called _____, often result in residual impairments of motor, sensory, emotional, and cognitive functioning that can have a _____ effect on sexuality. Stroke survivors frequently report a decline in the frequency of interest, _____, and sexual activity.

joints

chronic

interest

intercourse

Arthritis is a progressive, systemic disease that results in inflammation of the _____. Arthritis does not directly impair sexual response, but body image problems, depression, and _____ pain and fatigue may lessen a person's sexual _____. Arthritic impairment of hands, hips, knees, and arms may make masturbation difficult or impossible, and/or may interfere with certain _____ positions.

vascular

reproductive;
ovarian

prostate

Cancer and its therapies can impair hormonal, _____, and neurological function necessary for normal sexual function. Although all forms of cancer can affect sexual functioning, many people are most concerned by the effects of cancers of the _____ organs. Cervical, uterine, and _____ cancers all involve treatment that affects sexual functioning to some degree. The same is true for cancer of the _____ and of the testis.

Disabilities

motor

brain
desire

orgasm

People with spinal cord injuries (SCI) have reduced _____ control and sensation because the damage to the spinal cord obstructs the pathway between body and _____. Although the injury does not necessarily impair sexual _____, an SCI person may have impaired ability for arousal and _____.

Sensory
amplification

increase

_____ _____, the act of thinking about a physical stimulus, concentrating on it, and amplifying the sensation in your mind to an intense degree is one technique to _____ feelings of pleasure.

brain

muscular
intelligence

communicating

masturbation
intercourse

Cerebral palsy (CP) is caused by damage to the _____ before or during birth or during childhood; it is characterized by mild to severe lack of _____ control. A person's _____ may or may not be affected , although it is often mistakenly assumed that people with CP are mentally disabled because of their physical difficulty in _____. Genital sensation is unaffected by CP. Spasticity or deformity of arms and hands may make _____ difficult, and the same problems in hips and knees may make certain _____ positions painful or difficult.

self-esteem

sensory

Deafness or blindness that occurs in adolescence of adulthood may cause depression, lowered _____-_____, and social withdrawal during the adjustment period. If the _____ losses are a result of disease, the disease itself may have negative effects on sexual functioning.

70
learning

asexual

right

A person with an IQ around ____ is usually classified as mentally disabled. However, the _____ capabilities of such people vary greatly from one person to the next. Strong stereotypes imply that all mentally disabled people are unable to learn and are either _____ or unable to control their sexual impulses. A crucial point in sex education is that mentally disabled people have a basic _____ to sexual expression.

Coping and Enhancement Strategies

accepting

genital

Individuals and couples can best cope with the sexual limitations their illness or disability present by _____ the limitations and developing the possible options remaining to them. Expanding the definition of sexuality beyond _____ arousal and intercourse to include dimensions such as erotic thoughts and sensual touch is essential.

body

Illness and disabilities often affect a person's _____ image, and the text lists a number of suggestions for disabled individuals who wish to improve the image they have of their bodies.

communication

Finally, good _____ is especially important because the other partner is unlikely to know what the ill or disabled partner can or cannot do, or finds pleasing.

Matching

Match the illnesses or disabilities below with the appropriate descriptions. Note that each illness or disability may be used once, more than once, or not at all, but choose only **one** answer for each description.

a. multiple sclerosis
b. diabetes
c. heart attack
d. cerebrovascular accidents
e. arthritis
f. uterine cancer

g. cervical cancer
h. ovarian cancer
i. prostate cancer
j. testicular cancer
k. spinal-cord injury
l. cerebral palsy

_____1. also called strokes; people who have experienced this report a decline in sexual interest and activity

_____2. most common cancer of the female reproductive organs

_____3. adolescent women with this disease experience few sexual problems, but adult women do

_____4. retrograde ejaculation can sometimes occur as a result of this condition

_____5. is one of the most common forms of cancer in men ages 20–40

_____6. disease of brain and spinal cord that affects voluntary movement, vision and sensation

_____7. does not directly affect sexual response, but may result in body image problems

_____8. most men are unable to ejaculate or orgasm as a result of this, although many are able to experience erection

_____9. sexual problems following this are usually a result of anxiety

_____10. common treatment for this is an oophorectomy

_____11. most common disabling neurological condition for young adults in U.S.

_____12. genital sensation is unaffected, but assistance may be needed in preparing for sexual activity

_____13. moist heat prior to sex can help alleviate pain associated with this

_____14. one out of every eleven men after the age of 65 will develop this

_____15. disease of the endocrine system and leading organic cause of male erectile difficulties

_____16. causes more deaths than any other cancer of the female reproductive organs

Short Answer

1. What percent of people over age 65 have one chronic illness? What percent have two or more? (Obj. #1)

2. Describe some of the commonly held societal assumptions about sexual expression that discriminate against people who experience chronic illness or disability. (Obj. #2)

3. What do recent studies indicate concerning health care practitioners and the extent to which they provide sexual counseling to their patients? (Obj. #3)

4. Define multiple sclerosis and describe how common it is. (Obj. #4a)

5. How may multiple sclerosis affect sexual desire and function? (Obj. #4a)

6. Define diabetes. How may it affect sexual functioning in men? In women? (Obj. #4b)

7. What differences exist in women who develop diabetes in adolescence as opposed to adulthood? (Obj. #4b)

8. Relating it to exercise, describe the cardiac effects in men during masturbation and intercourse. (Obj. #4e)

9. What is the typical cause of any sexual problems that may be experienced following a heart attack? (Obj. #4c)

10. How may CVA negatively affect sexuality? (Obj. #4d)

11. Define arthritis and discuss how it may affect sexual expression. (Obj. #4e)

12. In general, describe the effects of cancer and its treatment that may affect sexual functioning. (Obj. #4f)

13. Which is more common — uterine or cervical cancer? (Obj. #4f)

14. What treatment alternative for cervical cancer may have fewer negative effects on sexual functioning than radiation therapy? (Obj. #4f)

15. Which type of cancer of the female reproductive organs results in more deaths than any of the others? (Obj. #4f)

16. What are the effects of prostatectomy on sexual functioning? (Obj. #4f)

17. How does treatment for testicular cancer affect sexual functioning and fertility? (Obj. #4f)

18. Distinguish between paraplegic and quadriplegic. (Obj. #5a)

19. How may SCI affect a man's sexuality? (Obj. #5a)

20. How may SCI affect a woman's sexuality? (Obj. #5a)

21. Cite research that indicates how many SCI men experience erections. (Obj. #5a)

22. Explain the technique of sensory amplification. In what situations is it used? (Obj. #5a)

23. What causes cerebral palsy? (Obj. #5b)

24. What are the effects of CP and what mistaken assumptions about people with CP are often made as a result of this? (Obj. #5b)

25. How does CP affect sexual functioning? (Obj. #5b)

26. What may people with CP and SCI need in order to facilitate sexual expression? (Obj. #5b)

27. List several ways in which blindness and deafness may affect a person's sexuality. (Obj. #5c)

28. List three stereotypes regarding sexual expression in mentally disabled individuals. (Obj. #5d)

29. List at least five suggestions for improving body image. (Obj. #6)

30. Discuss sexual coping strategies for each of the following illnesses or disabilities: (Obj. #6, #4a, b, d, e, #5b)

   a. multiple sclerosis

   b. diabetes

   c. CVA

   d. arthritis

   e. cerebral palsy

Multiple Choice

Select the best alternative. Check your answers with the answer key at the end of the chapter.
1. Approximately _____ percent of people over age 65 have two or more chronic diseases.
   a. 10
   b. 25
   c. 50
   d. 75

2. People with chronic illnesses or disabilities
    a. may be treated as children because of their dependency on others for care.
    b. may be seen as unattractive in comparison to the "Barbie and Ken" images of sexually active people in our society.
    c. may be perceived as asexual because of their condition.
    d. all of the above

3. _____ is a neurological disease of the brain and spinal cord.
    a. Multiple sclerosis
    b. Muscular dystrophy
    c. Diabetes
    d. Arthritis

4. Which of the following is affected in people who have MS?
    a. voluntary movement
    b. intellectual functioning
    c. hearing
    d. respiration

5. Nerve damage or circulatory problems from _____ can cause sexual problems.
    a. uterine cancer
    b. diabetes
    c. heart disease
    d. testicular cancer

6. Which of the following statements concerning men and diabetes is **false**?
    a. Loss of sexual desire is the most common sexual problem they experience as a result of their illness.
    b. Some diabetic men ejaculate into their bladders.
    c. Heavy alcohol use and poor blood sugar control increase the chance of erectile problems.
    d. It is the leading organic cause of erectile disorders.

7. Sexual problems following a heart attack are usually due to
    a. anxiety.
    b. a hormonal imbalance.
    c. vascular impairment.
    d. prescribed medication.

8. Cerebrovascular accidents, commonly called _____, often result in motor, sensory, and emotional impairments that may negatively affect sexuality.
    a. heart attacks
    b. aneurysms
    c. anginas
    d. strokes

9. If cervical cancer has spread beyond the cervix, which of the following would be the **most likely** treatment?
    a. surgery
    b. radiation therapy
    c. hormonal therapy
    d. drug therapy

10. _____ refers to loss of feeling and voluntary muscle function of the arms or hands, as well as the trunk and legs.
    a. Paraplegia
    b. Quadriplegia
    c. Cerebromuscular degeneration
    d. Muscular atrophy

11. In spinal cord injuries, injuries lower on the spine result in _____ while higher injuries cause _____.
    a. paraplegia; quadriplegia
    b. quadriplegia; paraplegia
    c. skeletal paralysis; skeletal deformity
    d. skeletal deformity; skeletal paralysis

12. According to various studies, what percentage of SCI men are able to experience erections?
    a. less than 10 percent
    b. approximately 25 percent
    c. well over 50 percent
    d. over 90 percent

13. Which of the following is the **best** example of sensory amplification?
    a. A woman who has lost all genital sensation is able to think about the inside of her arm, which is extremely sensitive, and transpose previously experienced genital sensations to this area, which can result in arousal and/or orgasm.
    b. Despite loss of all genital sensation as the result of a spinal cord injury, a man enjoys using a vibrator on his penis to enhance sexual pleasure.
    c. A woman with CP focuses on pleasurable genital sensations to distract her from knee and hip pain.
    d. You are listening to music you enjoy and you turn up the volume, but it is too loud and your eardrums rupture.

14. Which of the following incorrect assumptions is often made concerning individuals with cerebral palsy?
    a. They are mentally disabled.
    b. They are asexual.
    c. They have sexual desire but are unable to do anything about it.
    d. all of the above

15. Which of the following was one of the suggestions for improving body image?
    a. Ask people what they find physically attractive about you.
    b. Note your negative features in a mirror and think about how they can be minimized.
    c. Put up photographs of models or celebrities that you like.
    d. all of the above

Insight and Application

1. Think about specific individuals whom you have encountered in your life that have had various illnesses and disabilities. What incorrect assumptions, if any, did you make about the sexual nature and expression of these people, as well as other people with whom you have had more casual contact? How has your perspective changed, if at all, as a result of what you have read as well as your own life experiences?

2. How do you feel about institutions such as nursing homes or hospitals providing for the sexual needs of the residents? If you support this idea, what are some specific provisions regarding available facilities, staff training and development, etc. that would be important to establish?

Matching Answers

1. d	2. f	3. b	4. b	5. j	6. a	7. e	8. k
9. c	10. h	11. a	12. l	13. e	14. i	15. b	16. h

Multiple Choice Answers

1. c	2. d	3. a	4. a	5. b	6. a	7. a	8. d
9. a	10. b	11. a	12. c	13. a	14. d	15. a	

multiple sclerosis

diabetes

cerebrovascular accidents
(CVA)

arthritis

spinal cord injuries (SCI)

paraplegic

quadriplegic

sensory amplification

cerebral palsy (CP)

an inherited disease that occurs when the pancreas fails to secrete insulin. Nerve damage or circulatory problems resulting from diabetes can cause sexual problems	a neurological disease of the brain and spinal cord that affects vision, sensation and voluntary movement
a progressive, systemic disease that results in inflammation of the joints. It does not directly impair sexual response, but body image problems may diminish interest in sex	commonly called strokes, often result in residual impairments of motor, sensory, emotional and cognitive functioning that can have a negative effect on sexuality
a person with an injury lower on the spinal cord characterized by loss of feeling and voluntary muscle function of the trunk and legs	damage to the spinal cord that obstructs the pathway between body and brain, resulting in body paralysis that will vary according to the location of the injury
the method used by some disabled men and women to achieve maximum pleasure from a sensory input	a person with an injury higher on the spinal cord characterized by loss of feeling and voluntary muscle function of the arms or hands as well as the trunk and legs
	caused by damage to the brain that may occur before or during birth or during early childhood, it is characterized by mild to severe lack of muscle control

19

Sexually Transmitted Diseases

Introduction

The probability of you, your partner, or a potential partner experiencing at least one of the sexually transmitted diseases discussed in this chapter is quite high. Consequently, recognizing the various symptoms, being aware of treatment options available, and learning effective preventive measures is an investment in your future health care.

Objectives

After you study this chapter, you should be able to:

1. Cite statistics that indicate in what age groups sexually transmitted diseases will most commonly occur.

2. Discuss some of the factors that contribute to the rise in the incidence of sexually transmitted diseases.

3. Determine the characteristics that most vaginal infections have in common and what conditions may make a woman more susceptible to infection.

4. Describe the cause, incidence and transmission, symptoms and complications, and treatment alternatives for the following vaginal infections:
   a. bacterial vaginosis
   b. candidiasis
   c. trichomoniasis

5. Discuss chlamydial infection, making specific reference to the microorganism that causes it, the incidence and transmission, symptoms and complications and treatment alternatives.

6. Discuss each of the following sexually transmitted diseases, making specific reference to what causes the disease, what we know regarding incidence and transmission, symptoms and complications, and available treatment alternatives:
   a. gonorrhea
   b. nongonococcal urethritis
   c. syphilis
   d. pubic lice
   e. herpes
   f. viral hepatitis
   g. genital warts
   h. chancroid

7. Describe each of the following in reference to acquired immunodeficiency syndrome (AIDS):
   a. what causes it and how it is diagnosed
   b. when it was first recognized in the U.S. and around the world
   c. some of the serious diseases to which AIDS patients are vulnerable
   d. incidence and transmission
   e. symptoms and complications

    f.   treatment alternatives
    g. prevention

8.   Outline and describe seven strategies that can help reduce the likelihood of contracting a sexually transmitted disease.

Key Terms and Concepts

"Flash cards" listing key terms and concepts on one side and their corresponding definitions and explanations on the other side are provided at the end of the chapter.

Chapter Overview With Fill-Ins

After reading each of the major sections in the chapter, check your retention by **mentally** filling in each of the blanks in the corresponding sections below. Cover the answers in the margin as you go along, and write the answers in the space provided only when you are doing your final review.

sexually transmitted nonsexually	Diseases that can be transmitted through sexual interaction are called _____ _____ diseases. Some of these conditions can be spread _____ as well as through sexual contact (e.g., pubic lice, herpes, and genital warts). A number of factors may contribute to the high incidence of STDs: increasing
young birth control pills	sexual activity among _____ people; multiple sexual partners; increased use of _____ _____
condom	_____ and therefore, reduced use of vaginal spermicides and the _____ which can help protect against STDs;
symptoms	absence of obvious _____ in many of the diseases; and
guilt	finally, feelings of _____ and embarrassment, that often may prevent people from seeking treatment or informing their partners.

Common Vaginal Infections

Vaginitis common	_____ and leukorrhea are general terms applied to a variety of vaginal infections, which are far more _____ than some of the other STDs. Factors that increase the likelihood of
antibiotic	vaginal infection include _____ therapy, use of birth control pills, menstruation, pregnancy, wearing pantyhose and
nylon	_____ underwear, douching, and lowered resistance from stress or lack of sleep.
Bacterial vaginosis	_____ _____ is a superficial vaginal infection caused by a bacterium known as Gardnerella vaginalis. Males may harbor this organism as well as women, usually without
symptoms	_____. The predominant symptom in women is a foul-
flour paste	smelling, thin discharge that resembles _____ _____ in consistency. The treatment for bacterial
male	vaginosis is metronidazole (Flagyl), and _____ partners should be treated as well.

yeast

Candidiasis, also referred to as moniliasis or a _____ infection, is caused by a yeastlike fungus called Candida albicans. Symptoms are a white, clumpy discharge that looks like

cottage cheese

_____ _____, and often intense

itching

_____ and soreness of the vaginal and vulval tissues.

suppositories

Treatment consists of vaginal _____ or cream such as clotrimazole, nystatin, etc.

Trichomoniasis

_____ accounts for about one-fourth of all cases of vaginitis. When women have symptoms, it is usually a frothy yellow or white vaginal discharge with an unpleasant _____.

odor

Occasionally, men may have symptoms of penile discharge or

urethras

burning sensations in their _____, but most often they are asymptomatic. Both partners should be treated with metronidazole

Flagyl

(_____).

Chlamydial Infection

prevalent

Chlamydial infections are among the most _____ and the most damaging of all STDs. There are two general types of genital chlamydial infections in females: infections of the mucosa of the lower reproductive tract, commonly manifested as urethritis or

cervicitis
pelvic inflammatory

_____, and infections of the upper reproductive tract, which are expressed as _____ _____ disease (PID). In men, the organism is estimated to be the cause of

half

approximately _____ of the cases of epididymitis and nongonococcal urethritis. In addition, Chlamydia trachomatis causes

trachoma
blindness
sexual

_____, a contagious form of conjunctivitis. Trachoma is the world's leading cause of preventable _____. In the United States, the major mode of transmission is _____ relations. Chlamydial infection can potentially have very serious consequences for women and/or their newborn children, and to a

drugs

lesser degree, in men as well. A variety of _____ are commonly used to treat chlamydial infection.

Gonorrhea

genital-anal

Gonorrhea, caused by the bacterium Gonococcus, is a very common communicable disease and is transmitted by penile-vaginal, oral-genital, or _____-_____ contact. Typically, more men will experience symptoms than women, although it is not

asymptomatic

uncommon for men to be _____. In men, the two most common symptoms are a bad-smelling, cloudy discharge from the

penis; urination
cervix

_____ and burning sensations during _____. In women, the _____ may become inflamed without producing any observable symptoms; a greenish or yellowish discharge

Severe

usually results, but it is not readily detected. _____ complications may result in both men and women if left untreated.

Nongonococcal Urethritis

urethra

Any inflammation of the _____ that is not caused by gonorrhea is called nongonococcal urethritis (NGU). Symptoms are

gonorrhea; Women

similar to those of _____. _____ may be infected with either of the above organisms and be asymptomatic. Physicians may assume that any penile discharge is caused by

gonorrhea
erythromycin

_____, and so they may fail to diagnose NGU. A laboratory diagnosis should be made, and doxycycline or _____ usually clears up the condition.

Syphilis

spirochete

Syphilis is caused by a thin, corkscrew-like bacterium called Treponema pallidum (also called a _____). It is transmitted almost exclusively from open lesions of infected individuals to the mucous membranes or skin abrasions of sexual partners

oral-genital

through penile-vaginal, _____-_____, or genital-anal contacts.

four

If untreated, syphilis can progress through _____ phases of development. In the primary phase, syphilis is manifested in the

chancre

form of a painless sore called a _____, which appears at the site where the spirochete organism enters the body. During the

skin rash

secondary stage, a _____ _____ appears on the body, which may look terrible but usually does not hurt or itch. The

latent

_____ stage of syphilis may last for several years, during which time there are no observable symptoms of the disease. A small percentage of individuals who do not obtain treatment during

tertiary

the first three stages of syphilis are affected by the _____ stage later in life. The final manifestations of syphilis can occur

three

anywhere from _____ to forty years after infection and may include conditions such as heart failure, blindness, ruptured blood vessels, paralysis, skin ulcers, liver damage, and severe mental

penicillin

disturbance. The treatment for syphilis is _____, and individuals may be treated in any one of the four phases of the disease.

Pubic Lice

crabs

Pubic lice, commonly called "_____", are quite common and are frequently transmitted during sexual contact when two

pubic
one

people bring their _____ areas together. Pubic lice may live away from the body for as long as _____ day and may drop off onto underclothes, bedsheets, sleeping bags, etc. Eggs deposited by the female louse on clothing or bedsheets may survive

several; itching

for _____ days. Most people will start _____ if they get pubic lice, although other people experience little discomfort. Self-treatment can be done with A-200 pyrinate,

Kwell

available over-the-counter, or _____ lotion, which is available by prescription. All clothes and sheets that were used

washed

prior to treatment should be thoroughly _____.

Herpes

herpes simplex
five

mouth
genital
oral-genital

kissing

Herpes is caused by the _____ _____ virus (HSV). There are _____ different herpes viruses that infect humans, the most common being type 1 and type 2. Type 1 is of the type called "cold sores" or "fever blisters" that appear in the _____ or on the lips. Type 2 usually causes lesions on and around the _____ areas. Genital herpes appears to be transmitted primarily by penile-vaginal, _____-_____, or genital-anal sexual contact, while oral herpes may be transmitted by _____ or by oral-genital contact.

latex condoms
vaginal

autoinoculation

Research has shown that HSV-2 will not pass through _____ _____. However, condoms may break or come off, and when women are infected their _____ secretions containing the virus may wash over the male's scrotal area. People may also spread the virus from one part of their body to another by touching a sore and then scratching or rubbing somewhere else, a process known as _____.

papules
blisters

contagious; ten

cervix

Symptoms associated with HSV-1 and HSV-2 are quite similar. One or more small, red, painful bumps, called _____, usually appear, which rapidly develop into tiny painful _____ containing highly infectious virus particles. Soon the blisters rupture to form wet, painful open sores surrounded by a red ring. A person is highly _____ during this time. About _____ days after the first appearance of the papule, the open sore forms a crust and begins to heal, a process that may take as long as 10 more days. Sores on the _____ may continue to produce infectious material for as long as 10 days after the labial sores have completely healed.

dormant

After healing, herpes does not go away, but retreats up the nerve fibers leading from the infected site, where it may remain _____ or periodically flare up.

men

cervix
newborn

It is unlikely that _____ will experience any major physical complications of herpes. Women may experience two serious, although uncommon complications: cancer of the _____ and infection of the _____.

acyclovir

cure

One antiviral drug, _____, sold under the trade name Zovirax, is highly effective in the management of herpes, although there is currently no _____ for herpes.

Viral Hepatitis

liver

Hepatitis A
serum

Viral hepatitis is a disease in which _____ function is impaired by a viral infection. There are three major types of viral hepatitis: _____ _____ (formerly called infectious hepatitis), hepatitis B (formerly called _____ hepatitis), and non-A/non-B hepatitis.

common

Hepatitis A, which is the most _____ form of viral hepatitis in the United States, may be transmitted by blood or blood products,

semen

_____, vaginal secretions, and saliva. Manual, oral, or

anus

penile stimulation of the _____ are practices strongly associated with the spread of hepatitis B. Hepatitis B seems to be

fecal-oral

spread primarily through the _____-_____ route, which can be a problem when infected food handlers do not wash their hands properly after using the bathroom. _____-

oral-anal

_____ contact seems to be the primary mode for sexual transmission of Hepatitis A.

flu-like

Symptoms of viral hepatitis may vary from nonexistent to mild _____ symptoms to an incapacitating illness characterized by high fever, vomiting, and severe abdominal pains.

bed rest
dehydration
alpha interferon

At present, there is no specific therapy available for the various types of viral hepatitis, and treatment generally consists of _____ _____ and adequate fluid intake to prevent _____. Recent research has suggested that the drug _____ _____ can prevent destruction of liver cells in some hepatitis patients.

Genital Warts

human papilloma

Genital warts are caused by a virus called the _____ _____ virus (HPV).

epidemic

The incidence of genital warts has reached _____ proportions in recent years. Genital warts are primarily transmitted

oral-genital

by vaginal, anal, or _____-_____ sexual interaction. Warts may appear on the internal or external female genitals

foreskin

and on the shaft, glans, or _____ of the penis. Research has revealed a strong association between HPV infections and a vari-

cancers

ety of _____ of the cervix, vagina, vulva, penis and anus.

rare

Genital warts may spontaneously disappear, but this is _____. Many methods have been used for removing genital warts.

Chancroid

Africa

Chancroid is a bacterial infection that is widely prevalent in _____ as well as other tropical and semi-tropical regions of the world. It is one of the most common causes of genital

ulcers
United States

_____. Outbreaks have been occurring recently in several parts of the _____ _____. It is treated with antibiotics.

Acquired Immunodeficiency Syndrome (AIDS)

human
immunodeficiency
lymphocytes

immune

cancers

AIDS results from infection with a virus called _____ _____ virus (HIV). In many people, the AIDS virus specifically targets and destroys the body's CD4 _____, or "helper T cells", which, in healthy people, stimulate the _____ system to fight disease. The resulting impairment of the immune system leaves the body vulnerable to a variety of _____ and opportunistic infections.

vaginal

blood

unprotected

intravenous

birth

HIV has been found in the semen, blood, _____ secretions, saliva, tears, urine and breast milk of infected individuals and in any other bodily fluids that may contain _____. Most commonly, HIV enters the body through the exchange of bodily fluids during _____ anal or vaginal intercourse or oral-genital contact with an infected person, and via blood-contaminated needles shared by _____ drug users. The virus can also be transmitted from an infected woman to her fetus or infant before, during or shortly after _____ and via transfusions of infected blood.

multiple; unpro-
tected

Behaviors that place one at increased risk of HIV infection include having _____ sexual partners, engaging in _____ sex, sexual contact with people known to be at high risk, and sharing injection paraphernalia for IV drug use.

antibodies
contagious

Within a few months of being infected with HIV, most people develop _____ to the virus. Once infected with the virus, a person should be considered _____ regardless of whether clinical signs of HIV infection are present or not.

incubation

8; 11

death

Studies that estimate the _____ time for AIDS in adults (defined as the time between infection with HIV and the onset of one or more debilitating diseases associated with impairment of the immune system), have suggested that incubation periods range from _____ to _____ years or more. Once an AIDS patient develops a life-threatening illness, the disease tends to run a fairly rapid cause culminating in _____ for the vast majority of those afflicted.

ailments

The symptoms of HIV disease and AIDS are many and varied, and many of the symptoms may be associated with common everyday _____. People who develop AIDS experience many serious, life-threatening complications.

cure

immune
zidovudine

Although there is still no _____ for AIDS, a variety of drugs, which are still experimental, have been found to slow the deterioration of the _____ system. The most effective of these drugs is _____ (formerly called azidothymidine or AZT).

celibate; mono-
gamous
safer

The only certain way to avoid contracting AIDS sexually is either to remain _____ or to be involved in a _____ relationship with one mutually faithful, uninfected partner. If these conditions are not applicable, _____ sex practices (as described in detail in the chapter) would be advised for the person who takes his or her life and health seriously.

Prevention of Sexually Transmitted Diseases

abstinence; mono-
gamous

prevention

risk

medical

spermicides

multiple

genitals; wash

inform

Both _____, and being disease-free and _____ are two sure-fire ways to prevent STDs. Beyond that, the authors suggest a number of _____ guidelines: 1) assess your and your partner's _____ for transmitting STDs; 2) obtain _____ examinations prior to being sexually active in any way that is risky; 3) use condoms and _____; 4) avoid sexual activity with _____ partners; 5) inspect your partner's _____ prior to sexual activity; 6) _____ your and your partner's genitals before and after sexual contact; 7) obtain routine medical evaluations; and 8) _____ your partner(s) if you have an STD.

Matching

Match the STDs below with the corresponding descriptions. Each letter may be used once, twice or not at all, but choose only **one** answer for each blank.

a. bacterial vaginosis
b. candidiasis
c. trichomoniasis
d. chlamydial infection
e. gonorrhea
f. nongonococcal urethritis

g. syphilis
h. pubic lice
i. herpes
j. viral hepatitis
k. genital warts
l. chancroid

m. AIDS

_____1. The most common symptom in women is a frothy white or yellow vaginal discharge with an unpleasant odor. It is treated with the drug Flagyl.

_____2. This STD may be treated with a variety of topical applications, cauterization, freezing, surgical procedures, or a carbon dioxide laser.

_____3. The estimated incubation time of this disease is between 8 and 11 years.

_____4. This is the most common cause of vaginitis, and its main symptom is a flour-paste discharge that has a fishy, musty odor.

_____5. This is among the most prevalent and damaging of all STDs and may have severe consequences in men, women, and newborns.

_____6. This STD is frequently transmitted by two people rubbing pubic areas together, although it may be contracted by sleeping in an infected person's sheets or wearing his or her clothes.

_____7. One of the most notable symptoms of this STD is a yellowing of the skin as well as the whites of the eyes.

_____8. Also called a yeast infection, the white, clumpy discharge of this STD looks like cottage cheese.

_____9. Quite common in men, this STD manifests symptoms similar to those of gonorrheal infection and is commonly caused by chlamydial infections.

_____10. In rare cases, this disease may result in permanent joint damage. If it does not coexist with other infections, it is treated with cefixime or spectinomycin.

_____11. The initial outbreak of these painful blister-like sores will heal, but the virus will retreat to the nerve cells where it will remain, perhaps for a lifetime.

_____12. The second stage of this disease is typically characterized by a skin rash on the body.

_____13. This is caused by the bacterium Gardnerella vaginalis.

_____14. This causes trachoma, the world's leading cause of preventable blindness.

_____15. This is caused by a bacterium called Treponema pallidum.

_____16. Excessive amounts of dairy products and sugar in one's diet may result in this condition.

_____17. Although most prevalent in Africa and other tropical areas, there have been recent outbreaks in Texas, Louisiana and New York.

_____18. This, if left untreated, can result in severe mental disturbance, heart failure, paralysis, etc.

_____19. This is treated with Flagyl, and some men who are infected with it develop urethritis and cystitis.

_____20. When this invades the fallopian tubes, it is the primary preventable cause of female infertility and ectopic pregnancy.

Short Answer

1. Eighty-six percent of all STDs occur among which age group? (Obj. #1)

2. What percent of the U.S. population will acquire one or more STDs by age 30–35? (Obj. #1)

3. List four factors that may contribute to the high incidence of STDs. (Obj. #2)

4. Describe the normal vaginal environment. What factors may increase the likelihood of a vaginal infection? (Obj. #3)

5. Briefly summarize the cause, symptoms, and treatment alternatives for the three vaginal infections listed below: (Obj. #4)

	Cause	Symptoms	Treatment
a. bacterial vaginosis			
b. candidiasis			
c. trichomoniasis			

6. Discuss the consequences of chlamydial infection in men, women and children. (Obj. #5)

7. What are the symptoms of chlamydial infection in men and women? How is it diagnosed? (Obj. #5)

8. What other STDs commonly coexist with chlamydial infection? (Obj. #5)

9. Describe the symptoms of gonorrheal infection in men and in women. (Obj. #6a)

10. If gonorrheal infection is left untreated, what complications may develop in men? In women? In both sexes? (Obj. #6a)

11. What is the risk to an infant whose mother has gonorrhea? How may this be averted? (Obj. #6a)

12. Explain the problem in diagnosing and treating gonorrhea. (Obj. #6a)

13. Describe the symptoms of NGU in women and in men. (Obj. #6b)

14. What problem sometimes exists in diagnosing NGU in men? (Obj. #6b)

15. How may a pregnant woman who has syphilis transmit the disease to her unborn child? What are the effects on the infant? (Obj. #6c)

16. Describe the symptoms of syphilis at each of the following stages: (Obj. #6c)
    a. primary

    b. secondary

    c. latent

d.   tertiary

17. In what ways might an individual contract pubic lice? What is the treatment? (Obj. #6d)

18. Describe the two most common types of herpes viruses. (Obj. #6e)

19. How may herpes viruses be transmitted? (Obj. #6e)

20. What practices may help prevent the transmission of herpes? (Obj. #6e)

21. Describe the symptoms of oral and genital herpes. (Obj. #6e)

22. What happens to the herpes virus once it heals? (Obj. #6e)

23. What are the recurrence rates for herpes? (Obj. #6e)

24. Describe the prodromal symptoms of herpes. (Obj. #6e)

25. When is a person with herpes considered infectious? (Obj. #6e)

26. What factors may trigger reactivation of the herpes virus? (Obj. #6e)

27. What complications may arise from herpes infection in men? In women? (Obj. #6e)

28. What drug is effective in managing herpes? What are the advantages and drawbacks? (Obj. #6e)

29. In addition to using acyclovir, list five ways that a person may find symptom relief from herpes. (Obj. #6e)

30. What is viral hepatitis? (Obj. #6f)

31. Briefly describe the two most common types of viral hepatitis and how they are transmitted. (Obj. #6f)

32. List some of the symptoms of viral hepatitis. (Obj. #6f)

33. How is viral hepatitis treated? (Obj. #6f)

34. What is the incidence of genital warts? (Obj. #6g)

35. What are some of the complications associated with genital warts? (Obj. #6g)

36. Describe some of the available treatments for genital warts. (Obj. #6g)

37. What are the symptoms of chancroid? (Obj. #6h)

38. In what parts of the world is chancroid typically found? Where have outbreaks been reported recently? (Obj. #6h)

39. When is HIV infection diagnosed as AIDS? (Obj. #7a)

40. In what bodily fluids has the AIDS virus been isolated? (Obj. #7d)

41. Compare the modes of transmission of HIV in industrial vs. developing countries. (Obj. #7d)

42. List two reasons why HIV is transmitted more easily from men to women during intercourse. (Obj. #7d)

43. After being infected with HIV, how soon do most people test positive for the antibodies? (Obj. #7a)

44. Name the two blood tests that are most commonly used to screen for HIV infection. (Obj. #7a)

45. What is the incubation period for AIDS in adults? (Obj. #7d)

46. List at least six common symptoms of HIV disease. (Obj. #7c)

47. How did AIDS originate? (Obj. #7a, b)

48. When was AIDS first reported in the U.S.? In other parts of the world? (Obj. #7b)

49. What treatment alternatives are available to people with AIDS? (Obj. #7f)

50. The risk of contracting HIV is higher in individuals that have what other STDs? (Obj. #7e)

51. Aside from abstinence and monogamy, list at least five suggestions for reducing your risk of exposure to HIV. (Obj. #7d)

52. List seven steps for STD prevention. (Obj. #8)

Multiple Choice

Select the best alternative. Check your answers with the answer key at the end of the chapter.

1. Eighty-six percent of all STDs in the U.S. occur among which of the following age groups?
   a. 12–20-year-olds
   b. 15–29-year-olds
   c. 18–35-year-olds
   d. 21–38-year-olds

2. According to the text, one of the factors contributing to the high incidence of STDs is
   a. the lack of quality health care.
   b. the decreasing quality of latex condoms.
   c. the use of birth control pills.
   d. all of the above

3. Gardnerella vaginalis
   a. causes bacterial vaginosis.
   b. is not as common as trichomoniasis.
   c. is treated with vaginal suppositories.
   d. is characterized by a white, clumpy discharge that looks like cottage cheese.

4. The fishy odor of the vaginal discharge that is symptomatic of this infection can be especially pungent after intercourse.
   a. bacterial vaginosis
   b. candidiasis
   c. trichomoniasis
   d. pesce vaginalis

5. Wearing pantyhose and having a diet high in sugar are two factors that may make a woman susceptible to
   a. bacterial vaginosis.
   b. candidiasis.
   c. trichomoniasis.
   d. chlamydial infection.

6. _____ is characterized by a frothy, white or yellow discharge that has an unpleasant odor and is treated with Flagyl. Long-term infection may increase susceptibility to cervical cancer.
   a. Bacterial vaginosis
   b. Chlamydial infection
   c. Candidiasis
   d. Trichomoniasis

7. Chlamydial infection, if left untreated, may result in which of the following in women?
   a. urethritis
   b. cervicitis
   c. pelvic inflammatory disease
   d. all of the above

8. Chlamydia causes trachoma, the world's leading cause of
   a. cervical cancer.
   b. liver damage.
   c. preventable blindness.
   d. testicular cancer.

9. Which of the following statements regarding chlamydial infection is **true**?
   a. Chlamydial salpingitis is the primary preventable cause of female infertility.
   b. A woman with infections of the upper reproductive tract may experience a variety of symptoms.
   c. Penicillin is not effective in treating it.
   d. all of the above

10. If gonorrhea is left untreated in men, which of the following complications would be **least** likely to occur?
    a. epididymitis
    b. prostatic abscesses
    c. sterility
    d. penile abscesses

11. Men who contract NGU often manifest symptoms similar to those of a _____ infection.
    a. herpes
    b. gonorrheal
    c. syphilitic
    d. yeast

12. Currently, the incidence of syphilis
    a. has gradually been decreasing.
    b. has stayed approximately the same since 1960.
    c. has gradually been increasing.
    d. has increased dramatically.

13. During the latent stage of syphilis
    a. the infectious organisms continue to multiply.
    b. the infected individual is highly contagious after the first year has elapsed.
    c. a skin rash may develop.
    d. a person may experience heart failure, blindness, and even death.

14. The most common treatment for syphilis is
    a. penicillin.
    b. Flagyl.
    c. a blood transfusion.
    d. azidothymidine.

15. Which of the following statements concerning pubic lice is **false**?
    a. They are commonly called "crabs".
    b. They may survive on sheets and clothing.
    c. They are treated with A-200 pyrinate.
    d. They limit themselves to the genital areas.

16. Which of the following statements concerning herpes is **false**?
    a. HSV-1 usually infects the mouth or lips but may infect the genitals as well.
    b. HSV-2 will not pass through latex condoms.
    c. During the prodromal phase, the herpes blisters begin to crust over and heal.
    d. There are five different types of herpes viruses that infect humans.

17. Which of the following statements concerning herpes is **true**?
    a. The herpes virus may be eliminated by taking the drug acyclovir, also known as Zovirax.
    b. Being under emotional stress may trigger a herpes outbreak.
    c. One example of a prodromal symptom is a high level of anxiety.
    d. all of the above

18. A possible complication of a herpes infection in both men and women is
    a. damage to the joints if left untreated.
    b. sterility.
    c. severe eye infection.
    d. memory loss and disorientation.

19. Which of the following is **not** a possible complication of a herpes infection in women?
    a. ovarian cancer
    b. infection of the newborn
    c. severe eye infection
    d. cervical cancer

20. A suggestion for symptom relief from herpes is to
    a. drink large quantities of cranberry juice.
    b. wash frequently and dry the genital area with a blow dryer.
    c. apply a heating pad to the infected area to help minimize discomfort.
    d. keep the infected area moist with a topical lubricant to minimize drying and cracking.

21. A yellowing of the whites of the eyes is one of the most notable signs of
    a. third stage syphilis.
    b. trichomoniasis.
    c. AIDS.
    d. viral hepatitis.

22. _____ is the most common form of viral hepatitis in the United States.
    a. Hepatitis A
    b. Hepatitis B
    c. Hepatitis non-A/non-B
    d. Hepatitis C

23. The incidence of genital warts has been
    a. increasing dramatically.
    b. increasing slowly.
    c. stabilizing over the past five years.
    d. decreasing slowly.

24. Podophyllin is one of the treatments for
    a. viral hepatitis.
    b. candidiasis.
    c. genital warts.
    d. pubic lice.

25. AIDS was first reported in the U.S. in
    a. 1973.
    b. 1977.
    c. 1981.
    d. 1985.

26. Human immunodeficiency virus
    a. has been isolated from the breast milk of infected mothers.
    b. can readily be transmitted via saliva and urine.
    c. can be contracted as a result of donating blood.
    d. can be transmitted through casual contact (hugging, shaking hands, etc.).

27. The Western blot
    a. is the routine blood test that is initially given to individuals to detect the presence of AIDS antibodies.
    b. is a more costly blood test that is able to detect a silent HIV infection.
    c. is a type of Rorschach test that is administered to AIDS patients for clinical diagnosis and assessment.
    d. is a recently discovered drug therapy for AIDS patients that has not yet been approved by the FDA.

28. The time between infection with HIV and the onset of AIDS is referred to as
    a. the latent stage.
    b. reverse transcription.
    c. the incubation period.
    d. the prodromal phase.

29. HIV is diagnosed as AIDS
    a. seven years after initial infection with HIV has occurred.
    b. eleven years after initial infection with HIV has occurred.
    c. when the person infected with HIV develops a debilitating illness such as pneumonia or cancer.
    d. when the person infected with HIV has a specified number or less of helper T cells in his or her blood.

30. Which of the following is **not** one of the recommended suggestions for minimizing the possibility of contracting a sexually transmitted disease?
    a. washing the genitals before or after sexual contact
    b. inspecting your partner's genitals
    c. routine postcontact antibiotic therapy
    d. routine medical evaluations

31. In one survey of 400 college students, _____% of men and _____% of women said they would falsely claim that they had tested negative for HIV.
    a. 5; 10
    b. 10; 10
    c. 10; 2
    d. 20; 5

32. With which of the following STDs would a condom be **least** effective?
    a. herpes and genital warts
    b. herpes and trichomoniasis
    c. genital warts and bacterial vaginosis
    d. chlamydia and gonorrhea

Insight and Application

1. Prior to reading this chapter, what changes, if any, have you noticed in your sexual attitudes and behaviors over the past two to three years as a result of what you have read and heard concerning sexually transmitted diseases? Based on what you have read in the chapter, do you anticipate further changes in your sexual attitudes and behavior? If so, what do you think they will be? Give specific examples.

2. Assume that you have been sexually involved with a new partner for six months and things seem to be going well. At this point, your partner confides that he/she has genital herpes. Because the outbreaks are infrequent (approximately once a year) and because your partner is aware of health concerns and takes proper precautions, she/he made the decision to not share this information with you in the early stages of the relationship for fear of your reaction. Your partner has brought the subject up now because he/she has just begun experiencing prodromal symptoms and wants to abstain from genital sex for a while, so it is mandatory that this discussion not be postponed any further. What would be your reaction to this? How would you feel? What would you say and/or do? Do you think your partner's decision to refrain from discussing this with you six months ago was justified? Why or why not?

3. Have you ever contracted any of the sexually transmitted diseases discussed in this chapter? If so, what actions did you take — medically and insofar as your relationship with your partner? Based on what you have read and learned more recently, how would you have handled that situation differently, if at all? Give specific examples.

4. Review the list of prevention guidelines in the text. Which of these would you find difficult to implement, if any? Why?

Matching Answers

1. c	2. k	3. m	4. a	5. d	6. h	7. j	8. b
9. f	10. e	11. i	12. g	13. a	14. d	15. g	16. b
17. l	18. g	19. a	20. d				

Multiple Choice Answers

1. b	2. c	3. a	4. a	5. b	6. d	7. d	8. c
9. d	10. d	11. b	12. a	13. a	14. a	15. d	16. c
17. b	18. c	19. a	20. b	21. d	22. a	23. a	24. c
25. c	26. a	27. a	28. c	29. d	30. c	31. d	32. a

sexually transmitted diseases (STDs)	**bacterial vaginosis (BV)**
urethritis	**cystitis**
candidiasis	**trichomoniasis**
chlamydial infection	**pelvic inflammatory disease (PID)**
trachoma	**conjunctivitis**

a vaginal infection, usually caused by a bacterium called Gardnerella vaginalis, that may be the most common form of vaginitis among women in the U.S.	diseases that are transmitted by sexual contact
inflammation of the urethra or bladder, characterized by discomfort during urination	inflammation of the urethral tube
a form of vaginitis caused by a one-celled protozoan called Trichomonas vaginalis	an inflammatory infection of the vaginal tissues caused by the yeast-like fungus Candida albicans
invasive infections of the upper reproductive tract (uterus, pelvic cavity, etc.)	caused by the bacterial microorganism Chlamydia trachomatis, it is among the most prevalent and most damaging of all STDs
inflammation of the mucous membrane that lines the inner surface of the eyelid and the exposed surface of the eyeball	a chronic, contagious form of conjunctivitis caused by chlamydial infections

gonorrhea	**nongonococcal urethritis (NGU)**
syphilis	**chancre**
pubic lice	**herpes**
prodromal symptoms	**viral hepatitis**
genital warts	**acquired immunodeficiency syndrome (AIDS)**

an inflammation of the male urethral tube caused by other than gonorrhea organisms	a sexually transmitted disease that initially causes inflammation of mucous membranes
a raised, red painless sore that is symptomatic of the primary phase of syphilis	a sexually transmitted disease caused by a thin corkscrew-like bacterium called Treponema pallidum (also called a "spirochete")
a disease, characterized by blisters on the skin in the regions of the genitals or mouth, that is caused by a virus and is easily transmitted by sexual contact	parasitic insects that primarily infest the pubic hair and are transmitted by sexual contact
a disease in which liver function is impaired by a viral infection	symptoms that give advance warning of impending eruption
a catastrophic illness in which a virus invades and destroys the ability of the immune system to fight disease	viral warts that appear on the genitals and are usually transmitted through vaginal, oral or oral-genital sexual interaction

chancroid

a disease characterized by smaller bumps in the genital region that eventually rupture and form painful ulcers with a discharge

20

Atypical Sexual Behavior

Introduction

In this chapter, the authors use the label "atypical sexual behavior" to refer to the paraphilias, or the more uncommon types of sexual expression. Some of us have engaged in milder forms of some of the behaviors described, although to merit the labels discussed here one must usually engage in the behavior as a primary means of sexual arousal and expression. Being an unwilling recipient of some of these behaviors would be very upsetting and offensive to many people, which is why many of these behaviors are illegal.

Learning Objectives

After studying this chapter, you should be able to:

1. Define atypical sexual behavior and distinguish it from other labels such as deviant, perverted, abnormal, etc.

2. Explain each of the following considerations in discussing atypical sexual behavior:
   a. how these behaviors exist on a continuum
   b. what our knowledge base is regarding these various behaviors
   c. the impact of atypical sexual behavior both on the person exhibiting the behavior and on the recipient of the behavior

3. Define exhibitionism and discuss each of the following in regard to it:
   a. variations on this behavior
   b. what we know about the type of person who exhibits this behavior, and what some of the problems are with the available data
   c. theories regarding what influences the development of this behavior
   d. how likely exhibitionists are to engage in other illegal behaviors
   e. treatment alternatives available for people arrested for this behavior
   f. how to respond to exhibitionistic behavior

4. Explain what we know about the person who makes obscene phone calls, and the likelihood that this person will engage in other illegal sexual behaviors.

5. Outline several strategies for dealing with obscene phone calls.

6. Define voyeurism and discuss the problems in attempting to determine what qualifies as voyeuristic behavior.

7. Discuss common characteristics of voyeurs, the likelihood of voyeurs engaging in other serious offenses, and explain what factors may trigger voyeuristic behavior.

8. Define sadomasochistic behavior, sexual sadism and sexual masochism and discuss each of the following in reference to these behaviors:
   a. the complexity involved in labeling these behaviors
   b. available statistics that indicate how common these behaviors may be
   c. the behavioral and psychological dynamics involved
   d. social views regarding these behaviors
   e. reasons why people may choose to engage in these behaviors

9. Describe fetishism, making specific reference to the following:
   a. problems in defining it
   b. common fetish objects
   c. how it develops
   d. other offenses that may be associated with it

10. Distinguish transvestitism from female impersonation, cross-dressing by male homosexuals, and transsexualism.

11. Discuss each of the following in regard to transvestitism:
    a. the range of behaviors that may comprise it
    b. who is most likely to engage in this behavior, citing relevant statistics
    c. what studies reveal regarding partner response to this behavior
    d. factors associated with the development of transvestitism

12. Briefly define and discuss each of the following paraphilias that tend to be less common than the ones described previously:
    a. zoophilia
    b. necrophilia
    c. klismaphilia
    d. coprophilia and urophilia
    e. frotteurism

13. Briefly define each of the miscellaneous paraphilias referred to in table 20.1 in the text.

14. Discuss the controversy surrounding sexual addiction—what it is, how to categorize it and how to treat it.

Key Terms and Concepts

"Flash cards" listing key terms and concepts on one side and their corresponding definitions and explanations on the other side are provided at the end of the chapter.

Chapter Overview With Fill-Ins

After reading each of the major sections in the chapter, check your retention by **mentally** filling in each of the blanks in the corresponding sections below. Cover the answers in the margin as you go along, and write the answers in the space provided only when you are doing your final review.

paraphilia	The term _____ is currently used to describe sexual behaviors that have otherwise been labeled as deviant, perverted, aberrant, or abnormal. As these behaviors are not typically expressed by most people in our society, the authors use the term
atypical	_____ to describe these behaviors. Many of the behaviors
illegal	discussed are _____. Because many people who encounter
adversely	such acts are not _____ affected, many authorities view
minor	them as _____ sex offenses. However, recent evidence
progress	suggests that some people _____ from so-called "nuisance" offenses to more serious forms of sexual abuse, so their classification
reconsidered	as minor offenses may be _____.

Exhibitionism

indecent exposure

involuntary

20s
30s; married

insecure

limit

child molestation

therapy
antiandrogen

behavior

ignore

Often called _____ _____, exhibitionism refers to behavior where an individual (usually male) exposes his genitals to an _____ observer (usually an adult woman or female child). Based on limited available data, it would appear that most people who exhibit themselves are adult males in their _____ or _____, and over one-half are or have been _____. They are often shy, nonassertive people who feel inadequate and _____.

The majority of men who engage in exhibitionism _____ their illegal behaviors to exposing themselves. However, a minority of men may progress to more serious offenses, such as rape and _____ _____.

In the past several years, there has been a trend toward _____ as an alternative to incarceration. In addition, _____ drugs have been used to block inappropriate sexual arousal patterns. Research has revealed that men undergoing treatment for exhibitionism can sometimes modify their _____ and overcome their desire to engage in this activity.

The best response to exhibitionism is to calmly _____ it and to report such acts to proper authorities.

Obscene Phone Calls

exhibitionism

inadequate
anxiety

ignore
deafness
unlisted

The characteristics of people who make obscene phone calls seem to be similar to those of people who engage in _____.
According to research, these individuals are usually male, and they often feel _____ and insecure. When relating to the other sex, they frequently show greater _____ and hostility than people who engage in exhibitionism.

Advice for dealing with people who make obscene phone calls includes: do not overreact — gently hang up the phone and continue with what you were doing; _____ the phone if it rings again; feign _____; set the phone down and never return. You may also choose to get an _____ number.

Voyeurism

naked
strangers
sexual relations

risk

sociosexual

20s

Voyeurism refers to deriving pleasure from looking at the _____ bodies or sexual activities of others, usually _____, without their consent. To qualify as atypical sexual behavior, voyeurism must be preferred to _____ _____ with another, or indulged in with some _____, or both.

Most people inclined toward voyeurism have some of the same characteristics as people who expose themselves: poorly developed _____ skills and strong feelings of inferiority, especially toward potential sexual partners. They tend to be men in their early _____, and occasionally they will progress to other crimes, but that is typically not the case.

Sexual Sadism and Sexual Masochism

receiving; mental
aggressive

Sadomasochism is defined as obtaining sexual arousal through giving or _____ physical or _____ pain. Many people enjoy some form of _____ interaction during sexual sharing, for which the label sadomasochism seems inappropriate.

masochistic

People with _____ tendencies may be aroused by such things as being whipped, cut, pierced with needles, bound, spanked, humiliated, or forced to do filthy or _____ service.

degrading

less

There are some indications that people with sadistic tendencies are _____ common than their masochistic counterparts.

negative
misleading

Many people in contemporary Western societies view sadomasochism in a very _____ light. Several researchers maintain that these conceptions of sadomasochism are _____, because although there are a minority of individuals who engage in "heavy" sadomasochism, the majority of sadomasochism participants simply enjoy a form of sexual _____ which they voluntarily and mutually choose to explore.

enhancement

dominance

A recent review of sociological literature has confirmed that most people who engage in sadomasochistic activities are usually motivated by a desire to experience _____ and submission rather than pain.

self-awareness

Baumeister has theorized that sexual masochism may represent an attempt to escape from high levels of _____-
_____.

sex; pain

Clinical studies of sadomasochism participants sometimes reveal early experiences that may have established a connection between _____ and _____.

Fetishism

inanimate
body
exclusion
human

Fetishism occurs when an individual becomes sexually aroused by focusing on an _____ object or a part of the human _____. This term is only applicable when a person focuses on these things to the _____ of everything else. For some people, fetish objects serve as substitutes for _____ contact and are dispensed with if a partner becomes available.

classical

fantasy

orgasm

The most common way that fetishism is developed is by a kind of _____ conditioning, in which some object or body part becomes associated with sexual arousal. This would typically happen by incorporating the object or body part, often through _____, in a masturbation sequence where the reinforcement of _____ strengthens the fetishistic association.

burglary

Only rarely does fetishism develop into an offense that might harm someone, although _____ is the most frequent serious offense to be associated with fetishism.

Transvestitism

clothes
entire

one

men

female

heterosexual
tolerate

The term transvestitism applies to behaviors whereby an individual obtains sexual excitement from putting on the _____ of the other sex. Some people prefer to don the _____ garb of the other sex; more commonly, a person becomes aroused by wearing only _____ garment (e.g., panties or brassiere).

In the majority of cases, it appears that _____ are attracted to transvestitism, although some isolated cases of _____ transvestitism have been reported. Several studies indicate that cross-dressing occurs primarily among married men with predominantly _____ orientations. Recent data suggests that most wives only _____ rather than support the cross-dressing of their husbands.

conditioning
feminine

Like fetishism and some other atypical sexual behaviors, the development of transvestitism often reveals a pattern of _____. Occasionally, transvestitism is the behavior of the heterosexual male who is striving to explore the _____ side of his personality.

Other Atypical Behaviors

bestiality

transitory

preferred

Zoophilia, also called _____, involves sexual contact between humans and animals. Sexual contact with animals is commonly a _____ experience of young people to whom a sexual partner is inaccessible or forbidden. True zoophilia exists only when sexual contact with animals is _____ regardless of what other forms of sexual outlet are available.

corpse
men
dead
prostitutes

Necrophilia is when a person obtains sexual gratification by viewing or having intercourse with a _____. It appears to occur exclusively among _____. Due to problems associated with gaining access to _____ bodies, some men with necrophilic tendencies limit their contact to _____ who pose as corpses.

enemas

mothers

anal

Klismaphilia is when an individual obtains sexual satisfaction from receiving _____. Case histories of these individuals reveal that, as children, they were frequently given enemas by concerned and affectionate _____, and they learned to associate loving attention with the erotic pleasure of _____ stimulation.

feces
urine

Coprophilia and urophilia refer to activities in which people obtain sexual arousal from contact with _____ and _____, respectively.

Frotteurism

female; elevator
orgasm

masturbation

_____ may be a fairly common paraphilia that goes largely unnoticed. It involves an individual, usually a male, who obtains sexual pleasure by pressing and rubbing against a fully-clothed _____ in a crowded public place like an _____, bus, or subway. The man may achieve arousal and _____ during the act. More commonly, he incorporates the mental images of his actions into _____ fantasies at a later time.

Sexual Addiction: Fact, Fiction, or Misnomer?

nymphomania;
satyriasis; com-
pulsive

The idea that people may become dominated by insatiable sexual needs has been around for a long time, exemplified by the term _____, applied to women, and _____, or Don Juanism, applied to men. The concept of _____ sexuality achieved heightened legitimacy through several books written by Patrick Carnes. According to Carnes, many of the people who engage in many atypical as well as sexual victimization behaviors are

addiction

depression

high

ritualistic
despair

manifesting the outward symptoms of psychological _____, in which the feelings of _____, anxiety, loneliness, and worthlessness are temporarily relieved through a sexual "_____" not unlike the high achieved by drugs or alcohol. Carnes suggests that the addiction cycle progresses through four phases: preoccupation, _____ behaviors, expression of the sexual act, and _____.

compulsive

Although Carnes' conception of the sexual addict has received considerable attention, many sexologists do not believe that it should be a distinct category because it is rare and also similar to other _____ disorders, such as gambling and eating disorders. According to sexologist Eli Coleman, a person manifesting excessive sexual behavior typically has grown up in a home characterized by

intimacy

severe _____ dysfunction, such as child abuse or neglect.

treatment
self-help

Professional _____ programs as well as a number of _____-_____ groups for compulsive or addictive sexual behaviors have emerged throughout the nation.

Matching

Match the terms below with the appropriate descriptions. Each term may be used more than once, but choose only **one** answer for each blank.

a. exhibitionism
b. voyeurism
c. sadomasochism
d. fetishism
e. transvestitism
f. zoophilia
g. necrophilia
h. mysophilia
i. apotemnophilia
j. klismaphilia
k. coprophilia
l. urophilia
m. frotteurism

_____1. being sexually excited by the fantasy or reality of being an amputee

_____2. sexual arousal from contact with urine

_____3. female partners of men who engage in this activity tend to tolerate, rather than support it

_____4. burglary is the most frequent serious offense to be associated with this

_____5. Kinsey found that 22 percent of men and 12 percent of women in his study responded erotically to stories with these themes

_____6. obtaining sexual pleasure from rubbing against a fully clothed person (usually female) in a crowded place

_____7. some professionals believe that this behavior is more common among women than we suspect because they can engage in this behavior without detection

_____8. behavioral therapy as well as antiandrogens have been used to treat men who engage in this behavior

_____9. obtaining sexual gratification by having sex with a corpse

_____10. also called bestiality

_____11. Baumeister has hypothesized that this behavior may be an attempt to escape from high levels of self-awareness

_____12. sexual arousal from contact with feces

_____13. many professionals link this behavior with fetishism

_____14. men who engage in this are usually in their early 20s, and they have similar characteristics to men who expose themselves

_____15. obtaining sexual pleasure from receiving enemas

_____16. this behavior increases blood pressure, muscle tension and hyperventilation more so than other sexual activities, resulting in greater arousal from a physiological standpoint

_____17. becoming sexually aroused by something soiled or filthy

Short Answer

1. Define paraphilia. (Obj. #1)

2. What is John Money's explanation for why atypical sexual expression is more prevalent among men instead of women? (Obj. #2b)

3. Characterize the typical person who engages in exhibitionism. (Obj. #3b)

4. Briefly describe some of the explanations for exhibitionistic behavior. (Obj. #4c)

5. According to Gene Abel's 1981 research, what histories of other types of atypical sexual behaviors were found among rapists? (Obj. #3d)

6. What treatment alternatives are available to people who manifest exhibitionistic behavior? (Obj. #3e)

7. Describe the characteristics of people who make obscene phone calls. (Obj. #4)

8. What are some suggestions for dealing with obscene phone calls? For people who exhibit themselves? (Obj. #3f, 5)

9.   Briefly characterize the person who engages in voyeuristic behavior. (Obj. #7)

10. According to Hunt's research, what percentage of men and women reported obtaining sexual pleasure from sadomasochistic activities? (Obj. #8b)

11. According to one survey, what percentage of respondents engaged in bondage? (Obj. #8c)

12. What is autoerotic asphyxia, and why do some people engage in it? (Obj. #8c)

13. Why is the medical model of sadomasochism as a pathological condition being questioned? (Obj. #8c, d)

14. List four reasons why people might choose to engage in sadomasochistic activity. (Obj. #8e)

15. Describe Baumeister's theory of the function that sexual masochism serves. (Obj. #8e)

16. How does fetishism develop? (Obj. #9c)

17. With what more serious offense may fetishism be associated? (Obj. #9d)

18. Distinguish between transvestitism and transsexualism. (Obj. #10)

19. Describe the person who would be most likely to engage in transvestitism. (Obj. #11b)

20. According to various research studies, how do wives of men who engage in transvestitism respond to this behavior? (Obj. #11c)

21. Briefly describe the following atypical sexual behaviors: (Obj. #12a–e)
    a. zoophilia

    b. necrophilia

    c. klismaphilia

    d. coprophilia and urophilia

    e.   frotteurism

22. According to Patrick Carnes, what is sexual addiction? (Obj. #14)

23. List and briefly describe the four phases of sexual addiction as suggested by Patrick Carnes. (Obj. #14)

    a.

    b.

    c.

    d.

24. Why do some sexologists such as Eli Coleman disagree with the label "sexual addiction?" (Obj. #14)

25. List and briefly describe at least four of the miscellaneous paraphilias outlined in table 20.1 in the text. (Obj. #13)

Multiple Choice

Select the best alternative. Check your answers with the answer key at the end of the chapter.

1. Paraphilias are **best** defined as _____ sexual behaviors.
    a. illegal
    b. noncoital
    c. uncommon
    d. perverted

2. A person who becomes sexually aroused by exposing his genitals to a stranger is engaging in
    a. voyeurism.
    b. exhibitionism.
    c. fetishism.
    d. coprophilia.

3. Which of the following groups of adjectives would **best** describe a person who engages in exhibitionism?
    a. relatively young, shy, nonassertive
    b. relatively young, antisocial, aggressive
    c. middle-aged to older, potentially violent, hostile
    d. relatively young, self-confident, reckless

4. According to Abel's research, approximately _____ percent of the rapists on his sample had histories of other types of variant sexual behavior.
    a. 25
    b. 50
    c. 75
    d. 90

5. Which of the following statements concerning men who expose themselves is **false**?
    a. They are usually in their twenties or thirties.
    b. The majority of those men go on to commit more serious offenses.
    c. They usually have feelings of inadequacy and insecurity.
    d. all of the above

6. The characteristics of people who make obscene phones calls are similar to those who engage in
    a. fetishism.
    b. masochism.
    c. sadism.
    d. exhibitionism.

7. Watching X-rated movies or reading sexually explicit magazines is a mild form of _____, in which many people participate.
    a. exhibitionism
    b. frotteurism
    c. voyeurism
    d. masochism

8. A person who obtains sexual gratification from covertly observing people who are nude or engaging in sex is called a/an
    a. fetishist.
    b. sadist.
    c. voyeur.
    d. exhibitionist.

9. Obtaining sexual arousal through giving or receiving pain is called
    a. klismaphilia.
    b. frotteurism.
    c. fetishism.
    d. sadomasochism.

10. The results of Hunt's 1974 survey and Rubin's 1990 survey revealed that _____ of men and women engage in sadomasochistic activity with a partner.
    a. less than 10%
    b. 10%-25%
    c. 25%-40%
    d. 40%-60%

11. Which of the following statements concerning sadomasochism is **false**?
    a. Most people who engage in sadomasochism are usually motivated by pain.
    b. In Kinsey's survey, over 25 percent of both sexes reported erotic response to receiving love bites while having sex.
    c. Masochism is more common than sadism.
    d. A majority of people who engage in sadomasochistic activities may prefer one role or the other, but are comfortable in either role.

12. Among the majority of individuals that Weinberg and his colleagues interviewed, sadomasochism was definitely a _____ activity.
    a. nonconsensual
    b. consensual
    c. severely humiliating
    d. severely painful

13. Sadomasochistic activity may have which of the following effects?
    a. increased blood pressure
    b. hyperventilation
    c. increased muscle tension
    d. all of the above

14. Which of the following statements regarding autoerotic asphyxia is **false**?
    a. It is a very rare paraphilia.
    b. The purpose of engaging in this behavior is to enhance sexual arousal by reducing the supply of oxygen to the brain.
    c. It is a type of sexual masochism.
    d. Unlike other sadomasochistic activities, this behavior is always practiced alone.

15. Fetishism is **best** defined as
    a. obtaining sexual gratification, primarily or exclusively, from an inanimate object or part of the body.
    b. cross-dressing for purposes of sexual arousal.
    c. cross-dressing to make your appearance correspond with your sexual orientation.
    d. being dependent on pornography for sexual gratification.

16. The development of fetishism is typically an example of
    a. operant conditioning.
    b. classical conditioning.
    c. cultural conditioning.
    d. tactile conditioning.

17. Which of the following statements concerning transvestism is **false**?
    a. It exists primarily when people cross-dress to make their appearance correspond to their sexual identity.
    b. It occurs primarily among unmarried homosexual men.
    c. People who cross-dress are usually gender dysphoric.
    d. all of the above

18. Anthropologist Robert Munroe has noted that _____ tends to appear more often in cultures where men assume more economic responsibility than women.
    a. transvestism
    b. transsexualism
    c. fetishism
    d. homosexuality

19. Which of the following statements concerning transvestism is **true**?
    a. Most people who engage in transvestism are likely to seek therapy at some point.
    b. The practice of transvestism can be successfully altered with therapy.
    c. One explanation for the development of transvestism is that it is a heterosexual male's attempt to explore the feminine side of his personality.
    d. all of the above

20. Which of the following statements concerning zoophilia is **true**?
    a. According to Kinsey, approximately the same number of men and women reported having had sexual contact with animals.
    b. The animals most frequently involved in sex with humans are horses, rabbits, hamsters, and fish.
    c. It is commonly a transitory experience of young people for whom a sexual partner is not available.
    d. Males who engage in this activity usually have contact with household pets.

21. The term "necrophilia" refers to
    a. being dependent on violent pornography for sexual arousal.
    b. obtaining sexual gratification by having intercourse with a corpse.
    c. being sexually aroused by a person who is an amputee.
    d. obtaining sexual gratification from contact with feces.

22. Aporaphilia in which a person becomes sexually aroused from contact with feces is called
    a. coprophilia.
    b. klismaphilia.
    c. frotteurism.
    d. naturophilia.

23. When a person is sexually aroused by the fantasy or reality of being an amputee it is referred to
    a. mysophilia.
    b. narrotophia.
    c. acrotomophilia.
    d. apotemnophilia.

24. Which of the following statements is **true**?
    a. Don Juanism is one term for men who have insatiable sexual needs.
    b. The final phase of Carnes' cycle of sexual addiction is the sexual act itself.
    c. The term "satyriasis" is used to refer to a man who is bisexual.
    d. all of the above

25. Eli Coleman and others believe that excessive sexual activity reflects _____ rather than addiction.
    a. sexual dysfunction
    b. sexual compulsion
    c. a hormonal imbalance
    d. optimal health

Insight and Application

1. After reading this chapter, how have your attitudes changed, if at all, toward any of the sexual behaviors discussed?

2. Which of the atypical sexual behaviors discussed in the chapter do you find most acceptable? Least acceptable? Why?

3. Which of the atypical sexual behaviors discussed should be illegal? Under what circumstances? Why?

Matching Answers

1. i	2. l	3. e	4. d	5. c	6. m	7. e	8. a
9. g	10. f	11. c	12. k	13. e	14. b	15. j	16. c
17. h							

Multiple Choice Answers

1. c	2. b	3. a	4. b	5. b	6. d	7. c	8. c
9. d	10. b	11. a	12. b	13. d	14. d	15. a	16. b
17. d	18. a	19. c	20. c	21. b	22. a	23. d	24. a
25. b							

atypical sexual behavior

erotosexual differentiation

exhibitionism

voyeurism

sadomasochism

fetishism

transvestism

zoophilia (bestiality)

necrophilia

klismaphilia

the development of sexual arousal in response to various kinds of images or stimuli	sexual behavior that is not commonly expressed by the majority of people in our society
the act of obtaining sexual gratification by observing people who are undressed or engaged in sexual interaction without their consent	the act of exposing one's genitals to an unwilling observer
obtaining sexual excitement primarily or exclusively from an inanimate object or a particular part of the body	the association of sexual expression with pain
a paraphilia in which a person has sexual contact with animals	deriving sexual arousal from wearing clothing of the other sex
a very unusual variation of sexual expression in which an individual obtains sexual pleasure from receiving enemas	a rare sexual paraphilia in which a person obtains sexual gratification by viewing or having inter-course with a corpse

coprophilia	**urophilia**
frotteurism	**nymphomania**
satyriasis (Don Juanism)	**bondage**
sexual sadism	**sexual masochism**

a sexual paraphilia in which a person obtains sexual arousal from contact with urine	a sexual paraphilia in which a person obtains sexual arousal from contact with feces
a term, which most professionals refrain from using because of its pejorative nature, that refers to a woman who is dominated by insatiable sexual needs	a fairly common paraphilia in which a person obtains sexual pleasure by pressing or rubbing against another in a crowded public place
deriving sexual pleasure from being bound, tied up or otherwise restricted	a term, which most professionals refrain from using because of its pejorative nature, that refers to a man who is dominated by insatiable sexual needs
the act of obtaining sexual arousal through receiving physical or psychological pain	the act of obtaining sexual arousal through giving physical or psychological pain

21

Sexual Victimization

Introduction

There is a growing awareness of the high incidence of sexual victimization that occurs in our society. Men and women who survive rape, childhood sexual abuse, and sexual harassment are becoming more willing to speak out regarding their experiences, and our society is being forced to confront some of the cultural patterns that condone and even support sexual victimization. This chapter presents current research on both the perpetrators and victims of the coercive behaviors listed above and includes strategies for reducing the risk of rape, preventing child sexual abuse, and dealing with sexual harassment.

Learning Objectives

After studying this chapter, you should be able to:

1. Define all of the key terms and concepts for this chapter listed in the flash card section at the end of the chapter and be able to integrate them with all relevant material outlined below.

2. Discuss the difficulties in obtaining accurate statistics on the number of rapes and rape survivors in the U.S. and cite some of the variations in currently available statistics.

3. Identify and elaborate upon five false beliefs regarding rape.

4. Describe some changes in rape laws that have occurred in the past several years.

5. Citing relevant research, describe some of the psychosocial bases of rape.

6. Discuss what research has revealed regarding the impact of sexually violent and degrading media on the attitudes and behaviors of rapists and nonrapists.

7. Describe the characteristics of men who rape.

8. List and describe four different types of rapes and rapists.

9. Discuss recent research regarding acquaintance rape and sexual coercion, making specific reference to the following:
   a. how prevalent it is
   b. factors that might contribute to people engaging in unwanted sexual activity
   c. why some women may say "no" to sex when they mean "yes"

10. Discuss how frequently the rape of males occurs, who the perpetrators are, and what some of the problems are with the data in this area.

11. Discuss the possible situations or circumstances in which men might be raped.

12. Describe what the effects are on men who have been raped.

13. Explain the short-term and long-term effects of rape on female survivors, making specific reference to the following:
   a. rape trauma syndrome
   b. suggestions regarding how to respond to a partner who has been raped

14. List and briefly describe nine suggestions for reducing the risk of stranger rape.

15. List and briefly describe five suggestions for how to deal with threatening situations involving strangers.

16. List and briefly describe six suggestions for reducing the risk of acquaintance rape.

17. List and briefly describe seven ways in which a woman may take action if she has been raped.

18. Distinguish between pedophilia and incest, and discuss some of the differences in defining child molestation.

19. Discuss the sexual abuse of children, citing specific information and current research as it relates to the following:
    a. in what situations and under what conditions it most commonly occurs
    b. how prevalent it is and the problems with these statistics
    c. how incidence of abuse in girls compares to that of boys

20. Describe the factors that contribute to how severely the abuse affects the victim and what these effects might be.

21. Identify treatment programs available for child sexual abuse survivors.

22. Describe the characteristics of the person who sexually abuses children.

23. Discuss the controversy surrounding the issue of recovered memories of child sexual abuse.

24. List and describe ten suggestions for preventing childhood sexual abuse.

25. Explain what kinds of responses might be helpful in the event you discovered that your own child had been molested by an adult.

26. Define sexual harassment and describe two types of sexual harassment as provided by the EEOC guidelines.

27. Citing relevant statistics, discuss how common sexual harassment is among men and women.

28. Discuss the various forms that sexual harassment can take.

29. Discuss the effects of on-the-job harassment on victims.

30. Outline and describe six guidelines for dealing with sexual harassment in the workplace.

31. Discuss sexual harassment that may occur in an academic setting, making specific reference to the following:
    a. who the perpetrators are
    b. differences between harassment that occurs in an academic setting vs. the workplace
    c. how common sexual harassment is in this setting
    d. how to deal with sexual harassment in an academic environment

32. Cite examples of how and for what purposes wartime rape has been used.

33. Summarize statistics that indicate to what extent child sexual abuse is an international problem.

Key Terms and Concepts

"Flash cards" listing key terms and concepts on one side and their corresponding definitions and explanations on the other side are provided at the end of the chapter.

Chapter Overview With Fill-Ins

After reading each of the major sections in the chapter, check your retention by mentally filling in each of the blanks in the corresponding sections below. Cover the answers in the margin as you go along, and write the answers in the space provided only when you are doing your final review.

Rape

actual; threatened
Statutory

consent; Stranger
Acquaintance

The legal definition of rape varies from state to state; however, most laws define rape as sexual intercourse that occurs under _____ or _____ forcible compulsion that overcomes the earnest resistance of the victim. _____ rape refers to intercourse with a person who is under the age of _____. _____ rape is the rape of a person by an unknown assailant. _____ rape, or date rape, is committed by someone known to the victim.

8; 16
19; 30

Estimates of the percentage of rapes that women victims report to the police or other agencies range from _____ to _____ percent. Various contemporary surveys indicate that anywhere from _____ to _____ percent of women have experienced rape or attempted rape.

resist

coerced

fantasies
harm

victim

There are a number of false beliefs about rape: 1) the belief that women can always successfully _____ a rape attempt is false for several reasons; 2) the distorted perception that some men have that women want to be _____ into sexual activity, even to the extent of being raped; 3) the notion that many women "cry rape" is inaccurate; 4) although some women do have rape _____, in which they have control of the situation and they risk no threat of physical _____, it is a false belief that "all women want to be raped," as many novels and films suggest; and finally, 5) many women think "it could never happen to me," which is again inaccurate because any female is a potential _____.

violence

sexually
power

gratification

Many men incarcerated for rape offenses appear to have a strong tendency toward _____ that is often reflected in their act of rape. This fact , along with certain assumptions concerning male-female relationships, resulted in a number of feminist writers taking the position that rape is not _____ motivated, but rather an act of _____ and domination. However, recent research has made it clear that while this may be the case, rape is frequently motivated by a desire for sexual _____ as well.

erotic

violent

Research has indicated that mere exposure to _____ materials may not be the critical factor in increasing men's aggressiveness toward women, but rather the _____ nature of the material may have harmful effects on men's attitudes toward sex and women.

conservative
sexual
traditional
alcohol

Besides the different socialization processes that often distinguish rapists from nonrapists, other characteristics that have been linked to men who rape include: a tendency to hold rather _____ attitudes toward _____ topics; an adherence to _____ gender roles; a history of other types of sexual offenses; and _____ use.

four
anger; sadistic

The authors differentiate among _____ types of rapes and rapists: _____ rape, power rape, _____ rape and sexual gratification rape.

known
acquaintance; dating

prevalence

A majority of rapes are committed by someone who is _____ to the woman. A significant number of these _____ rapes take place in _____ situations. A number of recent studies provide solid evidence of the _____ of sexual coercion in dating situations.

females

Because the majority of people who are raped are _____, most of our knowledge about the short- and long-term effects of rape are taken from studies of women who have been raped. The emotional repercussions women experience following rape have been labeled

rape trauma
acute

groups

_____ _____ syndrome. There are usually two phases of rape trauma: the _____ phase and the long-term reorganization phase. Women often find that supportive counseling, either individually or in _____, can help them deal with the aftermath of rape.

judgment

decisions

sexual

There are several suggestions for how a male should respond to his partner's rape experience: do not question her _____ at the time of the rape; do not focus on your own shortcomings; listen to her; let her make all of the _____ concerning how to deal with the assault; provide empathy and support for weeks and even months following the rape; let her decide when and how to resume _____ activity.

Sexual Abuse of Children

Child

illegal
pedophilia
incest

_____ sexual abuse is defined as an adult engaging in sexual contact of any kind with a child. Such interaction is considered coercive and _____. Most researchers distinguish between nonrelative child sexual abuse, referred to as _____ or child molestation, and _____, which is sexual contact between two people who are related (one of whom is often a child).

socioeconomic

spouse
brother-sister
father-daughter

Although incest occurs at all _____ levels, it appears to occur with greater frequency in families disrupted by severe marital conflict, _____ abuse, alcoholism, unemployment, and emotional illness. Although _____-_____ and first cousin incest is most common, _____-_____ incest is more likely to be reported to authorities.

significance
appropriate
traumatizing
escape

The incestuous involvement of a father and his daughter often begins before the female child understand its _____. Later, when she discovers that the behavior is not _____ or finds her father's demands to be unpleasant and _____, it may be difficult for her to _____ from a well-established pattern of exploitative sexual activity.

incest

prevalence

It is difficult to accurately estimate the incidence of _____ or pedophilia for a number of reasons. However, numerous reports and surveys indicate the _____ of child sexual abuse is startling.

There is increasing evidence that child sexual abuse can have severely _____ long-term consequences such as: difficulty in forming _____ relationships, especially with men; _____ difficulties; low self-esteem, guilt, shame, and depression; a sense of alienation from others; a lack of trust in others; revulsion at being _____; drug and alcohol abuse; obesity; elevated _____ rates; and predisposition to being _____ in other ways.

damaging
intimate
sexual

touched
suicide
victimized

A variety of _____ programs have emerged to help survivors of child sexual abuse.

treatment

The pedophile offender is most commonly a _____ who is shy, lonely, sexually _____, possesses limited sexual knowledge, and is often very moralistic or _____. These offenders have often been _____ themselves during their own childhood. The man who engages in an incestuous relationship with his own child _____ many of the characteristics of the pedophile.

male
conservative
religious
victimized

shares

Preventing Child Sexual Abuse

The following list, drawn from the writings of a number of child abuse specialists, offers some suggestions for _____ child sexual abuse: 1) present prevention-oriented material to boys and girls when they are still very _____; 2) keep the discussion and concepts _____; 3) avoid making a discussion of child sex abuse _____; 4) carefully explain the differences between okay and not-okay touches; 5) encourage children to believe they have _____; 6) encourage children to tell someone right away if an adult has touched them inappropriately; 7) discuss some of the strategies adults might use to entice children; 8) discuss some of the strategies for getting away from _____ situations; 9) encourage children to state clearly to the offender that they will _____ a responsible adult about what went on; and 10) discuss the (129) _____ aspects of touch and sexuality between two adults who care for each other.

preventing

young
simple
frightening

rights

dangerous

tell
pleasurable

Sexual Harassment

The definition of sexual harassment is "any unwanted sexual attention of a sexual nature from someone at the _____."

workplace

In 1980, the Equal Employment Opportunity Commission issued guidelines derived from the _____ _____ Act that imposed liability on companies for sexual harassment by supervisors unless the company takes immediate and appropriate action. These guidelines emphasize that both verbal and physical harassment are _____. Two kinds of sexual harassment are "_____ _____ _____" and "hostile or offensive environment."

Civil Rights

illegal
quid pro quo

widespread 42; 15	A number of studies have indicated that sexual harassment is extremely _____. A survey of more than 20,000 federal employees found that _____ percent of the women and _____ percent of the men had been sexually harassed. Other surveys of women indicate an even greater incidence.
financial physical psychological six	A person who quits or is fired as a result of sexual harassment faces the prospect of severe _____ difficulties, as well as a variety of adverse emotional and _____ effects. Many victims also report a variety of _____ effects. The text outlines _____ guidelines for dealing with sexual harassment in the workplace.
academic	Sexual harassment may also take place in an _____ environment. Several surveys indicate that significant percentages of both male and female students have experienced sexual harassment.
report	The authors advise students to _____ this if they encounter it — as opposed to dropping the class or dropping out of school — so that the inappropriate actions may be curtailed.

Short Answer

1. List five common false beliefs about rape and briefly describe why the beliefs are inaccurate. (Obj. #3)

    a.

    b.

    c.

    d.

    e.

2. Of 114 imprisoned rapists, what percentage did not see themselves as rapists? (Obj. #3)

3.   List four recent reforms in rape laws. (Obj. #4)

4.   What has been the problem with some of the past studies on men who rape? (Obj. #5, 7)

5.   In addition to having power and control over women, what motivates some men to rape women? (Obj. #5, 6)

6.   Briefly summarize the results of Peggy Reeves Sanday's research. (Obj. #5)

7.   What are some of the characteristics of a rape-prone society? (Obj. #5)

8.   Describe the relationship between sexually violent media and some rapists' behaviors. Cite research to support your answer. (Obj. #6)

9.   What are the effects of sexually violent media versus sexually degrading media? (Obj. #6)

10. In general, what are some of the other characteristics of men who rape? (Obj. #7)

11. What were the results of Gene Abel's study of rapists who had never been identified by the criminal justice system? (Obj. #7)

12. List and briefly characterize the four types of rapes and rapists. (Obj. #8)

13. What are some reasons for engaging in unwanted sexual acts where physical force is not used? (Obj. #11b)

14. List four reasons why rape has taken place during war times. (Obj. #32)

15. In what situations and by whom may men be raped? (Obj. #10, 11)

16. Explain why men might get erections and women might lubricate and be orgasmic while they are being sexually molested. (Obj. #33, 34)

17. List some reasons why women may say "no" to sex when they really mean "yes." (Obj. #9c)

18. List and briefly describe the two phases of rape trauma syndrome. (Obj. #13a)

19. What types of sexual problems were most common among rape survivors? Least common? (Obj. #13a)

20. List at least four suggestions for how a man might effectively respond to his partner after she has been raped. (Obj. #12b)

21. List at least five strategies for reducing the risk of stranger rape. (Obj. #14)

22. List five strategies for reducing the risk of acquaintance rape. (Obj. #16)

23. What can a woman do if she has been raped? (Obj. #17)

24. Describe some of the family conditions associated with incest. (Obj. #19)

25. What is the most common type of incest? (Obj. #19)

26. How may a father coerce his daughter into sexual contact with him? (Obj. #19)

27. Explain one difficulty in interpreting statistics on the overall incidence of child abuse. (Obj. #19)

28. How common is incest in Europe as compared to the United States? (Obj. #14b)

29. Describe some of the long-term effects of sexual abuse on the child and what factors influence the severity of these effects? (Obj. #20)

30. Describe the profile of the person who sexually abuses children. (Obj. #22)

31. Briefly summarize the controversy surrounding the issue of recovered memories of child sexual abuse. (Obj. #23)

32. List at least five suggestions for preventing child abuse. (Obj. #24)

33. List and briefly describe the two kinds of sexual harassment. (Obj. #26)

34. In a study of 24,000 federal employees, what percent of men and women surveyed had been sexually harassed? (Obj. #27)

35. List three forms of sexual harassment. (Obj. #28)

36. Describe some of the emotional, physical, and financial effects of sexual harassment. (Obj. #29)

37. List at least three options for dealing with sexual harassment in the workplace. (Obj. #30)

38. How does sexual harassment in the academic environment differ from sexual harassment in the workplace? (Obj. #31a-d)

39. What do the authors suggest that students do if they experience sexual harassment? (Obj. #31d)

Multiple Choice

Select the best alternative. Check your answers with the answer key at the end of the chapter.

1. _____ refers to intercourse with a person who is under the age of consent.
   a. Power rape
   b. Stranger rape
   c. Statutory rape
   d. Pedophilia

2. Psychological mechanisms such as _____ and _____ may be used to avert memories of childhood sexual abuse.
   a. denial; projection
   b. repression; cognitive avoidance
   c. projection; reaction formation
   d. cognitive avoidance; displacement

3. One reason that the notion that "women can always successfully resist rape if they really want to" is false is that
   a. the assailant has the elements of surprise and intimidation on his side.
   b. men are usually physically larger and stronger than women.
   c. a woman's shoes and clothing may inhibit her ability to escape.
   d. all of the above

4. Peggy Reeves Sanday's research indicated that American women are _____ as likely to be raped as are women in certain other societies.
   a. five times
   b. fifty times
   c. one hundred times
   d. several hundred times

5. According to Malamuth, which of the following is the best predictor of a man's inclination to engage in rape?
   a. his own experience of sexual abuse as a child
   b. his perception of peer group acceptance of rape
   c. the type of athletic activities he participated in
   d. the nature and extent of his moral or religious training

6. Which of the following statements concerning sexual gratification rape is false?
    a. It is likely to be impulsive.
    b. The majority of date rapes fit into this category.
    c. Power and anger are usually eroticized in this type of rape.
    d. This is probably the most common kind of rape.

7. Which of the following was not listed as a characteristic of men who rape?
    a. recovering drug addict
    b. alcohol use
    c. conservative attitudes toward masturbation
    d. adherence to traditional gender roles

8. Which of the following is one of the reasons men and women gave for engaging in unwanted sex acts where physical force was not used?
    a. enticement
    b. desire to be popular
    c. partner questioning one's sexuality
    d. all of the above

9. Which of the following is a characteristic of the acute phase of rape trauma syndrome?
    a. reacting in a controlled or expressive manner
    b. frequent changes in place of residence
    c. refraining from sexual contact
    d. sexual difficulties

10. One long-term study of rape survivors revealed that _____ percent avoided sexual contact for six months to a year after the assault.
    a. 20
    b. 40
    c. 60
    d. 80

11. A woman may report having various sexual problems during the _____ phase of rape trauma syndrome.
    a. acute
    b. reorganization
    c. primary
    d. adjustment

12. The explanation for why a man might have an erection while he was being sexually assaulted is that
    a. he has probably had prior "rape fantasies" that are now coming true.
    b. he probably has some underlying masochistic desires.
    c. he is sexually attracted to his assailant.
    d. sexual responses can occur in situations that cause high levels of anxiety.

13. The profile of the pedophile typically **does not** include
    a. someone with good social skills.
    b. a religious person.
    c. someone with conservative sexual attitudes.
    d. a male who is middle-aged or older.

14. Which of the following patterns appears to be a precursor to rape and other violent sexual acts?
    a. masturbating to deviant sexual fantasies
    b. conflicts regarding gender identity
    c. a history of interpersonal as well as sexual dysfunction
    d. conflicts regarding sexual orientation

15. Which of the following is **not** an example of incestuous behavior?
    a. sexual contact between mother and son
    b. a 21-year-old man having intercourse with a 16-year-old girl
    c. sexual contact between uncle and niece
    d. sexual contact between first cousins

16. Which of the following statements concerning brother-sister incest is **true**?
    a. It is the most common form of incest.
    b. It is not uncommon for siblings to look favorably upon their experiences.
    c. It is frequently not reported or discovered.
    d. all of the above

17. Father-daughter incest
    a. usually involves physical force on the part of the father.
    b. may bring the daughter special recognition or privileges.
    c. usually begins in late adolescence.
    d. is most common.

18. Which of the following was **not** listed as one of the characteristics of men who engage in incest?
    a. violent
    b. emotionally immature
    c. conservative
    d. unemployed

19. Which of the following statements **most accurately** reflects current knowledge and understanding regarding recovered memories of child sexual abuse?
    a. Research indicates that human memory is so fallible that recovered memories are very likely to be false or inaccurate.
    b. The legitimacy of recovered memories has been supported by several research studies.
    c. "Repressed memories" may be inadvertently planted by overzealous or poorly trained psychotherapists.
    d. All of the above.

20. Which of the following was one of the suggestions given for preventing child sexual abuse?
    a. Avoid complicated discussions and keep explanations simple.
    b. Carefully explain the differences between okay and not-okay touches.
    c. Encourage children to believe that they have rights.
    d. all of the above

21. Approximately _____ percent of child sex abuse victims are younger than age seven.
    a. 10
    b. 25
    c. 40
    d. 60

22. Which of the following statements is **false**?
    a. A survey of federal employees found that 12 percent of the women and 5 percent of the men surveyed had been sexually harassed.
    b. Sexual harassment includes physical and verbal harassment.
    c. An increasing number of larger companies are establishing programs that clarify for their employees exactly what sexual harassment is.
    d. all of the above

23. If you are a victim of sexual harassment on campus, it is suggested that you
    a. drop the class.
    b. find another faculty advisor.
    c. report the harassment.
    d. transfer to another school.

24. Janelle's coworker constantly makes lewd remarks about her body and makes other sexist comments or derogatory sexual remarks in her presence. This is called _____ harassment.
    a. quid pro quo
    b. hostile or offensive environment
    c. corporal
    d. exploitative

Insight and Application

1. Think of specific films, television programs, novels, and media images that perpetuate and support the "rape culture" discussed in the text. Give specific examples of these. How do these messages and role models influence relationships between the sexes?

2. Have you personally experienced any of the various types of sexual victimization discussed in this chapter? If so, how have you dealt with those experiences? What kind of personal or professional help have you sought, if any? How closely have your experiences paralleled the information presented in the text?

3. Has anyone close to you (partner, family member or friend) experienced any of the types of sexual victimization discussed in this chapter? If so, how did you respond/react to the person's experience? If you had it to do over again, would you respond differently? If so, how?

4. What kind of "child sexual abuse prevention" information did you receive when you were growing up, if any? If you could recreate that part of your history, what kinds of information and/or examples would have been helpful to you, and at what age(s)?

Multiple Choice Answers

1. c	2. b	3. d	4. d	5. b	6. c	7. a	8. d
9. a	10. b	11. b	12. d	13. a	14. a	15. b	16. d
17. b	18. a	19. d	20. d	21. b	22. a	23. c	24. b

rape

statutory rape

stranger rape

acquaintance rape
(date rape)

anger rape

power rape

sadistic rape

sexual gratification rape

rape trauma syndrome

acute phase

intercourse with a person
under the age of
legal consent

---

sexual intercourse that
occurs without consent
as a result of actual or
threatened force

---

forced sexual assault by a
friend, acquaintance or date

---

rape of a person by an
unknown assailant

---

rape in which the primary
goal is to exert control
over another human being

---

rape that is characterized by
the use of physical violence
far in excess of the amount
necessary to force sexual
submission

---

rape in which the primary
goal is sexual gratification;
most acquaintance rapes
probably fit into this
category

---

rape in which power
or anger, or both,
may be eroticized

---

the first phase of rape trauma
which begins immediately
following the rape and may
last up to several weeks; it
includes a range of emotional
and physical symptoms

---

the emotional repercussions
women experience following
rape or attempted rape

long-term
reorganization phase

child sexual abuse

pedophilia
(child molestation)

incest

sexual harassment

sexual contact of any kind between an adult and a child (inappropriate touching, oral-genital stimulation, coitus, etc.)	the second phase of rape trauma which may last for up to several years; it includes a range of fearful and/or negative feelings and behaviors
sexual contact between two people who are related, one of whom is often a child	nonrelative child sexual abuse
	unwanted sexual advances from individuals in the workplace or an academic setting

22

Sex For Sale

Introduction

This chapter examines two topics in which sex and money converge: pornography and prostitution. The controversial social and legal aspects of each are explored.

Learning Objectives

After studying this chapter, you should be able to:

1. Define pornography and explain some of the problems in establishing a contemporary definition of it.

2. Discuss the legal controversies surrounding pornography as they relate to the following:
    a. evaluating what is obscene from a legal standpoint
    b. freedom of speech
    c. regulating the dissemination of pornography
    d. sexual discrimination

3. Describe recent actions that school boards and their appointed committees have taken regarding books banned from classroom use.

4. Describe the effects of sexually explicit materials, making specific reference to the following:
    a. the outcome of President Johnson's Commission on Obscenity and Pornography
    b. the limitations of research results in this area
    c. three types of sexually explicit materials
    d. the effects of the exposure to violent pornography
    e. the effects of exposure to degrading pornography
    f. the extent to which pornography affects intimate relationships between men and women
    g. the process and outcome of the 1986 U.S. Attorney General's Commission on Pornography
    h. China's laws regarding sexually explicit materials

5. Define prostitution and discuss the ways in which it has manifested itself throughout history.

6. Identify the characteristics of the female prostitute's typical customer.

7. Describe some characteristics of the typical prostitute and explain some of the motivations for being a prostitute.

8. Explain how AIDS is a concern for prostitution, and citing relevant statistics, discuss the extent to which AIDS is a problem in the U.S. as opposed to parts of Africa.

9. List and briefly describe three types of female prostitutes.

10. Define the role that a brothel has played in prostitution.

11. List and briefly describe five types of male prostitutes.

12. Discuss the various people, agencies, businesses and institutions that benefit economically from prostitution.

13. Discuss teenage prostitution and child pornography, making reference to the following:
    a. what prompts some teenagers to become prostitutes
    b. common characteristics in the lives and backgrounds of teenage prostitutes
    c. according to one study, who the children are that are used in child pornography
    d. how federal laws have affected child pornography
    e. what many consumers of child pornography have in common
    f. how children who are involved in child prostitution are affected socially, emotionally, and psychologically

14. Explain the controversy that exists in this country regarding the legal status of prostitution, and in doing so, distinguish between legalization and decriminalization.

15. Describe how female Taiwanese prostitutes differ from those in the United States.

Key Terms and Concepts

"Flash cards" listing key terms and concepts on one side and their corresponding definitions and explanations on the other side are provided at the end of the chapter.

Chapter Overview With Fill-Ins

After reading each of the major sections in the chapter, check your retention by **mentally** filling in each of the blanks in the corresponding sections below. Cover the answers in the margin as you go along, and write the answers in the space provided only when you are doing your final review.

Pornography

visual

Generally speaking, pornography is written, visual, or _____ materials of a sexual nature that are used for the purposes of sexual arousal.

obscene
free speech
dissemination
discriminates

The legal controversies related to pornography have centered on four issues: the evaluation of what is _____; the constitutional right of _____ _____; regulations concerning the _____ of sexually explicit materials; and the extent to which pornography _____ against women.

sexually explicit

decreased

sex offenses

In the late 1960s, President Johnson appointed a Commission on Obscenity and Pornography to study the effects of _____ _____ material. The commission found that after pornography was legalized in Denmark in the late 1960s, sales of pornography to Danes _____ in the years after legalization. The commission noted that legalization and increased availability of pornography did not result in an increase of reported _____ _____, although a cause-and-effect relationship is difficult to establish.

violent
humiliating
erotica

Much of the current research on the effects of pornography separates sexually explicit materials into three groups: _____ and aggressive pornography, degrading and _____ pornography, and mutually consenting and pleasurable _____.

---

violent	Research has indicated that exposure to _____ pornography in young volunteer subjects may lead to increased
aggressive	tolerance for sexually coercive or _____ behavior, to greater acceptance of the myth that women want to be
raped; hostility	_____, and to increased _____ toward a female accomplice in laboratory studies. Exposure to violent pornography
rape	also reduces sensitivity to _____ victims.
degrading; similar	Many of the studies examining the effects of nonviolent but _____ pornography show results _____ to the effects of exposure to violent pornography.
violent	Most researchers have found that the _____ nature of material, whether it is sexual or not, is associated with
aggressive	_____ tendencies in men.
intimate	Besides the questions about the effects of violent or degrading pornography are concerns about its impact on _____ relationships between men and women. One criticism of pornography
unrealistic performance responsive	is that it contributes to _____ expectations about sexuality; it often stresses _____ and conquest rather than pleasure. In addition, women are often portrayed as intensely _____ to just about any stimulation from men.
violent; caused	The 1986 U.S. Attorney General's Commission on Pornography Report concluded that _____ pornography _____ sexually aggressive behavior toward women and that
degrading	_____ pornography fosters accepting attitudes toward rape and has some causal relationship to sexual violence. Many of the report's conclusions and recommendations have generated
controversy	considerable _____.

Prostitution

money	Prostitution refers to the exchange of sexual services for _____. Although prostitution has existed throughout history, the significance and meaning of prostitution have
varied	_____ in different times and societies. Customers of prostitutes are usually white, middle-aged, middle-class, and
married	_____. They patronize prostitutes for various reasons. No single theory can explain the motivation for being a prostitute,
46; 60	although studies have found that prostitutes have a ____ to ____ percent incidence of childhood sexual abuse.
AIDS Africa 85	_____ is a concern with prostitution. In parts of _____, sex with prostitutes is a primary mode of transmission. In Kenya, a study found that ____ percent of 1000 prostitutes tested in Nairobi were infected with the AIDS virus. In
lower	general, rates in the United States are much _____ and vary greatly from one geographic area to another.
streetwalkers brothels	There are several different types of female prostitutes who service male customers: _____, women who work in _____ or massage parlors, and call girls.

gigolos

kept
heterosexual

heterosexual

economic; criminal

Men who provide sexual services for women in exchange for money and gifts are called _____. Male prostitutes who cater to other men can be classified into different groups: hustlers, call boys, _____ boys, and peer-delinquent prostitutes. Some male prostitutes consider themselves to be _____. They have concurrent female sexual partners and usually return to a _____ lifestyle after a brief career in prostitution.

Most men and women who sell sexual services view their work as an _____ opportunity. However, pimps, the _____ justice system, referral agents, and hotel operators all benefit financially from prostitution as well.

Short Answer

1. Why is a contemporary definition of pornography difficult to establish? (Obj. #1)

2. List and briefly describe the three categories of sexually explicit materials that are currently being researched. (Obj. #4c)

   a.

   b.

   c.

3. List the three criteria used by the Supreme Court for evaluating obscenity. (Obj. #2a)

4. Give some examples of books that have been banned from classroom use or the library by various school boards. (Obj. #3)

5.   Freedom of speech is guaranteed under which constitutional amendment? (Obj. #2b)

6.   Briefly summarize the findings of President Johnson's Commission on Obscenity and Pornography regarding the following: (Obj. #4a, b, d, e)

   a.   the effects of legalization of pornography in Denmark

   b.   how imprisoned sex offenders' exposure to pornography compared to other prison inmates and non-prison populations

   c.   the effects of exposure to pornography on college students

   d.   The Commission's recommendations

7.   What were the conclusions of the 1986 U.S. Attorney General's Commission on Pornography Report? (Obj. #4g)

8.   List some of the criticisms of the report's conclusions and recommendations. (Obj. #4g)

9.   What year were sexually explicit materials banned in China? How are offenders punished? (Obj. #4h)

10. How is dissemination of pornography regulated? (Obj. #2c)

11. Why are some people opposed to laws establishing pornography as a form of sexual discrimination? (Obj. #2d)

12. What were the results of the study in which men and women were repeatedly exposed to pornography? (Obj. #2d, 4f)

13. In one study, what percentage of women said they had been upset by being asked to do something their male partners had seen or red in pornographic materials? (Obj. #2d, 4f)

14. Briefly summarize the research findings on the effects of degrading pornography. (Obj. #4e)

15. Briefly summarize the researching findings of the effects on violent pornography. (Obj. #4d)

16. Describe the typical background of the teenage prostitute. What percent have been victims of sexual abuse? (Obj. #13a, b)

17. Where are pornographers able to find children who will participate in making pornographic videotapes, etc.? (Obj. #13c)

18. What is the current status of commercially produced child pornography? (Obj. #13d)

19. Briefly summarize the role of prostitution in: (Obj. #5)

    a.   ancient Greece

    b.   medieval Europe

    c.   England during the Victorian era

20. Characterize the customers of female prostitutes. (Obj. #6)

21. Compare the problem of AIDS and prostitution in Africa and the United States. What percent of prostitutes in Kenya were infected with HIV? (Obj. #8)

22. How do the family backgrounds of Taiwanese prostitutes compare to those of U.S. prostitutes? (Obj. #15)

23. How do Taiwanese parents respond to a daughter's decision to become a prostitute? (Obj. #15)

24. List and briefly describe the three types of female prostitutes who service male customers: (Obj. #9)

    a.

    b.

    c.

25. Briefly describe the following: (Obj. #11)

    a.   gigolos

    b.   hustlers

    c.   call boys

    d.   kept boys

    e.   peer-delinquent prostitutes

    f.   pimps

26. List and briefly describe four different groups of people that benefit financially from prostitution: (Obj. #12)

    a.

    b.

    c.

    d.

27. Briefly state the arguments for maintaining the status of prostitution as a criminal offense. (Obj. #14)

28. List several arguments for the legalization of prostitution. (Obj. #14)

29. List several arguments for the decriminalization of prostitution. (Obj. #14)

30. What is COYOTE? (Obj. #14)

Multiple Choice

Select the best alternative. Check your answers with the answer key at the end of the chapter.

1. The legal controversies about pornography center on what is to be legally defined as
    a. erotic.
    b. obscene.
    c. degrading and humiliating.
    d. violent.

2. Current federal law regarding obscene materials prohibits all of the following **except**
    a. broadcasting obscene materials.
    b. private possession of obscene materials.
    c. mailing obscene materials.
    d. importing obscene materials.

3. Most pornography dissemination statutes stem from
    a. the Comstock Act.
    b. the West Coast Society for the Suppression of Vice.
    c. the John Birch Society.
    d. COYOTE.

4. Which of the following was a finding of the 1970 commission report on pornography?
    a. Legalization and increased availability of pornography in Denmark caused an increase in the sale of pornography to Danes.
    b. Imprisoned sex offenders had more exposure to pornography than other prison inmates or non-prison populations.
    c. Significant, long-lasting changes in behavior were evident in college students who were exposed to pornography.
    d. none of the above

5. Central to both violent and degrading pornography is the depiction of
    a. aggression or brutality.
    b. people who are there out of a sense of shared pleasure.
    c. unequal balance of power.
    d. degradation and humiliation.

6. Exposure to nonviolent but degrading pornography demonstrates _____ exposure to violent pornography.
    a. more adverse effects than
    b. fewer adverse effects than
    c. similar effects to
    d. There has been no research examining this issue.

7. One study of college students and the general population found that after repeated exposure to pornography
    a. women and men became more innovative in their sexual interaction with their partners.
    b. men became sexually more demanding and women became more submissive.
    c. women and men became less satisfied with the sexual performance of their partners.
    d. women and men found their partners to be more physically appealing.

8. _____ percent of a randomly selected group of women said they had been upset by being asked to do something their male partner had seen in pornographic pictures, movies, or books.
   a. 10
   b. 20
   c. 30
   d. 40

9. One reason that researchers criticized the Meese Commission's report on pornography is that
   a. it ignored the detrimental effects of violence, whether accompanied by sexually explicit materials or not.
   b. it focused on sexually explicit materials that were violent and ignored the effects of materials that were degrading and humiliating.
   c. it ignored the results of the Denmark study.
   d. it was a sophisticated rehash of the 1970 Commission report and reached similar conclusions without taking into account the results of more recent research.

10. Which of the following statements concerning prostitution is **true**?
   a. There are times throughout history when it flourished and other times when it was nonexistent.
   b. In medieval Europe, it was viewed in an extremely negative light.
   c. Customers of prostitutes are typically young, single, blue-collar workers.
   d. The significance of prostitution has varied in different times and societies.

11. A common pattern in the backgrounds of female prostitutes is a history of
   a. sexual abuse.
   b. being raised in a single-parent family.
   c. early experimentation with drugs and alcohol.
   d. excessive masturbation.

12. Almost _____ percent of teenage runaways who come to emergency shelters have been sexually molested or subjected to severe physical abuse.
   a. 90
   b. 70
   c. 50
   d. 30

13. This type of female prostitute is usually managed by a "madam".
   a. woman who works in a brothel
   b. call girl
   c. kept girl
   d. streetwalker

14. _____ often work in small groups and use homosexual prostitution as a vehicle for assault and robbery.
   a. Streetwalkers
   b. Peer-delinquent prostitutes
   c. Hustlers
   d. Gigolos

15. When laws against prostitution are enforced,
   a. the customer is most likely to be punished.
   b. the prostitute is most likely to be punished.
   c. both the prostitute and the customer receive equal punishment.
   d. the pimp is most likely to be punished.

16. Regulation in terms of licensing and taxation would most likely occur if prostitution were
    a. legalized.
    b. institutionalized.
    c. decriminalized.
    d. litigated.

Insight and Application

1. What were your reactions to the various research results on the effects of sexually explicit materials? What is your subjective assessment of the ways in which violent pornography, degrading pornography, and erotica affect intimate relationships between men and women, if at all?

2. Do you think prostitution should be legalized, decriminalized, or remain illegal? Why? Consider the ramifications of your decision in the community in which you live. What kinds of issues would be important to take into account?

Multiple Choice Answers

1. b	2. b	3. a	4. d	5. c	6. c	7. c	8. a
9. a	10. d	11. a	12. b	13. a	14. b	15. b	16. a

pornography

prostitution

brothel

gigolos

streetwalker

call girl

hustler

call boy

kept boy

peer-delinquent
prostitutes

the exchange of sexual services for money	visual and written materials of a sexual nature that are used for purposes of sexual arousal
men who provide sexual services for women in exchange for money and gifts	a house in which a group of prostitutes works
a type of female prostitute who is at the top of the prostitution hierarchy; she generally earns more than other types of prostitutes and also provides social services to her customers	a type of female prostitute who services male customers; she solicits customers on the street or in bars
a male prostitute who caters to homosexual men; he earns more money than hustlers, and provides social as well as sexual services to his customers	a male prostitute who caters to homosexual men; he makes contact with his customers on the streets or in gay bars
male prostitutes who work in small groups and use homosexual prostitution as a vehicle for assault and robbery	a male prostitute who is partially or fully supported by an older male

pimps   **COYOTE**

obscene

the prostitutes' union (Cast Off Your Old Tired Ethics) which acts as a collective voice for prostitutes' concerns	men who "protect" prostitutes (usually streetwalkers) and live off their earnings
	a term that implies a personal or societal judgment that something is offensive

TO THE OWNER OF THIS BOOK:

I hope that this study guide has been helpful for you in your study of human sexuality. In order to improve future editions of this material, your feedback is essential. I would appreciate it if you would respond to the following questions and return the completed questionnaire to me. Thank you for your help!

School and address: _____

Department: _____

Instructor's name: _____

1. What did you like most about the *Study Guide for Crooks and Baur's Our Sexuality,* Sixth Edition?

_____

_____

2. What did you like least about it? _____

_____

_____

3. Were all of the chapters of the book assigned for you to read? _____

   If not, which ones weren't? _____

4. Did you find that the *Study Guide* promoted active learning? _____

5. Which sections of the *Study Guide* were most helpful to you? _____

_____

   Why were they helpful? _____

_____

6. Which sections of the *Study Guide* were least helpful to you? _____

_____

   Why were they not helpful? _____

_____

_____

7. Was the material in the *Study Guide* consistent with that in the textbook? _____

   If it was not, please describe: _____

_____

8. Do you have any other suggestions for us to consider for the next edition?_____

_____

_____

Optional:

Your name: _____ Date: _____

May Brooks/Cole quote you, either in promotion for *Study Guide for Crooks and Baur's Our Sexuality,* or in future publishing ventures?

Yes: _____ No: _____

Sincerely yours,

Lauren Kuhn